Frank McAlpine

Our Album of Authors

A Cyclopedia of Popular Literary People

Frank McAlpine

Our Album of Authors
A Cyclopedia of Popular Literary People

ISBN/EAN: 9783337226466

Printed in Europe, USA, Canada, Australia, Japan

Cover: Foto ©Thomas Meinert / pixelio.de

More available books at **www.hansebooks.com**

OUR
Album of Authors,

A Cyclopedia of Popular Literary People,

BY

FRANK M'ALPINE,

EDITOR OF "TREASURES FROM THE POETIC WORLD," "TREASURES
FROM THE PROSE WORLD" AND "POPULAR
POETIC PEARLS."

Sold Only by Subscription.

ELLIOTT & BEEZLEY,
PHILADELPHIA, CHICAGO, CINCINNATI.
1885.

COPYRIGHT, 1885,
ELLIOTT & BEEZLEY.

MANUFACTURED BY
ELLIOTT & BEEZLEY'S PUBLISHING HOUSE,
PHILADELPHIA, CHICAGO, AND CINCINNATI.

PREFACE.

OUR ALBUM OF AUTHORS gathers into one volume a knowledge of the men and women who have made the standard literature of the world. Our text-books are too brief for the general public. Our encyclopedias are too expensive for the masses; besides they contain hundreds of minor authors who have added no new thoughts or noble impulses to the literature of our race.

General readers have not the time to crush a mountain of quartz to get a grain of gold, or to hunt the sands of the earth to find a single diamond, or to search through forty centuries that have been prolific of authors to find the thoughts and the impulses of those who form the chief literary constellation of the ages.

OUR ALBUM OF AUTHORS takes the reader over the entire field, and introduces him to the representative men and women in the various departments of literature. It presents only a few minor writers, and these were selected either because they are very popular, or because the reader may learn a valuable lesson from their lives and writings.

This volume will be valuable to those wishing to make up a library, as it gives a list of books published by standard authors and names each author's best works. It will be valuable to teachers for reference and study, because it not only gives extended sketches of the best authors, but it gives the critical estimation of each author's writings. It will be valuable to parents, because it carries their children into the society of good books, and makes them acquainted with the men and women of the grandest, purest, and noblest thoughts. It calls attention to the fact that there is no royal road to greatness in any department of life, but that the crown is gained only after years of patient, ceaseless, and earnest toil. It shows that true nobility has come from lowly birth, and that success has been gained in spite of circumstances. Such lessons, with the examples given, will urge the young to greater efforts, and to higher aims in life. In short, OUR ALBUM OF AUTHORS will be most valuable to all who love the society of noble lives and elevated thoughts.

As a few words of earnest advice or remonstrance which a boy hears at the right time, from a man whom he respects, may affect that boy's character for life, so a good book, placed in his hands at the right time, may mould his character and give direction to the remainder of his life.

With earnest wishes for the greatest good of the greatest number, this volume enters upon its mission.

FRANK McALPINE.

CONTENTS.

Addison, Joseph	11
Agassiz, Louis J. R.	16
Alcott, Louisa May	19
Aldrich, Thos. Bailey	20
Audubon, John James	22
Bancroft, George	24
Black, William	28
Boker, George H.	30
Brown, Chas. Farron	31
Browning, Elizabeth Barrett	33
Browning, Robt.	38
Bryant, Wm. Cullen	39
Bulwer-Lytton	46
Bunyan, John	52
Burns, Robt.	54
Byron, Lord	60
Carlyle, Thos.	67
Carleton, Will	69
Cary, Alice and Phœbe	74
Campbell, Thos.	77
Chaucer, Geoffrey	80
Clemens, Samuel L.	84
Coleridge, Samuel Taylor	88
Cooper, Jas. Fenimore	95
Cowper, William	100
Dante, Alighieri	105

CONTENTS.

DE QUINCEY, THOS.	112
DICKENS, CHAS.	115
DISRAELI, BENJ.	123
DRAKE, JOSEPH R.	126
DRYDEN, JOHN	127
ELIOT, GEORGE	132
EMERSON, RALPH WALDO	137
EVERETT, EDWARD	143
FRANKLIN, BENJ.	148
GIBBON, EDWARD	156
GOETHE, JOHANN WOLFGANG VON	162
GOLDSMITH, OLIVER	169
GRAY, THOMAS	175
HALLECK, FITZ-GREENE	178
HAWTHORNE, NATHANIEL	182
HARTE, FRANCIS BRET	190
HEMANS, FELICIA DOROTHEA	193
HOLMES, OLIVER WENDELL	198
HOOD, THOMAS	204
HOLLAND, JOSIAH GILBERT	211
HUGO, VICTOR	216
HUNT, LEIGH	221
INGELOW, JEAN	224
IRVING, WASHINGTON	226
JONSON, BEN	231
JOHNSON, SAMUEL	233
KEATS, JOHN	239
LAMB, CHAS.	241
LAMARTINE	246
LONGFELLOW	252
LOWELL	261
MACAULAY, THOS. B.	271
MANN, HORACE	280

CONTENTS.

Milton, John	283
Mitchell, Donald G.	288
Miller, Joaquin	292
Moore, Thos.	294
Motley, John L.	301
Montgomery, James	304
Payne, John H.	309
Poe, Edgar Allen	310
Pope, Alexander	314
Prescott, Wm. H.	319
Read, Thos. B.	322
Ruskin, John	324
Saxe, J. G.	328
Scott, Sir Walter	331
Schiller	340
Shakespeare, Wm.	344
Shelley, P. B.	348
Sigourney, Mrs.	354
Southey, Robt.	355
Spenser, Edmund	361
Stowe, Harriet Beecher	366
Stedman, E. C.	369
Swift, Jonathan	370
Taylor, Bayard	372
Taylor, B. F.	377
Tennyson, Alfred	378
Thackeray, W. M.	385
Watts, Isaac	390
Whittier, John G.	394
Whitman, Walt	401
Willis, N. P.	409
Wordsworth	411
Young, E.	414

INDEX TO PORTRAITS.

ADDISON, JOSEPH	13
BANCROFT, GEORGE	25
BROWNING, ELIZABETH BARRETT	35
BRYANT, WILLIAM CULLEN	41
BULWER-LYTTON	47
BURNS, ROBERT	57
BYRON, LORD	61
CARLETON, WILL	71
CARY, ALICE AND PHŒBE	75
CHAUCER, GEOFFREY	81
CLEMENS, SAMUEL L.	85
COLERIDGE, SAMUEL TAYLOR	89
COOPER, JAS. FENIMORE	97
COWPER, WILLIAM	103
DANTE, ALIGHIERI	107
DICKENS, CHAS.	119
DRYDEN, JOHN	129
ELIOT, GEORGE	133
EMERSON, RALPH WALDO	139
EVERETT, EDWARD	145
GOETHE, JOHANN WOLFGANG VON	163
GOLDSMITH, OLIVER	171
HALLECK, FITZ-GREENE	179
HAWTHORNE, NATHANIEL	183
HARTE, FRANCIS BRET	191

HOLMES, OLIVER WENDELL	199
HOOD, THOMAS	205
HOLLAND, JOSIAH GILBERT	213
HUGO, VICTOR	217
IRVING, WASHINGTON	227
JOHNSON, SAMUEL	235
LAMARTINE	247
LONGFELLOW	253
LOWELL	263
MILTON, JOHN	285
MITCHELL, DONALD G.	289
MOORE, THOS.	297
PAYNE, JOHN H.	308
POE, EDGAR ALLEN	311
POPE, ALEXANDER	315
RUSKIN, JOHN	325
SAXE, JOHN GODFREY	329
SCOTT, SIR WALTER	333
SCHILLER	341
SHAKESPEARE, WM.	345
SHELLEY, P. B.	349
SOUTHEY, ROBERT	357
SPENSER, EDMUND	363
STOWE, HARRIET BEECHER	367
TAYLOR, BAYARD	373
TENNYSON, ALFRED	379
THACKERAY, W. M.	387
WATTS, ISAAC	391
WHITTIER, JOHN G.	395
WHITMAN, WALT	403
WORDSWORTH	413

OUR
ALBUM OF AUTHORS.

JOSEPH ADDISON.

JOSEPH ADDISON was born at Milston, Wiltshire, England, May 1, 1672, and he died in Holland House, June 17, 1719. His father was Lancelot Addison, Dean of Lichfield. Joseph had ample opportunity to acquire an education. He passed through several schools, including the Charter-House. At the age of fifteen, he went to Oxford, where "he was entered a student of Queen's College," but in two years Addison was elected a scholar of Magdalen College. In 1693 he took his master's degree. During the next eleven years he devoted himself entirely to study, observation and writing. Although his productions in this period gained him local fame, yet they added nothing toward his permanent celebrity. There are three distinct features in Addison's life work. He appears as poet, essayist and politician. We can become acquainted with him best by studying his work in each department separately. His first intention was to prepare for the ministry, but his ability attracted the attention of the Whig party, to which he belonged, and its leaders sought to prepare him for political work. Upon recommendation of Lord Somers, Addison obtained a pension of £300 per annum, to enable him, as he acknowledges in a memorial address to the crown, "to travel, and qualify himself to serve His Majesty." In the summer of 1699 he crossed into France, where he learned the French language. At the close of

1700 he went into Italy. "The classic ruins of Rome, the 'heavenly figures' of Raphael, the river Tiber, and streams 'immortalized in song,' and all the golden groves and flowery meadows of Italy," seem to have raised his fancy and brightened his expression. Addison next went to Switzerland, where he learned of his appointment as envoy to Prince Eugene, then engaged in the war in Italy. But the death of King William in 1702 put an end to the Whig supremacy, and Addison lost his pension. He pursued his travels, however, through most of Germany and Holland, returning to England in 1703. Upon his return Addison was engaged to celebrate in verse the battle of Blenheim. He so pleased the lord-treasurer, Godolphin, by this poem, that he was appointed commissioner of appeals. In 1705, the same year that "The Campaign" appeared, he published an account of his travels, entitled "Remarks on Several Parts of Italy," and dedicated it to Lord Somers. Early in 1706, by recommendation of Lord Godolphin, Addison was appointed Under Secretary of State. "In 1709, when the Marquis of Wharton was appointed Lord Lieutenant of Ireland, our poet accompanied him as secretary and was made keeper of records, with a salary of £300 a year." In the same year Addison was elected a member of parliament for Cavan. This position he held for several years. His name appears frequently in the journals of the two sessions, but he wielded no particular influence in that body. Finally, in 1717, he received his highest political honors by being appointed Secretary of State, but he held the office for only a short time. "He wanted the physical boldness and ready resources of an effective public speaker, and was unable to defend his measures in parliament." He retired from office with a pension of £1,500 per annum. We cannot look on Addison as being great in political matters, hence we turn back to his literary life.

In this department no man of his day exerted a wider or better influence. He was distinguished at Oxford for his Latin poetry. His first appearance in English verse was an address to Dryden. The youthful poet thus sang the praises of his great master, and the veteran writer honored the poem with a position in the third volume of his "Miscellanies." In the next volume of this collection, Dryden published Addison's translations in tolerable heroic couplets, of "all Virgil's Fourth Georgic, except the story of Aristæus."

JOSEPH ADDISON

Next appeared "Essay on Virgil's Georgics." This effort was complimented by Dryden, by prefixing it to his own translation of the poem.

In 1694 Addison published "Account of the Great English Poets." This poem contains about 150 lines, and consists of sketches of Chaucer, Spencer, Cowley, Milton, etc. While animated in language and versification, and full of poetic fire, yet the poem shows much ignorance of the old English poetry. In 1695 he published a composition praising contemporary great men, and celebrating the great events of his time. This piece was addressed "To the King." This poem produced no particular sensation, and, indeed, possessed no great merit. In 1699 appeared quite a collection of his Latin verses at Oxford. These exhibited considerable characteristic humor, and attracted the attention of some foreign scholars. We have now to pass over the incidents of his life rapidly till about 1709, when Steele commenced to publish the "Tatler," to find writings which we most admire. The period over which we have thus passed with a bound is not a blank. It was filled with political effusions, sweet hymns, and some choice writings; but his most admired works are his delightful contributions to the "Tatler," the "Spectator," and the "Guardian." To the "Spectator" Addison contributed his celebrated criticism on "Paradise Lost," besides numerous papers upon the theory of literature, and his comprehensive essays, "On the Pleasures of the Imagination." To Addison, further, belong those essays which rise into the region of moral and religious meditation, and tread the elevated ground with a step so graceful as to allure the reader irresistibly to follow; sometimes, as in the "Walk through Westminster Abbey," enlivening solemn thought by gentle sportiveness; sometimes flowing on with an uninterrupted sedateness of didactic eloquence; and sometimes shrouding sacred truths in the veil of ingenious allegory, as in the majestic "Vision of Mirza." Perhaps the best of all his papers are the "Mountain of Miseries;" "Shallum and Hilpa," an antediluvian novel; the "Reflections by Moonlight on the Divine Perfections." His best poems are the tragedy of "Cato," and his numerous hymns.

Addison married the Countess-Dowager of Warwick, in 1716, only three years before his death. The lady, having forfeited her jointure by the marriage, brought her husband nothing but the right to occupy Holland House. He is said to have "married discord in a noble wife." As in Dryden's union with Elizabeth Howard, he received "the heraldry of hands, not of hearts." The closing year of Addison's life was marked by his alienation from Steele, his oldest friend. This was caused by the divisions in the Whig party. Steele attacked the Peerage Bill in a paper called the "Plebeian," and Addison answered him in the "Old Whig." This brought on an angry word-contest between the old friends. Addison seems to have regretted this quarrel, hence he ordered his executor, Tickell, not to publish the "Old Whig" in the posthumous collection of his works. Asthma accompanied by dropsy put an end to Addison's life work, at the close of his forty-seventh year, and his remains now repose in the Poets' Corner of Westminster Abbey. An American edition of his works has been published in six volumes. William Mathews, LL. D., in his "Literary Style," exclaims, "What an urbanity reveals itself in the almost perfect manner, so easy and high-bred, courteous, not courtier-like, as Bulwer says, of the gentle Addison!"

LOUIS J. R. AGASSIZ.

Louis John Rudolph Agassiz was born near the eastern extremity of the lake of Neuchatel, Switzerland, May 28, 1807 and he died in the New World, December 14, 1873.

Agassiz's father was a Swiss Protestant clergyman of good abilities.

Young Agassiz commenced his education at home, then, after spending four years in the gymnasium of Bienne, completed his elementary studies at the academy of Lausanne. Before leaving the latter school, he had become noted for his special love of the natural sciences, and for his eminent ability in pursuing them.

Agassiz decided to take up medicine as a profession, because of the close relation between the science of medicine and the natural sciences. In order to prepare himself for his chosen profession, he studied at the universities of Zurich, Heidelberg, and Munich. At the last named place, he took his degree of doctor of medicine. While pursuing his medical studies, he improved all the opportunities afforded to strengthen and extend his knowledge of natural history.

Up to this time, Agassiz had given no special study to the line of investigation which afterward formed the principal part of his life-work. He was led into the study of ichthyology by the following circumstance: Spix and Martius returned from their famous Brazilian tour about 1820, with a fine collection of fresh water fishes. Spix died before he had worked out the history of these fishes, hence it became necessary for another naturalist to describe them. Though but little more than a youth just from his academic studies, Agassiz's reputation was such that he was selected for the work. His attention thus turned to the study of fishes, he threw the energy of his great powers into that branch of investigation, and won immortal fame. His published works commenced in 1828, while he was but twenty-one years of age. This first work was a description of a new species which he had found. In 1830 he enlarged his plans, and commenced a "History of the Fresh Water Fishes of Central Europe." The investigations were conducted successfully, and the first part of the work appeared in 1839.

Encouraged by the success of his publications, Agassiz undertook the task of studying and classifying the fossil fishes that abound in the stratified rocks of his native mountains. The work was carried forward with his accustomed enthusiasm. Five magnificently illustrated volumes, the results of his researches in the new field, appeared at intervals between 1833 and 1844. This work made him known to foreign naturalists, and laid the foundation of his greatness. In the progress of his work, he found it necessary to make his classifications upon a new basis. It will hardly be expected that we give a description of his classifications here. Suffice it to say that parts of his system have been retained by recent ichthyologists, though under some modifications. His researches in fossils were very valuable, and he early gave to geologists several important and correct generalizations.

The British Association for the Advancement of Science wisely came to the aid of the intrepid young zoologist, by replenishing his overtaxed resources. The late Earl of Ellesmere, known in his youth as Lord Francis Egerton, purchased the original drawings made to illustrate the five volumes brought out by Agassiz in 1833-44. These drawings were chiefly the work of the renowned Dinkel, numbering 1,290; and all that were necessary for the prosecution of his work, the generous earl left in the hands of Agassiz. While thus engaged, he visited England for the purpose of studying the rich stores of fossil fishes with which that country abounds. He was young, enthusiastic, quick in perceiving peculiarities of new fossils, and he possessed a remarkably faithful memory.

Besides numerous and generously illustrated volumes recording his investigations in England, Scotland, Wales, Switzerland and among the Alpine glaciers, which added greatly to his fame, he was honored in 1838, with the professorship of natural history at Neuchatel.

In 1846 he visited the United States for the purpose of investigating the natural history and geology of this country, and of lecturing on zoology at the Lowell Institute. The pecuniary and scientific advantages offered him in the New World induced him to remain here for the rest of his life. In 1847 he was appointed professor of zoology and geology in Cambridge University. This position he left in 1851 for the professorship of comparative anatomy at Charlestown, but returned to Cambridge in 1853. Volume after volume recorded his work in the New World. In 1865 he visited Brazil, an account of which was published by Mrs. Agassiz. In 1871 he visited the southern shores of the North American continent.

For some time he had hoped to establish a permanent school for the study of zoological science among the living specimens. Such an institution he was enabled, through the liberality of Mr. John Anderson, to establish. That gentleman gave Agassiz the island of Penikese, on the east coast, together with $50,000 as an endowment fund. Another American friend gave him a fine yacht of eighty tons burden, to be employed in marine dredging in the surrounding seas. But he was unable to complete his plans, for he died in 1873. It is difficult to over-estimate the advantages which American science would have gained had Agassiz lived to carry out his plans. In his last letter, written but a few days before his death, he expressed a strong desire to live four years longer, that he might complete his work. He was one of the most remarkable men that ever lived; and "his daring conceptions were only equaled by the unwearied industry and genuine enthusiasm with which he worked them out."

LOUISA MAY ALCOTT.

Miss Alcott was born at Germantown, Pennsylvania, in 1833.

Her father was Amos Bronson Alcott, an American educator of considerable note. The father commenced as a local trader, and carried his trunk about among the planters of Virginia. Having acquired an education from books loaned to him, he commenced teaching school. In 1828 he removed to Boston, and established a school for young children of five years of age. The school would succeed to-day, but then it was in advance of the age, and it failed. Finally his ability attracted attention abroad, and James P. Greaves, of London, a fellow-laborer of Pestalozzi, the immortal educator of Switzerland, invited him to come to England. Before Alcott's arrival, however, Mr. Greaves died, but he was received very cordially by the friends of the new departure in education. In honor of the American educator, their school at Ham, near London, was named the "Alcott House." Returning to America he was active in conversational and literary pursuits. He published two books, "Tablets," 1868, and "Concord Days," 1872.

Thus we see that Miss Alcott comes from a thoughtful, industrious parent. She is also a cousin of the eminent educator and author, Dr. Wm. A. Alcott, who died in Massachusetts, in 1859. Dr. Alcott visited about

20,000 schools to assist in revising and improving the school work. He published upwards of one hundred books and pamphlets on literary and educational topics. His name is identified permanently with some of the most valuable reforms in education, morals, and physical training, which the present century has witnessed. The labor performed by him without asking for compensation is almost unparalleled.

From such parentage, and guided by such relatives, it is not surprising that Miss Louisa May Alcott performed her life-work most satisfactorily. She commenced writing fairy tales in her teens. In 1855, her first volume, "Flower Fables," appeared. Her next literary work consisted of stories written for the Boston journals. "Hospital Sketches," published in 1863, won for her a general reputation. These sketches were written in the South, while she was acting in the capacity of volunteer nurse in the army. From 1863 to 1864 she wrote for the "Atlantic Monthly;" and in 1865 appeared "Moods," her first novel. "Little Women," perhaps her most popular work, was published in 1867. She published "An Old Fashioned Girl" in 1869, and "Little Men" in 1871. She has also published "Work," "Morning Glories," etc.

All of her works have had immense sales, and are deservedly popular. She is one of the best story writers of the age. Her language is simple and elegant, and her style easy and attractive.

THOMAS BAILEY ALDRICH.

T. B. ALDRICH was born in Portsmouth, New Hampshire, in 1836.

He had commenced to prepare himself for college when his father died. This event caused him to change his plans, and enter the counting-house of his uncle, a merchant in New York. In the three years that he remained with his uncle, he won some reputation by his verses contributed to the New York journals. His poems were collected into a volume entitled "The Bells," and published in 1855. The title of the book was taken from his poem "The Bells," which was regarded as his best production. The success of his poem "Baby Bell," published in 1856, was wonderful. It was copied all over the country. The fame which he had thus acquired induced him to abandon mercantile pursuits, and adopt literature as a calling.

Aldrich's life as an author has been one of continued prosperity. He contributed numerous and interesting articles to "Putnam's Magazine," the "Knickerbocker," and the weekly newspapers. In the papers, he first published "Daisy's Necklace, and What Came of it." This prose poem was afterward published in book form, and it attained great popularity.

In 1856 Aldrich joined the editorial staff of the "Home Journal," then under the charge of N. P. Willis and Geo. P. Morris. This relation he held for three years, writing constantly; and many of his articles became great favorites.

He has been an incessant literary worker, as will be seen by the following synopsis of his most important productions: "The Ballad of Baby Bell, and other poems," published in 1856; "The Course of True Love never did Run Smooth," 1858; "Pampinea and other Poems," in 1861; "Out of his Head, a Romance in Prose," 1862; a collection of poems, 1863; a volume of poems published in Boston in 1865; "The Story of a Bad Boy," published first in "Our Young Folks," and afterward, in 1870, in book form. "The Story of a Bad Boy" attracted wide attention.

Aldrich has been editor of "Every Saturday" from its foundation, and he has contributed articles to the "Atlantic Monthly" and other magazines.

He occupies a high position as a lyric poet, and also as a novelist. Nothing grand in poetry has been attempted by him, but he has performed all that he has undertaken with much beauty, and almost perfection. Among his finest poems are "Friar Jerome's Beautiful Book," "The Face Against the Pane," and "Baby Bell." Among his best novels are "The Story of a Bad Boy," "Marjorie Daw and other People," and "Prudence Palfrey."

The following stanza illustrates the charming beauty of his style:

    Have you not heard the poets tell
    How came the dainty Baby Bell
      Into this world of ours?
    The gates of heaven were left ajar;
      With folded hands and dreamy eyes,
      Wandering out of Paradise,
    She saw the planet like a star,
      Hung in the glistening depths of even,
    Its bridges running to and fro,
    O'er which the white-winged angels go,
      Bearing the holy dead to heaven;
    She touched a bridge of flowers—those feet,
    So light they did not bend the bells
    Of the celestial asphodels!
    They fell like dew upon the flowers;
    Then all the air grew strangely sweet;
      And thus came dainty Baby Bell
      Into this world of ours.

JOHN JAMES AUDUBON.

AUDUBON was born in Louisiana, in 1781; and after a short illness, he died at his home in New York, on the banks of the Hudson, January 27, 1851.

His parents were French Protestants, who settled in Louisiana while that province was yet a French colony.

In his youth he was very fond of observing the appearance and habits of birds, and of delineating them from nature. At the age of fifteen he was sent to Paris, where he spent about two years in study, and in the drawing-school of David. Having completed his mission abroad he returned home, settled on a plantation in Pennsylvania, and soon married.

For the next fifteen years, he took annual tours into the primeval forests of America. These journeys were long and hazardous, and far from home and family, but they resulted in a portfolio containing 200 sheets filled with colored delineations of about 1,000 birds. With this portfolio, he set out for Philadelphia, but while absent from the city on business, the manuscript was entirely destroyed by rats. As it contained the fruits of several years of severe toil, the loss was a sad one, and the shock caused almost a fatal sickness. Upon his recovery, however, his native energy asserted itself, and Audubon again set out for the woods with gun and game-bag, pencils and drawing-book. For about three years he roamed through the recesses of the forests. His portfolio again filled he returned to his family, who in the meantime had gone to Louisiana.

After a short sojourn there, he set out for the Old World, to exhibit to the ornithologists of Europe the riches of America in that department of natural history.

In 1826 he arrived at Liverpool, where his delineations of American birds created considerable interest, and his ability was immediately recognized. Audubon gave public exhibitions of his work in the Royal Institute of Liverpool, and also at Manchester and Edinburgh. In all of these exhibitions his work was greatly admired.

He was advised to bring out his work in large quarto, as the most convenient size; "but finally he decided that his book should eclipse every other ornithological publication. Every bird was to be delineated of the size of life, and to each species a whole page was to be devoted; consequently, the largest 'elephant folio' paper was to receive the impression." This increased the expense of the original work to one thousand dollars per copy, hence, at first, his subscribers were few. "The exceptionally high character of the work, however, gradually became known, and a sufficient number of subscribers was at length obtained in England and America, during the ten or twelve years that the work was going through the press, to indemnify him for the great cost of the publication." A very meager allowance was Audubon's reward for his skill and labor bestowed upon this extraordinary work. But it established the author's reputation, and brought better reward for his future publications. Cuvier declares that Audubon's works are the most splendid monuments which art has erected in honor of ornithology.

Audubon spent considerable time in visiting England, Scotland, France, Canada, and the various states of the United States to gather information in his favorite study. He finally brought out his first work in popular form, and it had an excellent sale.

His "American Ornithological Biography" filled five large octavo volumes, and his "Birds of America," seven volumes. Continuing his work, he brought out "The Quadrupeds of America" in atlas folio, and his "Biography of American Quadrupeds," in 1850.

Audubon united estimable mental qualities with a deep sense of religion. "His conversation was animated and instructive, his manner unassuming, and he always spoke with gratitude to heaven for the very happy life he had been permitted to enjoy."

GEORGE BANCROFT.

BANCROFT was born at Worcester, Mass., Oct. 3, 1800.

His father, the Rev. Dr. Aaron Bancroft, was a minister of much ability, and a man of fine literary taste. Dr. Bancroft prepared an excellent "Life of Washington," which he published in 1807. Without doubt, the tastes of the father had something to do with the literary tendencies of his son.

George Bancroft's education was ample. He was early trained in an academy at Exeter; and at the age of thirteen he entered Harvard College. From this institution he graduated with distinction. Later he studied for two years in the University of Gottingen, Germany. Upon completing his studies in college, Bancroft entered the church, but his strong literary inclination prevailed, and he took up his pen. While in Europe he received the

GEORGE BANCROFT.

degree of Doctor of Philosophy. He also formed the acquaintance of Humboldt, and other noted men, and traveled over a great portion of Europe.

He returned to the United States in 1822, and taught in Harvard University for about one year. He opened a school at Northampton in 1823. About the same time he published a volume of poems, and translated quite extensively from the German, chiefly the historical manuals of Professor Heeren.

At this time, Bancroft began to gather material for his "History of the Colonization of the United States." The three volumes of this part of his famous "History of the United States" appeared from 1834 to 1840. The work showed an energetic and lively style, and an occasional democratic prejudice. As a reward for the strong American tendencies of his thoughts, he was appointed collector of the port of Boston, in 1838, by President Van Buren. In 1844 his party ran him for governor of Massachusetts, and, although defeated, he received the largest vote ever before given by his state. While the canvass was progressing, he was absent from the state, engaged on his history. The standing which he had thus gained recommended him most favorably, and in 1845 President Polk made him Secretary of the Navy. In the succeeding year, his literary reputation secured for him the appointment as minister plenipotentiary to England. In 1849, while in England, Oxford conferred upon him the degree of Doctor of Laws. His appointment gave universal satisfaction.

His literary labors were greatly aided by the kindness of the British government in giving him access to the State Paper Office, and to collections in the museum, and various private collections. He also had access to the State Records of Paris, where he received valuable aids. Upon returning to the United States, he took up his residence in New York, in 1849. From that time his life was given almost entirely to work on his "History," the last volume of which was brought out in 1873. The period between 1849 and 1873 was interrupted by his appointment, in 1867, as minister to Prussia, in 1868, as minister to the German Confederation, and in 1871 as minister to the German Empire. Thus we see that he was appropriately honored by his countrymen.

The first volume of "Bancroft's History" appeared in 1834, and the tenth and last in 1873, covering, as will be seen, a period of thirty-nine years. Upon completion, it became very popular in this and foreign countries. It has been translated into various languages.

Bancroft has taken up his residence in Washington, and is engaged in revising his great work. It is said that the revision will be complete this year (1885), when the great historian will lay down his pen for the last time. He can afford to cease from his labors; for his life has been full of honors; and his pen has erected a monument to his ability that will endure through all time. His labors have brought him an ample fortune. He is a hearty lover of his country, and of the founders of her independence; and his country certainly reciprocates by cherishing the memory of the noble historian of her TRIALS, TRIUMPHS and GLORY.

WILLIAM BLACK.

WILLIAM BLACK, claimed by many to be the most popular living novelist, was born in Glasgow, Scotland, in November, 1841. In early life, he was a close student, and was most attracted by the study of botany. He was early trained for a painter, which possibly aids him greatly in making the beautiful word-pictures we so often find in his writings. Black is a close observer of nature, and uses natural objects and phenomena to good advantage in his works.

On his book-shelves are found his favorite authors. They are Heine, Alfred de Musset, Thackeray, and George Sand. The particular works of the last two authors which he most admires are "Esmond" and "Consuelo." Marcus Aurelius must not be forgotten as one of his constant literary companions. At the same time, he is a miscellaneous reader. One can see that his books of modern poetry, politics, history, and travel are not merely ornamental. A journalist for some years as well as a novelist, Mr. Black has found it necessary to be thoroughly acquainted with the current literature of his time, as well as with those classic authors of the past whose wisdom and power are the splendid heritage of the present. Upon a table near his fire-place always lie a few books, the latest "Harper's," an American newspaper, etc.

His literary career may be briefly stated as follows: His first essays in literature were some contributions to a Glasgow newspaper on Ruskin, Kingsley, and Carlyle. Then he wrote a series of sketches in imitation of Christopher North for the "Weekly Citizen," the staff of which he subsequently joined, and entered thoroughly into the labors of journalism. In 1864 he went to London with a view to advancement in his profession; two years later, he represented the "Morning Star" as correspondent during the Prusso-Austrian war. Later he became editor of the "London Review," and afterward assistant editor of the "Daily News," a position he relinquished in 1875 to devote his sole time to fiction, thus picking up the threads of a career he had dropped in 1868, when he published his first novel—"Love or Marriage." He has published the followings works: "In Silk Attire," 1868; "A Daughter of Heth," 1871; "The Strange Adventures of a Phaeton," 1872; "Kilmeny" and "Princess of Thule," 1873; "The Maid of Killeena," and "Three Feathers," 1875; "Lady Silverdale's Sweetheart, and Other Stories," 1876. Since 1876, he has published "Madcap Violet," "Green Pastures and Piccadilly," Macleod of Dare," "Sunrise," "Shandon Bells," and "Judith Shakespeare." The last two works were published in "Harper's," in 1882-4. Considering Black's age, the above record is an excellent one. His pen is still busy, and we may expect many noble works from this young Scotch genius.

A little criticism upon the manner of closing one of his novels is thus related by himself: "A short time after the terrible news of the shooting of President Garfield reached this country, a prominent American gentleman, Mr. Carnegie, called upon me, and among other things he said: 'Just before I left home I saw President Garfield. Informing him that I was coming to England, he said, "You will see Black; tell him he ought not to have made 'Macleod of Dare' end tragically—life itself is full of tragedy.' This could only have been a few weeks before he was shot.'" Black acknowledges that Garfield's words, together with the death that followed so soon, made a deep impression upon him. He justifies himself, however, in dealing with the phases of life from his own standpoint, and refuses to be influenced by critics.

A friend of Black thus writes of his personal appearance: "I have seen him under most conditions, and have always found him the same pleasant, sympathetic companion, the same thoughtful, unostentatious, quick-witted gentleman. Tightly built, lithe of limb, strong in arm, capable of great physical endurance, the novelist is nevertheless below the medium height. Short, black hair, a thick brown mustache, a dark hazel eye, a firm mouth, a square forehead, Black gives you the idea of compact strength—a small parcel, so to speak, well packed."

He is well posted upon all the current topics of the day, and has well-formed opinions. He is a ready conversationalist, but understands, at the same time, the most effective use of silence. He is popular in both the New and Old World, and if he continues to improve in his writings, he will certainly rival the great masters of fiction.

His present home is at Brighton, where he lives splendidly by the fruits of his pen. We shall watch his career with unusual interest.

GEORGE H. BOKER.

GEORGE H. BOKER was born in Philadelphia in 1824. At the age of eighteen he graduated at Princeton College. Law was his chosen profession, but after he had completed his legal studies he never entered upon the practice of law. Literature had greater charms for him, hence, like Bryant, he followed the royal path of letters.

In 1847 he published the "Lessons of Life, and other Poems," a volume which was well received. Turning next to the stage, he wrote "Calaynos, a Tragedy." "Calaynos" extended his reputation in America, and, crossing the ocean, was successfully played in London. He also wrote "Anne Boleyn," and the tragedies of "Leonor de Guzman" and "Francesca da Rimini." In 1856 Boker published two volumes of "Plays and Poems," at Boston. These volumes are excellent additions to the best grade of American literature. "His dramas are conceived in the highest style of dramatic art, and rise almost to the dignity of classics." During the late war he produced many stirring patriotic poems, which were collected into a volume, and published at Boston in 1864, as "Poems of the War."

As a recognition of his merit, he was appointed minister resident at Constantinople in 1871, and was afterwards transferred to St. Petersburg.

"The Ivory Carver," "The Black Regiment," and the "Ballad of Sir John Franklin," are most excellent productions, and are familiarly known to nearly every one. As a dramatic and lyric poet, Boker's excellence is acknowledged.

CHARLES FARRER BROWN.

C. F. BROWN was born at Waterford, Maine, April 26, 1834, and, after an unusually successful career as author and public lecturer, he died at Southampton, England, March 6, 1867.

Brown commenced active life as a printer, and worked at the art preservative in Maine, in Boston, and finally in Cleveland, where he became reporter for a daily newspaper. He first learned printing as a trade. His ability, however, soon attracted attention, and he was invited to take the pencil as a reporter. In that capacity he wrote a letter purporting to come from a traveling showman. The letter appeared in 1858, over the nom de plume of Artemus Ward, and attracted considerable attention. Artemus Ward soon became a familiar name in American literature. His writings were humorous and purely original in style. They were copied far and wide, thus spreading the fame of the author. In 1860 Artemus Ward went to New York, where he took the editorial management of "Vanity Fair," a humorous publication. Upon the failure of the "Fair," he entered the lecture field in 1861. His lectures were humorous and very popular. In 1862 appeared "Artemus Ward: His Book." The success of this book called three others from his pen, as follows: In 1865, "Artemus Ward among the Mormons;" 1866, "Artemus Ward among the Fenians;" and 1867, "Artemus Ward in England."

In 1866 he had gone to England, where he lectured with success, his fame as a humorist having crossed the ocean before him. While there, he became a contributor to "Punch." He died of consumption, at the age of thirty-three; or if 1836, as given by some authors, is the date of his birth, he died at thirty-one.

Considering his age, his career was remarkable. In the few years of his life he wrote four books, and lectured in various parts of the United States and England. His last work, as will be seen by comparing the dates, was written in the year of his death. All writers express but one opinion of him, and that is that he was one of the most celebrated humorists of his time.

ELIZABETH BARRETT BROWNING.

Mrs. BROWNING was born in London, England, in 1809, and she died at Casa Guidi, Florence, June 29, 1861.

Her father, Mr. Barrett, was an English country gentleman. Possessing some means, he helped his daughter to acquire an excellent classical education; and, possessing considerable ability, he became, as she says, her public and her critic.

"Her studies were early directed to the poets of antiquity, and, under the guidance of her blind tutor, Boyle, whose name she always warmly cherished, she mastered the rich treasures of Æschylus. The sublime Grecian possessed for her a charm which was only equaled by the fascination held over her wondering spirit by Shakespeare." While she was profoundly versed in Greek literature, and intimately acquainted with all the Attic writers in tragedy and comedy, she was thoroughly versed in pure and undefiled English. In her extensive correspondence with contemporaries, she shows a thorough knowledge of English literature, from Chaucer to her own time.

Physically she was very delicate, but nature made up for her fragile frame by giving her a superior mental and spiritual organization. Miss Mitford, her intimate friend, describes her as a "slight, delicate figure, with a shower of dark curls falling on each side of a most expressive face, large tender eyes, richly fringed by dark eyelashes, and a smile like a sunbeam." Such, in brief, is a description of the attainments and person of the lady who, according to E. C. Stedman, was not only "the greatest female poet that England has produced, but more than this, the most inspired woman so far as known, of all who have composed in ancient or modern tongues or flourished in any land or clime."

Almost before her childhood had passed, she showed remarkable preferences for the arts, but especially for the poetic art. Some of her poems written before she was fifteen, show strong marks of genius, and are worthy of preservation. Her first publication was an "Essay on Mind, and other Poems." This, it is said, was written in her seventeenth year. In 1833 appeared her excellent translation of "Prometheus;" 1838, her second volume of original poetry, "The Seraphim, and other poems;" and in 1839, "The Romance of the Page."

While thus busily engaged in her work, she met with a personal calamity. A blood-vessel burst in her lungs, which forced her to remain at home in close confinement for some time. At length her physician ordered that she be removed to a milder climate. In company with friends she went to reside at Torquay. At that place an accident occurred which saddened her life, and gave a deeper hue of thought and feeling to her poetry. Her favorite brother and two friends were taking a pleasure ride on a small vessel, when the boat sank, and all on board were drowned. The shock caused a severe sickness, from which she never entirely recovered. It was a year before she was able to be removed to her father's house in London. For many years she remained in a darkened chamber, and received no visitors except her own family and a few devoted friends. While thus secluded from the outward world, she read extensively the valuable books in almost every language.

In 1844 she came forth from her seclusion in two volumes of "Poems by Elizabeth Barrett." The melancholy thought showed traces of the sadness of much of her former life.

In 1846, her thirty-seventh year, she was married to Robert Browning, a noted English poet. In hopes of finding health, Mr. Browning removed to Italy. His wish was gratified, for under the sunny skies of Florence, his wife found the health which had forsaken her in her native land. In her adopted home she remained till her death.

The revolutionary outbreak in 1848, furnished the theme for her next work. "Casa Guidi Windows" is a poem relating to the impressions that were made upon her mind by the events which she saw from the windows of

ELIZABETH BARRETT BROWNING.

her house in Florence. It shows great warmth of feeling for the Italians. In 1856 "Aurora Leigh" was published. This is a novel in blank verse, which the poetess declared to be her most mature work. While the poem is full of splendid passages, yet as a whole it is not considered satisfactory. It contains a prodigality of genius, with discordant mixture of material. Notwithstanding the lack of unity, which is so essential for a poem of such magnitude, a large number of critics consider "Aurora Leigh" the chief source of Mrs. Browning's fame. But perhaps an equal number look upon "Casa Guidi Windows" as "containing her ripest growth and greatest intellectual strength." Indeed the circumstances under which this poem was written, were such as to call out her best efforts. She was looking from her window, and beholding the Italians struggling for freedom. Being in full sympathy with them, her utterances were in accordance with her heart—they were lavish and unrestrained. In 1860 appeared her last publication, "Poems Before Congress," which evinced her deep interest in the people of Italy. She died in the following year, and a marble tablet in front of the villa of the Brownings records that in it wrote and died Elizabeth Barrett Browning, who, by her songs, created a golden link between Italy and England, and that in gratitude Florence had erected that memorial. "Last Poems," published in 1862, contained the literary remains of the priestess of English poetry.

Some of her poems are especially admired. "Cowper's Grave," "The Cry of the Children," "A Child Asleep," and "He Giveth His Beloved Sleep," are jewels that shine with the brilliancy of the sun.

"The position of Mrs. Browning as a poet is now yielded. Her genius was perhaps as great as that of any poet of her generation, but circumstances retarded its highest possible development. In certain intellectual qualities she was inferior to Tennyson, and the author of 'Sordello,' but in others she was their superior. Be her exact niche, however, what it may, she occupies a favored place in English literature, and is undoubtedly one of the few leading poets of the nineteenth century. Her poetry is that which refines, chastens, and elevates. Much of it is imperishable, and although she did not reach the height of the few mighty singers of all time, she has shown us the possibility of the highest forms of the poetic art being within the scope of woman's genius."

ROBERT BROWNING.

ROBERT BROWNING was born at Camberwell in Surrey, England, in 1812, and educated at the London University. He is also a Fellow of Balloil College, Oxford.

At the age of twenty-four, Browning attracted public attention by his poem of "Baracelsus." Considering the age of the author, it was a remarkable poem. In 1837 his tragedy of "Stafford" was brought on the stage. His next work was brought out in 1841. "Sordello" was a thin volume, but is esteemed the richest puzzle to all lovers of poetry which was ever given to the world.

His next works were in dramatic form, the most popular being "Pippa Passes." "Pippa is a girl from a silk factory, who passes the various persons of the play at certain critical moments, in the course of her holiday, and becomes, unconsciously to herself, a determining influence on the fortunes of each." Of his eight plays, the one given above, and "A Blot on the Scutcheon," "King Victor and King Charles," "Colombe's Birthday," "Luria," "The Return of the Druses," are the best.

He wrote the two dramatic sketches, "A Soul of Tragedy" and "In a Balcony." The plays and sketches mentioned are superior productions both in conception and execution.

In 1855 he added greatly to his reputation by publishing a volume of fifty poems, entitled "Men and Women." Another volume of character sketches entitled "Dramatis Personae," appeared in 1864. The most extensive of all his works, "The Ring and the Book" was published in 1868. This poem is in four volumes of blank verse. It is an Italian story of the seventeenth century. Its merits and faults are equally great, and yet it amply repays the reader for all time given to its perusal. In 1871 appeared "Balaustion's Adventure, including a Transcript from Euripides;" 1871, "Prince Hohenstiel-Schwangau, Savior of Society;" 1872, "Fifine at the Fair;" 1873, "Red Cotton Night-Cap Country;" 1875, "Aristophanes' Apology, including a Transcript from Euripides, being the last Adventure of Balaustion;" 1875, "The Inn Album."

Obscurity, and eccentricities of style and expression are Browning's chief defects. In spite of these defects, the pure poetic gold predominates in his writings, and he has proven strong poetic powers alike in thought, description, passion, and conception of character. While his extended poems are marred by obscurity, most of his shorter poems are particularly happy and beautiful. Among these may be mentioned, "The Pied Piper of Hamelin," "A Child's Story," "How They Brought the Good News from Ghent to Aix," "Evelyn Hope," "My Lost Duchess," and numerous descriptions of the sunny South. These are among the very best of their kind.

Robert Browning stands at the head of what is known as the psychological school of poetry. Latterly his merits have been more readily acknowledged in his native country; and for nearly forty years he has been recognized by the world as one of our most original and intellectual poets.

WILLIAM CULLEN BRYANT.

BRYANT was born at Cummington, Hampshire County, Massachusetts, November 3, 1794, and, after an unusually long and active literary life, he died in New York, June 12, 1878.

His father was Peter Bryant, a physician of considerable literary culture, and a person who had traveled quite extensively. The father took a unusual interest in the culture of his children, and he was amply rewarded for all his pains. There is an unauthenticated tradition that the first Bryant of whom there is any account in America, came over in the Mayflower. Mr. Stephen Bryant came over from England, and was settled at Plymouth, Massachusetts, in 1836. Stephen's son Ichabod was the father of Philip Bryant, and Philip, of Peter, the father of William Cullen.

Bryant's mother was Miss Sarah Snell, of Mayflower stock, being a descendant of John Alden. Thus our poet has an honorable and cultured ancestry. Strict Puritanical discipline was the order of the day, hence the young poet's life did not fall in pleasant places, so far as recreations were concerned. While the children were held with a steady hand, their educational and moral interests were considered with conscientious earnestness.

For some time after his birth young Bryant was very frail, and the chances for living seemed decided against him. His head was of such enormous size as to cause his father much uneasiness. Dr. Bryant decided that the size of William's head must be reduced. He thought to accomplish the desired result by giving the babe a cold bath daily. Accordingly two of his students took the child each morning and plunged it, head and all, into a clear, cold spring that bubbled from the ground near the house. Whether the size of the head was reduced or not, we are unable to tell, but the world of popular literature has ample cause to rejoice over the massive size of Bryant's head and heart and mind. In 1810, at the age of sixteen, he entered Williams College, in Williamstown, Massachusetts, where he studied for two years. He soon distinguished himself for his attainments in language and polite literature. In 1812 he withdrew from college and entered upon the study of law. After three years of preparation he was admitted to the bar in 1815. He practiced first at Plainfield, and afterward at Great Barrington. Bryant attained high standing in the local and state courts, but his tastes inclined him rather to literature than the law.

Bryant's literary record commenced when he was only ten years of age, and even before that age he communicated lines to the local papers. "With a precocity rivaling that of Cowley or Chatterton, Bryant, at the age of thirteen, wrote a satirical poem on the Jeffersonian party, which he published

WILLIAM CULLEN BRYANT.

in 1808, under the title of "The Embargo." By referring to history, you will notice that the English orders in council had been issued in retaliation for the decrees of Napoleon. The above action of foreign powers led Jefferson to lay an embargo on American shipping. This formed the subject of Bryant's satire, "The Embargo." This poem and "The Spanish Revolution" were published in 1808, and passed to a second edition in the succeeding year. The age of the author was called in question, and his friends came forward with proofs that the lad was only thirteen when he wrote the satire. "The Genius of Columbia" was written in 1810, and "An Ode for the Fourth of July," in 1812. When he was only eighteen years of age he wrote the imperishable poem, "Thanatopsis."

In the "Bryant Homestead Book," of 1870, is written the following: "It was here at Cummington, while wandering in the primeval forests, over the floor of which were scattered the gigantic trunks of fallen trees, moldering for long years, and suggesting an indefinitely remote antiquity, and where silent rivulets crept along through the carpet of leaves, the spoil of thousands of summers, that the poem entitled 'Thanatopsis' was composed. The young poet had read the poems of Kirke White, which, edited by Southey, were published about that time, and a small volume of Southey's miscellaneous poems; and some lines of those authors had kindled his imagination, which, going forth over the face of the inhabitants of the globe, sought to bring under one broad and comprehensive view the destinies of the human race in the present life, and the perpetual rising and passing away of generation after generation who are nourished by the fruits of its soil, and find a resting-place in its bosom." When the poem was sent to the "North American Review," Richard H. Dana was so surprised at its excellence that he doubted whether it was the product of an American. Bryant also contributed several prose articles to the "Review." While in the practice of his profession he wrote some of his finest poems. Of these we will name lines "To a Waterfowl," "Green River," "A Winter Piece," "The West Wind," "The Burial-Place," "Blessed are they that Mourn,", "No Man Knoweth his Sepulchre," "A Walk at Sunset," and "The Hymn to Death." While Bryant was writing "The Hymn to Death," his father was dying at the age of fifty-four. In the same year he married Miss Frances Fairchild, and also published his first collection of verse. In 1821 Bryant wrote "The Ages," and delivered it before the Phi Beta Kappa Society of Harvard College. At that time, our poet was recognized as a writer of great merit. From that time till he left his profession and took up his pen for a support, he wrote about thirty poems. We here name some of them: "The Indian Girl's Lament," "An Indian Story," "Monument Mountain," "The Massacre at Scio," "Song of the Stars," "March," "The Rivulet," "After a Tempest," "Hymn to the North Star," "A Forest Hymn," and "June." We pause here to quote Bryant's wish that he might die

"In flowery June
When brooks send up a cheerful tune,
And groves a joyous sound;"

and to remark that in that beautiful month he passed to his rest.

This brings our poet to 1825, when, through the efforts of Mr. Sedgwick and Mr. Verplanck, he was appointed assistant editor of the "New York Review" and "Atheneum Magazine." Bidding adieu to courts and law books, he became a follower of Apollo. In 1825 Bryant removed to New York to enter upon his new duties. The "Review" did not prosper, and in one year it was merged into the "New York Literary Gazette." In a few months this magazine was consolidated with the "United States Literary Gazette," which in turn passed into the "United States Review." These publications were not profitable, although they contained the writings of such men as Bryant, Halleck, Willis, Dana, Bancroft, and Longfellow. Our poet next connected himself with the "Evening Post," and remained with that journal till his death. Between 1827 and 1830 he assisted in the editorial management of the "Talisman," a very successful annual, and also contributed the tales of "Medfield," and "The Skeleton's Cave" to a book entitled "Tales of the Glauber Spa." A complete edition of his poems was published in New York in 1832, and in England about the same time. The English edition was brought out through the influence of Washington Irving, who wrote a laudatory preface. John Wilson praised the work in an article in "Blackwood's Magazine." This volume established Bryant's reputation abroad, and made him almost as popular in England as in America.

In 1834, the poet, rich in fame, sailed for Europe. He traveled through France, Italy, and Germany. Returning to his native land, he spent several years in literary work, when in 1845 he again crossed the ocean. In 1849 he made his third journey abroad, and extended his travels into Egypt and Syria. He also traveled extensively over the various parts of the United States and Cuba. The letters written by him in his wanderings were collected into book form, and entitled "Letters of a Traveler." In 1857 and 1858 he again visited Europe, and, as the result of this journey, soon appeared "Letters from Spain and other Countries." A new and complete edition of his poems was printed in 1855; and in 1863 appeared a volume of new poems entitled "Thirty Poems." In 1870 appeared his translation of the "Iliad," and in 1871 of the "Odyssey." These great epics were translated into English blank verse, which were considered the best English version in print. In 1876 Bryant and Sydney Howard Gay commenced a "History of the United States," but the work was not complete when the poet died. The book was to extend through four finely illustrated volumes.

"Bryant was frequently called upon to pay public tributes to the memory of Americans. On the death of the artist, Thomas Cole, in 1848, he pronounced a funeral oration; in 1852 he delivered a lecture upon the life and writings of James Fenimore Cooper; and in 1860 he paid a similar tribute to his friend Washington Irving; he made an address on the life and achievements of S. F. B. Morse, on the occasion of the dedication of his statue in Central Park, New York, in 1871; addresses on Shakespeare and Scott on similar occasions in 1872; and one on Mazzini in 1878; on his return from which, a fall resulted in his death."

Bryant's prose writings are marked by pure and vigorous English, and he stands in the front rank as a poet. We quote from Professor Wilson's review of the poet's first volume, published in England: "The chief charm of Bryant's genius consists in a tender pensiveness, a moral melancholy, breathing over all his contemplations, dreams, and reveries, even such as in the main are glad, and giving assurance of a pure spirit, benevolent to all living creatures, and habitually pious in the felt omnipresence of the Creator. His poetry overflows with natural religion—with what Wordsworth calls the religion of the woods. This is strictly applicable to 'Thanatopsis' and 'Forest Hymn;' but Washington Irving is so far right that Bryant's grand merit is his nationality and his power of painting the American landscape, especially in its wild, solitary and magnificent forms. His diction is pure and lucid, with scarcely a flaw, and he is master of blank verse."

We cannot close this sketch better than by showing the poet's devotion to his country in his own words: "We are not without the hope that those who read what we have written, will see in the past, with all its vicissitudes, the promise of a prosperous and honorable future, of concord at home, and peace and respect abroad; and that the same cheerful piety which leads the good man to put his personal trust in a kind Providence, will prompt the good citizen to cherish an equal confidence in regard to the destiny reserved for our beloved country."

BULWER-LYTTON.

EDWARD GEORGE EARLE LYTTON BULWER-LYTTON was born May 25, 1805; and he died at Torquay, on the 18th of January, 1873, and is buried in Westminster Abbey.

His father was General Bulwer, of Hayden Hall and Wood-Dalling, Norfolk, England. His mother was of the ancient family of Lytton, of Kneedworth, county of Hertfordshire. We see from the above that Edward came from noble parents, and from two lines of honored ancestry. General Bulwer died when Edward, the youngest of three sons, was but two years old, and thus the mother had the full care, and the education, of the children to provide for.

The mother was a lady of culture and refinement. Her even temper and tenderness were remarkable, and her memory was ever held most sacred

LORD LYTTON.

by her gifted son. In dedicating his works to her, he said—"From your graceful and accomplished taste I early learned that affection for literature which has exercised so large an influence over the pursuits of my life; and you who were my first guide, were my earliest critic."

Edward was not sent to the public schools, but he received a thorough education from his mother and private teachers whom she employed. In later life he was honored by various schools. Oxford conferred upon him the degree of D. C. L. in 1853.

His literary work began when he was only thirteen, and at fifteen he published a volume of poems entitled "Ismael, an Oriental Tale, with Other Poems." In 1825, at Cambridge, he won the chancellor's medal with a poem on "Sculpture." At the time he wrote the prize poem he was a fellow-commoner of Trinity Hall. He spent the long vacations in wandering over England, Scotland and France. His literary record extends over more than half a century, and during that time he was most active. As Scott said of Byron, there was "no reposing under the shade of his laurels—no living upon the resources of past reputation—his foot was always in the arena, his shield hung always in the list." In 1826 he printed "Weeds and Wild Flowers," a collection for private circulation; and in 1827 appeared "O'Neil, or a Rebel," a romance in heroic couplets, of the patriotic struggle in Ireland. "The Siamese Twins," printed in 1831, and his juvenile poems, he afterward ignored.

In addition to what has already been given, the following is an outline of his work: "Falkland," his first romance, appeared anonymously in 1827; "Pelham," 1828, a brilliant novel full of witty paragraphs; "The Disowned," 1828, a novel that did not attain great popularity; "Devereux," 1829; "Paul Clifford," 1830; "Eugene Aram," and "Godolphin," 1833; "The Pilgrims of the Rhine," and "The Last Days of Pompeii," 1834; "Rienzi," 1835; "Athens, Its Rise and Fall," 1836; "Ernest Maltravers," 1837; "Leila," "Calderon," and "Alice, or The Mysteries," being a sequel to "Ernest Maltravers," 1838.

In addition to his literary work, Bulwer became editor of "The New Monthly," as successor to Campbell, in 1833. "The Monthly Chronicle" he projected in 1838. To this magazine he contributed the fantastic "Zicci," but the magazine expired before the story was completed. The story was afterwards developed into "Zanoni," a romance of which the author was especially proud. It was not, however, fully appreciated by the public.

In the most busy period of his life, while books were flowing from his pen in almost a steady stream, he was a member of parliament. He disclosed eminent ability in governmental matters. In 1831 he was returned for St. Ivens; and he sat in parliament for Lincoln from 1832 to 1841. He spoke in favor of the Reform Bill, and was instrumental in securing the reduction of newspaper stamp duties.

Bulwer contributed a strong political pamphlet on the crisis in 1834. His leading political aim was to aristocratize the community. He sought to elevate the masses in character and feeling to the standard of the aristocracy. Thus he would make "superior education, courteous manners, and high honor," instead of wealth and pedigree, the special features of honored English citizenship.

Between 1838 and 1841 he turned aside to try his hand at play writing. "The Lady of Lyons," "Richelieu," and "Money" appeared within the three years, and they have kept the stage ever since. It is said that no Englishman not himself an actor has written so many permanently successful plays.

From 1841 to 1852 he had no seat in parliament. Upon succeeding to his mother's estate in 1843, he took her name, and was afterward known as Bulwer-Lytton, or as he is now popularly known, Lord Lytton. "Before 1849, when he opened a new vein with "The Caxtons," he produced five works in his familiar style: "Night and Morning," 1841; "Zanoni," 1842; "The Last of the Barons," the most historically solid, and perhaps the most effective of his romances, 1843; "Lucretia, or the Children of the Night," 1847; "Harold, The Last of the Saxon Kings," 1848. In this period, also, Lytton was making a desperate effort to win high rank as a poet. He published a volume of poems in 1842. Besides a volume of translations from Schiller in 1844, he published "The New Timon," a satire, in 1845, and "King Arthur," a romantic epic. The keen-edged satire, "St. Stephen's," a gallery of parliamentary portraits from the time of Queen Anne, was not published till in 1860. "The Lost Tales of Miletus," and a translation of Horace's "Odes," were Lytton's last essays in verse.

In 1848 he took up a new style in "The Caxtons," in which he sustained himself nobly. "My Novel" appeared in 1853, and "What Will He Do With It?" in 1858. The sub-title of "My Novel" is "Varieties of English Life." "A Strange Story" was contributed to "All the Year Round" in 1862. "A serial story of the kind made a new call on his resources, but he was equal to it, and fairly rivaled the school of Dickens in the art of sustaining thrilling interest to the close." In 1872-73 "The Parisians" appeared in "Blackwood's Magazine," and "The Coming Race" was written anonymously. These two works were published by his son and successor in the title, as the romance of "Kenelm Chillingly." Upon his death, in 1873, Lord Lytton had an historical romance, "Pausanius the Spartan," partly written. Thus he died, after having written about fifty separate works.

In addition to the work which we have already described, we will write a paragraph upon his return to parliament. In 1852 he returned as a member from Hertfordshire, and sat on the conservative side. He was colonial secretary in Lord Derby's government from 1858 to 1859; and in 1866 he was raised to the peerage as Baron Lytton. He was not a great orator, but he was an earnest and valuable worker and writer.

His son, the present Lord Lytton, has, with a just pride, said of his father, "Whether as an author, standing apart from all literary cliques or coteries, or as a politician, never wholly subject to the exclusive dictation of any political party, he always thought and acted in sympathy with every popular aspiration for the political, social, and intellectual improvement of the whole national life."

JOHN BUNYAN.

JOHN BUNYAN, the most popular religious writer in the English language, was born at Elstow, about a mile from Bedford, England, in the year 1628; and he died Aug. 31, 1688. His father was a tinker, a hereditary caste of the lowest grade of people in England. They wandered about the country in a kind of gipsy-life, and " were generally vagrants and pilferers." Bunyan's father was of a better grade than most of the tribe. Having gained some means, he quit his wandering life and settled in a fixed residence where he could send his son to the village school. Here the boy learned to read and write. His scholastic training, however, was extremely meager, and his manuscript was full of errors in grammar and orthography. John's boyhood belongs to the period in English history when the Puritan spirit was in its highest vigor. The boy's powerful imagination and sensibility amounted almost to a disease, hence it is not surprising that, under Puritanic influence, he should have been haunted by religious terrors. Even before he was ten years old, he had fits of remorse and despair, and in his dreams he imagined that fiends were trying to fly away with him. The common belief is that Bunyan was a very wicked character in his early life,—that he was a worthless contemptible profligate, and the most thoughtless wretch on the face of the earth. Nothing could be farther from the truth than is the above opinion. In his writing, as a devout man, he bemoans the exceeding sinfulness of his early life. His strong regrets for his sins have misled public opinion, while in reality, at the age of eighteen, he was a person of gravity and innocence. Outside of the most austerely puritanical circles, he would have been considered a person of reasonably good habits. The worst that can be said of him is that he had formed the habit of swearing, but a single reproof from a lady "cured him so effectually that he never offended again." At the age of seventeen the tinker's son enlisted in the Parliamentary army. An event occurred in the decisive campaign of 1645, which gave a lasting color to his thoughts. One of Bunyan's comrades having taken Bunyan's place was killed by a shot from the town. Bunyan considered that he was saved by special interposition of Providence. The glimpses which he caught of the pomp of war, served him a good turn, in furnishing material from which to draw illustrations of sacred things. After a few months of army life he returned home and married. His wife brought him a few pious books. One by one he broke off from all habits and modes of life that were objectionable to the Puritans. He became constant in his attendance at prayers and sermons. Upon turning his naturally excitable mind wholly toward religious subjects, he was haunted by a succession of visions and thoughts that seemed likely to drive him to suicide or insanity. A few circumstances will illustrate his condition. He said, "If I have not faith, I am lost; if I have faith, I can work miracles." Then to test his faith, he was tempted to cry to the mud-puddles near his house, "Be ye dry," and to stake his hopes of eternity on the result. Again he was possessed with the notion that the day of grace for his time was passed, and he was a few months too late in his efforts to become a Christian. At times he doubted whether the Turks were not right and the Christians wrong. While doubts and uncertainties and fantasies were flitting through his mind, " he was troubled by a maniacal impulse which prompted him to pray to trees, to a broomstick and to the parish bull. Next the deepest clouds surrounded him. Hideous forms floated before him, and sounds of cursing were in his ears. He had a curiosity to commit the unpardonable sin, to utter blasphemy, and to renounce his share of the benefits of the redemption. In this mental condition, he envied the beasts and trees, and the stones of the streets. Bunyan feared that he had committed the sin against the Holy Ghost." His body, though cast in a sturdy mould, and though still in the highest vigor of youth, trembled, whole days together, with fear of death and judgment. Finally the clouds broke, and Bunyan enjoyed peace, but it was several years before his overstrained nervous system was fully restored. He joined the Baptist society at Bedford, and after some time passed as a member of the congregation, he began to preach. Bitter persecutions soon overtook him. After he had preached about five years, the Restoration occurred, and the dissenters were greatly oppressed. Bunyan was flung into Bedford jail in 1660, where he remained almost continuously for twelve years. On several occasions he could have purchased his liberty by promising to leave England, or quit preaching. "If you let me out to-day, I will preach again to-morrow," was his reply. His only books while in prison were the Bible and "Fox's Book of Martyrs." Bunyan spent much time in controversy, but gradually he came to understand in what direction lay his strength, and "Pilgrim's Progress" stole silently into the world. Probably this book has had a greater sale than any other book published excepting only the Bible. The second part of the book appeared in 1684, but the exact date of the first part we do not know. The "Holy War" soon followed. These two works are the best allegories ever placed in print. So popular did the author become with the lower and middle classes, that he was commonly called "Bishop Bunyan," and many Puritans are said to have begged with their dying breath that their coffins might be placed as near as possible to the coffin of the author of "Pilgrim's Progress."

ROBERT BURNS.

Robert Burns was born in a cottage near Ayr, January 25, 1759, and on the 21st of July, 1796, he passed away.

His father, William Burns, was a small farmer, who had to work hard, but who used every means in his power to train up his children properly. Carlyle thus refers to the poet's father: "He was a man of thoughtful, intense character, as the best of our peasants are, valuing knowledge, possessing some, and open-minded for more, of 'keen insight and devout heart,

ROBERT BURNS

friendly and fearless; a fully unfolded man seldom found in any rank of society, and worth descending far in society to seek. . . . .
Had he been ever so little richer, the whole might have issued otherwise. But poverty sunk the whole family even below the reach of our cheap school system, and Burns remained a hardworked plow boy." Robert was taught English well, which formed a foundation "on which to erect the miracles of genius." His books were few, including the "Spectator," Pope's works, Allen Ramsey, and a collection of "English Songs." Later, of course, his library grew so as to include numerous standard works. What books he had were thoroughly studied, and "his mind grew up with original and robust vigor."

In their extreme poverty, Burns was obliged to work early and late, to assist in the support of his father's family. At the same time, he was so passionately fond of books, that he would eat his meals with one hand while holding his book in the other. He would carry volumes to the fields to read in spare moments. "I pored over the collection of songs," he tells us, "driving my cart or walking to labor, song by song, verse by verse, carefully noting the true, tender, sublime or fustian." While yet following the plow, he gathered "round him the memories and the traditions of his country till they became a mantle and a crown," and he was inspired to wish—

"That I for poor auld Scotland's sake
Some useful plan or book could make,
Or sing a sang at least."

Oh, Burns, auroral visions are gilding your horizon as you walk in glory, if not in joy, "behind your plough upon the mountain side." Soon will the country murmur of you from sea to sea, and "poor auld Scotland" shall live in perennial glory in the songs which you have sung.

In Robert's twenty-fifth year his father died. The poet and his brother Gilbert continued to run the farm, but they were scarcely able to make a living. "Meanwhile he became intimate with his future wife, Jean Armour, but her father discountenanced the match," and Burns decided to seek refuge in exile. He engaged as book-keeper to a slave estate in Jamaica, and had taken passage for the West Indies, when he wrote his lines ending—

"Adieu, my native banks of Ayr."

Before the ship started, however, the wonderful success of his first volume, which was published at Kilmarnock, in June, 1786, withheld him from his project, and changed the current of his life. This volume contained "The Twa Dogs," "The Author's Prayer," "Address to the Deil," "The Vision," and "The Dream," "Halloween," "The Cotter's Saturday Night," lines "To a Mouse," "To a Daisy," "Man was made to Mourn," "Epistle to Davie," and some of his most popular songs. "This epitome of a genius so marvelous and so varied, took his audience by storm." Robert Heron tells us that old and young, grave and gay, learned and ignorant, were alike transported.

While this edition brought the author only £20, yet it "introduced him to the *literati* of Edinburgh, whither he was invited, and where he was welcomed, feasted, and admired and patronized." In 1787 the second edition of the "Poems" brought Burns £400. This sum enabled him to travel through England and the East Highlands. In 1788 "he took a new farm at Ellisland on the Ninth, settled there, married, lost his little money, and wrote, among other pieces, "Auld Lang Syne," and "Tam O'Shanter." He was appointed excise officer of the district, in 1789, at a salary of £50; but in 1791 he removed to a similar position at Dumfries worth £70. In 1792 the poet wrote about one hundred songs to supply the "Melodies of Scotland" with accompaniments. The best of these songs will continue to ring in the ear of every Scotchman as long as time lasts.

For his contributions to this work, Burns' wife received a shawl, and he received £5 and David Allan's picture representing "The Cotter's Saturday Night." He wrote an indignant letter, and never afterward composed for money.

But he was growing prematurely old, and his nights of festivity hastened the closing hour. His hands commenced to shake, his appetite failed, and his spirits sank into a deep gloom. He, wrote in April, 1796, "I fear it will be some time before I tune my lyre again. By Babel's stream I have sat and wept. I have only known existence by the pressure of sickness and counted time by the repercussion of pain." On the fourth of July his condition was pronounced critical. A tremor pervaded his frame, his tongue was parched, and his mind delirious; but soon the golden cord was loosed, and his spirit took its flight. He was buried July 26, with military honors, as belonging to the Dumfries Volunteers. The sun shone brightly on that day, and while the earth "was heaped up, and the green sod was laid over him, the immense crowd stood gazing for some minutes' space, then melted silently away."

Burns had faults. Like Byron and Poe, he was given to feasts and festivities. But with all his faults he had fine poetic sensibilities. He frequently regretted his weaknesses, by wishing that he could "lie down in his mother's lap and be at peace." In early youth his constitution was broken and his nerves over-strained by hard work. For three weeks at a time he groaned under the miseries of a diseased nervous system, and of headaches. The following circumstance will illustrate his excellent parts: Burns' brothers and sister were living on the farm and supporting their aged mother. They had become involved, and upon his return from Edinburgh the poet gave the children £180 to save the family from ruin. "I give myself no airs on this," said he, "for it was mere selfishness on my part. I was conscious that the wrong scale of the balance was pretty heavily charged, and I thought that throwing a little filial and fraternal affection into the scale in my favor, might help to smooth matters at the grand reckoning."

Sir Walter Scott tells us of having seen Burns shed tears over a print representing a soldier lying dead in the snow, his dog sitting in misery on one side, on the other his widow with a child in her arms.

Burns compares himself to an Æolian harp, strung to every wind of heaven. His genius flows over all living and lifeless things with a sympathy that finds nothing mean or insignificant. An uprooted daisy becomes in his page an enduring emblem of the fate of artless maid and simple bard. He disturbs a mouse's nest and finds in the "tim'rous beastie" a fellow mortal doomed, like himself, to "thole the winter's sleety dribble," and draws his oft repeated moral. He walks abroad and, in a verse that glints with the light of its own rising sun before the fierce sarcasm of the "Holy Fair," describes the melodies of a "simmer Sunday morn." He loiters by Afton Water and "murmurs by the running brook a music sweeter than its own." He stands by a roofless tower, where "the howlet mourns in her dewy bower," and "sets the wild echoes flying," and adds to a perfect picture of the scene, his famous vision of "Libertie." In a single stanza he concentrates the sentiments of many "Night Thoughts."

> "The pale moon is setting beyond the white wave,
> And time is setting wi' me, O."

Burns is Scotland condensed in a personality. "Let who will make her laws, Burns has made her songs, which her emigrants recall by the long wash of Australasian seas, in which maidens are wooed, by which mothers lull their infants, which return through open casements unto dying ears,—they are the links, the watchwords, the masonic symbols of our race."

LORD BYRON.

GEORGE NOEL GORDON BYRON was born at Holles Street, London, Jan. 22, 1788, and he died while in the service of the Greeks, at Missolonghi, April 19, 1824.

It may not be uninteresting to note the ancestry of Byron. His father was Captain John Byron of the Guards, a profligate officer, who eloped to France with a divorced lady, and then married again in order to gain money to pay his debts. His grand-uncle, whom our author succeeded in the title, killed a neighbor in a drunken brawl, was tried before the House of Lords, and acquitted; and he then conducted himself so badly as to gain the appellation of "wicked Lord Byron." The poet's grandfather was Admiral Byron, known as "Foul-weather Jack," who had as little rest on sea as the poet on land, and who had the virtues without the vices of the race. The family of Byrons distinguished themselves in the field; seven brothers fought in the battle of Edgehill. No literary branches of any note grew from the family

tree of the Byrons till the birth of our author, excepting that in the reign of Charles II there was a Lord Byron who wrote some good verses. One writer has tried to find a poetic ancestry for our author by connecting the Byrons of the 17th century with the family of Sidney. Byron's mother was Catherine Gordon, heiress of Gight in Aberdeenshire. "The lady's fortune was soon squandered by her profligate husband, and she retired to the city of Aberdeen, to bring up her son on a reduced income of about £130 per annum. The little lame boy, endeared to all in spite of his mischief, succeeded his grand-uncle, William, and became Lord Byron, in his eleventh year." The happy mother sold off her effects and went with her son to Newstead Abbey. This estate had been conferred on Sir John Byron by Henry VIII, and Charles I had ennobled the family as a reward for high and honorable service in the royal cause during the Civil War.

While Byron came from an honored and noble ancestry, yet he was unfortunate in his parentage. Deserted by his father, he was left to the uncertain training of a mother who was moved by the extremes of indulgent fondness and vindictive disfavor. In her fits of anger, he was her "lame brat," and her discipline consisted in throwing things at him; while in her pleasant moods he was her "darling boy," and the recipient of her kisses. Between these extremes she lost all control over him. He became self-willed and resisted all efforts to control him by sullen resistance or defiant mockery. This characteristic followed him through life, and, without doubt, may be traced to his parental training.

Upon succeeding to the title of Lord Byron, the youth was sent to the school at Dulwich, and from thence to Harrow. In 1805 he was removed to Trinity College, Cambridge, where he studied for about two years. His school life was not particularly brilliant. He gained large stores of general information, but made little progress in his classical studies. The head master of the school at Harrow received him as a "wild northern colt," very much behind his age in Greek and Latin. According to his own account, he was always rebelling and getting into mischief; yet he managed to keep up his reputation for general information by reading every history he could get hold of, and by studying the English classics. Perhaps the most profitable time of his life was the year's vacation spent at Southwell with the Pigotts. The genial encouragement which they gave him expanded his poetic impulses and marked the dawn of his genius. While at Harrow he had been busy scribbling verses, and the admiration expressed by the Pigotts led him to publish a collection entitled "Hours of Idleness." Upon his return to Cambridge, he found his volume well received. The applause which it gained encouraged him to make literature a profession. He accordingly made a careful examination of himself, including his acquirements. The rest of his college life was spent in collecting his powers to make a grand struggle for fame.

In 1808 a savage attack was made upon him through the *Edinburgh Review*. It is said that Byron never acted except under the influence of love or defiance. The attack in the *Review* stirred our poet to action, and "English Bards and Scotch Reviewers," a scorching satire, was the result. It is understood that Lord Brougham wrote the criticism, but Byron's reply was a complete punishment of the objects of his wrath. This was Byron's first literary battle, and he could have said, as did the hero of Lake Erie, "We have met the enemy, and they are ours." With the wreath of triumph still fresh on his brow, the young lord started, in 1809, for a tour of the continent. For two years he wandered over Spain, Albania, Greece, Turkey and Asia Minor.

For some time after his return, he lived at Newstead very unhappily, but he busied himself correcting the proof sheets of "Childe Harold." Finally he went to London to enter politics. He took his seat in the House of Lords, and spoke two or three times on important measures. In the spring of 1812 the first two cantos of "Childe Harold" appeared in print. It gained an instantaneous and wide-spread popularity. "I awoke one morning," he said, "and found myself famous." "The effect was not confined to England; Byron at once had all Europe as his audience, because he spoke to them on a theme in which they were all deeply concerned. He spoke to them, too, in language which was not merely a naked expression of their most intense feeling; the spell by which he held them was all the stronger that he lifted them with the irresistible power of song above the passing anxieties of the moment." A moment's call upon our historic memories will show why " Childe Harold " pleased all Europe. It appeared about the time Napoleon set out for Moscow. It was with difficulty that an English army could defend itself in Portugal, and the English nation was trembling for its safety. The movements of the dreaded Bonaparte were being watched by all eyes, and every state in Europe was shaking to its foundation. At such a time as this, " Childe Harold " "entered the absorbing tumult of a hot and feverish struggle, and opened a way in the dark clouds gathering over the contestants through which they could see the blue vault and the shining stars."

In his second canto, Byron turned from the battlefields of Spain,

<blockquote>With blood-red tresses deepening in the sun,
And death-shot glowing in his fiery hands—</blockquote>

to "august Athena," "ancient of days," and the "vanished hero's lofty mound," thus placing before the world the departed greatness of Greece.

Young Lord Byron became the lion of the hour, and the center of London society. In 1813 he produced "Giaour," and "The Bride of Abydos;" 1814, "Corsair," and "Lara;" 1816, "Siege of Corinth" and "Parisina." Omitting the rest of his social life till the close of this sketch, we will now finish, in brief, the record of his principal literary work. Leaving England, he spent the remainder of his life at Geneva, Venice, Ravenna, and in other parts of the continent.

In 1816 appeared the third canto of " Childe Harold " and the " Prisoner of Chillon;" 1817, "Manfred," the "Lament of Tasso," and "Beppo;" 1818, "Ode to Venice," "Mazeppa," and completed "Childe Harold;" 1820 translated the first canto of "Morgante Maggiore," the "Prophesy of Dante," translation of "Francesca de Rimini," "Marino Faliero," and "The Blues." From 1821 to 1823 he finished " Don Juan," and wrote " Sardanapalus," "Letters on Bowles," "The Two Foscari," "Cain," "Heaven and Earth," "Werner," "Deformed Transformed," "The Age of Bronze," and "The Island."

Having been appointed by the Greeks commander-in-chief of an expedition against Lepanto, he was about to enter upon his duties, when he was taken sick. All efforts to save him failed, and he died in 1824.

Byron's love disappointments were numerous; but in 1815 he married Miss Milbanke, a northern heiress, and daughter of Sir Ralph Milbanke. Ida, an only daughter, was born in the following December. Lady Byron left him in about one year, and refused to return. Their union seems to have been unfortunate, as they were not adapted to each other. His " Farewell to Lady Byron " was written in sincerity and bitterness of heart, and it is a poem of much tenderness. The thick gloom and the numerous misfortunes that settled upon Lord Byron, caused him to leave his native land forever, and quiet trouble in the pleasures and stirring scenes of the continent.

In many respects Byron's life is but a repetition of the life of Burns,— the one a lord, the other a peasant, but both singularly brilliant and yet unfortunate; loved and yet despised, and both dying from excesses in the very prime of life. It is difficult to write of such men; for their biographers usually paint their portraits by putting in all the shadows and leaving out most of the lights. This principle of biography we cannot adopt. We must consider Byron as one of the remarkable literary men of his day. His genius will be a source of wonder and delight to all who love to contemplate the workings of human passion in solitude and society, and the rich effects of taste and imagination.

When we see his uncontrolled passions lifted into great surging billows, like the wild unrest of the ocean, and then see him penning his farewell to his wife and child, while the tears are falling like rain upon the paper as he writes, we cannot find it in our heart to write unkindly of him. We simply repeat what Joaquin Miller said of

BURNS AND BYRON.

In men whom men condemn as ill
I find so much of goodness still,
In men whom men pronounce divine
I find so much of sin and blot,
I hesitate to draw a line
Between the two, where God has not.

THOMAS CARLYLE.

CARLYLE was born December 4, 1795, in the village of Ecclefechan, in Annandale, Scotland. His birthplace is a fine pastoral district, famous in Border stories, and rich in ancient castles and Roman remains.

Carlyle's father was a farmer. He refers to his mother as being affectionate, pious, and more than ordinarily intelligent.

He commenced his studies in the grammar school of Annan, and afterwards went to Edinburgh University. At the latter place he began to study for the church, but changed his mind before completing the academical course.

Having excelled in mathematics, he became a teacher of that branch successively at Annan, Kirkcaldy, and Fifeshire. In 1818 Carlyle went to Edinburgh, where he had the range of the University Library, and where he wrote a number of short biographies and other articles for the Edinburgh Encyclopædia.

In 1823 he published the "Life of Schiller" in the "London Magazine," and afterwards, in 1825, in book form. In 1824 he translated Legendre's "Geometry," prefixing an essay on Proportion, and translated Goethe's "Wilhelm Meister." In 1825 Carlyle married Jane Welsh, a lineal descendant of John Knox. The lady possessed a small property in Dumfriesshire, and after about three years' residence in Edinburgh she and Mr. Carlyle retired to her estate. Before leaving Edinburgh, however, he had published four volumes of "Specimens of German Romance," and written essays on "Jean Paul" and "German Literature."

While in his country residence, Carlyle wrote papers for the "Foreign Review." He also wrote his "Sartor Resartus," which after being rejected by several publishers, appeared in "Fraser's Magazine" in 1833-'34. In 1834 he quit his quiet retreat for a house in a suburb of London. His reputation as a critical and popular writer being fully established, he entered the lecture field. In 1837 he delivered a series of lectures on "German Literature," and on the "History of Literature, or the Successive Periods of European Culture." In 1839 his subject was "Revolutions of Modern Europe," and in 1840, "Heroes and Hero Worship." These lectures added greatly to Carlyle's popularity. The author's next book appeared in 1837, being "The French Revolution," a history. This is the ablest of all the author's works, and is indeed one of the most remarkable books of the age. The first perusal of it forms a sort of era in a man's life, and fixes forever in his memory the ghastly panorama of the Revolution, its scenes and actors. His next two works were political. The first, "Chartism," appeared in 1839, and the second, "Past and Present," 1843. In 1845 he published "Oliver Cromwell's Letters and Speeches, with Elucidations," in two volumes. The work was admirably done, and was of special service to history. His next work was a series of political tracts, entitled "Latter-day Pamphlets," which appeared in 1850; and in 1851 he published the "Life of John Sterling," an affectionate tribute to the memory of a friend.

The first portion of Carlyle's great work, "Life of Frederick the Great," appeared in 1858, and the laborious history was completed in six volumes in 1865. In 1866 he was elected Lord Rector of Edinburgh University; and in the same year, he met with a severe loss in the death of his wife. She had been his loving companion for forty years, and had been a valuable aid in his literary work. His publications after the death of his wife, were only short articles upon the topics of the day. In addition to what we have already described, Carlyle collected, in 1838, his contributions to the "Reviews," and published them in five volumes, entitled "Miscellanies." The volumes included his masterly essays on great literary characters, as Voltaire, Mirabeau, Johnson and Boswell, Burns, Sir Walter Scott, etc. Carlyle's fame is continually extending, and editions of his works have reached a sale of 30,000 copies. "His greatest and most splendid successes have been won in the departments of biography and history. The chief interest and charm of his works consist in the individual portraits they contain, and the strong personal sympathies or antipathies they describe. He has a clear and penetrating insight into human nature; he notes every fact and circumstance that can elucidate character, and having selected his subject, he works with passionate earnestness till he produces the individual or scene before the reader, exact in outline according to his preconceived notion, and with marvellous force and vividness of coloring." He is justly placed among the greatest literary characters. The hand of time shall never erase the writing which Thomas Carlyle has written upon the wall of the nineteenth century.

He died in London, England, February 5, 1881, at the advanced age of eighty-five years.

WILL CARLETON.

What Robert Burns did for the Scottish cotter and the Reverend William Barnes has done for the English farmer, Will Carleton has done for the American—touched with the glamour of poetry the simple and monotonous events of daily life, and shown that all circumstances of life, however trivial they may appear, possess those alternations of the comic and pathetic, the good and bad, the joyful and sorrowful, which go to make up the days and nights, the summers and winters, of this perplexing world. Like his prototypes, he infuses into his work the most eloquent and touching pathos, constantly relieved by irresistible touches of jocularity, and twines the mingled thread of mirth and sorrow with a dexterity that enthralls the reader. Poetry, publishers tell us, is little read nowadays. Fashion ordains the purchase of Edwin Arnold's or Browning's latest productions, but there are few modern poetical productions that show by their well-thumbed pages and shabby covers that they have moved the hearts by their pathos, or stirred them as the trumpet-like lines of Macaulay and Aytoun did a generation since. One of these few is Carleton—who sprung suddenly into popularity and took his place at a bound in the front rank of those writers who have achieved success by their sympathetic treatment of the homeliest subjects.

In 1871 the poet's corner of the "Toledo Blade" contained a poem on which the diffident author had not ventured to set a price, modestly supplying it as a gratuitous contribution. Its success was phenomenal. The vigilant eye of George William Curtis saw at once the merit of the poem, and "Harper's Weekly" promptly republished "Betsey and I Are Out," with numerous characteristic illustrations. The authorship, which had been claimed by scores of pretenders, was by this definitely attributed to Will Carleton, then only about twenty-five, and employed as editor of the "Detroit Weekly Tribune."

He was born in 1845, near Hudson, Michigan, where his father,—one of the pioneers of Lenawee County,—had cleared a farm, on which five children were born to him and reared in the usual pursuits of farm life. Under the wise guidance of his parents Will developed an amazing appetite for learning and plodded daily five miles to obtain tuition at the nearest high school. At the age of sixteen he utilized his attainments in teaching others, and thus secured the means of defraying his expenses at Hillsdale College, whence he graduated June 17, 1869, delivering on that occasion his exquisite poem "Rifts in the Cloud," republished in "Farm Legends," which is well worthy committal to memory by aspiring students. He had previously acquired considerable popularity by the production of a political poem entitled "Fax," and some other stirring poems, notably one, "Forward," in which occurs the line

"A million men have lived good corses all their lives,"

published under the *nom de plume* of "Paul Pillow"; he added to his reputation by the production of the beautiful lines, "Cover them Over," which has ever since been a favorite recital on Decoration days. "How Betsey and I Made Up" confirmed the popularity obtained by "Betsey and I Are Out," since which time Mr. Carleton's pen has been industriously engaged in the production of "Farm Ballads" (1873), "Farm Legends" (1875), "Farm Festivals" (1881), "Young Folks' Centennial Rhymes" (1876), his

WILL CARLETON.

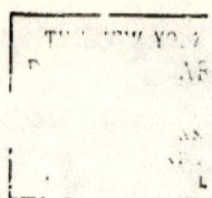

last production (1885) being "City Ballads," most probably the result of his residence in Chicago and Brooklyn. This book is dedicated "to Adora, friend, comrade, lover, wife."

Mr. Carleton's writings are more varied than many would anticipate from the homely tone of the verses which have made him famous. The poem, "Three Links of a Life," is full of dramatic power and abounds in rare and felicitous descriptive word-painting. For example:

"When the rough-clad room was still as sleek,
Save the deaf old nurse's needle-click,
The beat of the grave clock in its place,
With its ball-tipped tail and owl-like face,
And the iron tea-kettle's droning song
Through its Roman nose so black and long,
The mother lifted her baby's head,
And gave it a clinging kiss and said:

. . . .

"'Although thou be not Riches' flower,
    Thou neat one,
Yet thou hast come from Beauty's bower
    Thou sweet one!
Thy every smile's as warm and bright
As if a diamond mocked its light;
Thy every tear's as pure a pearl
As if thy father was an earl,

Thou neat one, thou sweet one!'

. . . .

"The midnight rested its heavy arm
Upon the grief-encumbered farm;
And hoarse-voiced Sorrow wandered at will,
Like a moan when the summer's night is still;
And the spotted cows, with bellies of white,
And well-filled teats all crowded awry,
Stood in the black stalls of the night,
Nor herded nor milked, and wondered why.
And the house was gloomy, still, and cold;
And the hard-palmed farmer, newly old,
Sat in an unfrequented place,
Hiding e'en from the dark his face;
And a solemn silence rested long
On all, save the cricket's dismal song."

A good example of his pathetic power is afforded by his poems, "The Good of the Future" and "The Joys that Are Left." They possess the merit of being free from vagueness and obscurity affected by most metaphysical verse-makers. The springs of human interest are played upon naturally, yet with the quaintness and geniality characteristic of the writer, whose future work will no doubt maintain him in the rank of the leading writers of the century.

ALICE AND PHOEBE CARY.

ALICE was born in the Miami Valley, eight miles north of Cincinnati, Ohio, April 26, 1820, and she died in New York, February 12, 1871.

PHŒBE was born near Cincinnati, September 4, 1824, and her life work closed by her death at Newport, R. I., July 31, 1871.

Their parents were people of considerable culture. The education of Alice and Phœbe was limited to the meager opportunities of a newly settled country. Alice commenced writing verses at the age of eighteen years. For ten years she contributed prose and verse to newspapers. Her sketches of rural life, first published in the "National Era," under the signature of "Patty Lee," attracted considerable attention. In 1849 the "Poems of Alice and Phœbe Cary" appeared in book form in Philadelphia.

In 1850 the sisters removed to New York and devoted themselves entirely and successfully to literary work. Alice became a constant contributor to leading literary periodicals. She also continued to write poems and novels, which appeared in book form. Her published volumes, besides the one mentioned above, are "Clovernook Papers," in two series, published in 1851 and 1853; "Clovernook Children," 1854; "Hagar, a Story of To-Day," 1852; "Lyra, and Other Poems," 1853; enlarged editions, including "The Maiden Flascala," 1855; "Married, not Mated," 1856; "Pictures of Country," 1859; "Lyrics and Hymns," 1866; "The Bishop's Sons," 1867; "The Lover's Diary," 1867; and "Snow Berries, a Book for Young Folks," 1869.

Phœbe's poems were more independent in style and more buoyant in tone than those of her sister. One of her first poems, printed in 1842, attracted much attention. Her works, besides her contributions to her sister's volumes, are "Poems and Parodies," 1854; "Poems of Hope, Faith

PHŒBE AND ALICE CARY.

and Love," 1868; and most of the "Hymns for all Christians," compiled in 1869, by Rev. Dr. Deems.

The writings of Alice and Phœbe are "marked with great sweetness and pathos," and their home became a noted resort for their literary friends.

CAMPBELL.

THOMAS CAMPBELL was born in Glasgow, Scotland, July 27, 1777, and he died at Boulogne, July 15, 1844, at the age of sixty-seven. He was buried in Westminster Abbey.

He came from the respectable family of Kirnan, in Argyllshire. His father had settled in Glasgow, but having failed in business, was unable to support his son in college. Thomas was, therefore, obliged to resort to private teaching in order to continue in school. Notwithstanding the amount of additional labor thus entailed, he made rapid progress in his studies, and attained considerable distinction at the university over which it was his fortune, in after years, to preside. He very early gave proofs of his aptitude for literary composition, especially in the department of poetry; and so strong was his addiction to these pursuits, that he could not bring himself seriously to adopt the choice of a profession. We are told by his biographer, Dr. Beattie, that "the imaginative faculty had been so unremittingly cultivated that circumstances, trifling in themselves, had acquired undue influence over his mind, and been rendered formidable by an exaggeration of which he was at the moment unconscious. Hence, various difficulties, which industry might have overcome, assumed to his eye the appearance of insurmountable obstacles. Without resolution to persevere, or philosophy to submit to the force of necessity, he drew from everything around him, with morbid ingenuity, some melancholy presage of the future."

We find him at the age of twenty in Edinburgh, attending lectures at the university, soliciting employment from the book-sellers, and not unknown to a circle of young men then resident in the Scottish metropolis, whose names have become historic. Among these were Walter Scott, Henry Brougham, James Jeffrey, Dr. Thomas Brown, John Leyden and James Grahame, the author of the "Sabbath." He also became acquainted with Dr. Robert Anderson, editor of a collection of British poets, a man of extreme enthusiasm and kindness of disposition, who early appreciated the remarkable powers of Campbell, and encouraged him to proceed in his literary career.

In 1799, his poem, "The Pleasures of Hope," was published. For more than three-fourths of a century, the poem has maintained, nay, increased, its popularity. Within that time, the public has adopted and abandoned many favorites—names once famous and in every mouth have gradually become forgotten and unregarded—poetical works of greater pretension, which were once considered as master-pieces of genius and inspiration, have fallen into neglect; but this poem by the boy Campbell remains a universal favorite. He disposed of the copyright of "Pleasures of Hope" for £60, but the publishers generously gave him £50 extra for each new edition of two thousand copies. Also in 1803 they permitted him to publish a quarto subscription copy, by which he realized £1,000.

Campbell went abroad, and passed some time on the continent, without any definite aim. His means were soon exhausted, and he was reduced to extreme poverty. Returning to Britain, his reputation soon gained him literary employment, but his tardiness in fulfilling engagements soon placed him in bad repute among the strong publishers, who hesitated often in offering him work. But he was constantly popular with the public, and an occasional poem from his pen found its way into print. In 1802 he wrote "Lochiel's Warning," and "Hohenlinden," two excellent poems known to everybody. A critic declares the latter one of the grandest battle pieces ever written. "In a few verses, flowing like a choral melody, the poet brings before us the silent midnight scene of engagement, wrapped in the snows of winter, the sudden arming for the battle, the press and shout of charging squadrons, the flashing of artillery, and the final scene of death. 'Lochiel's

Warning' being read in manuscript to Sir Walter (then Mr.) Scott, he requested a perusal of it himself, and then repeated the whole from memory—a striking instance of the great minstrel's powers of recollection, which was related by Mr. Campbell himself. In 1803 the poet repaired to London, and devoted himself to literature as a profession. He resided for some time with his friend, Mr. Telford, the celebrated engineer. Telford continued his regard for the poet throughout a long life, and remembered him in his will by a legacy of £500." In the meantime he married, and in 1805, through the influence of Mr. Fox, received a government pension of £200 per annum. Later Mr. Southey bequeathed him what amounted to nearly £1,000. The pension was given as a tribute to him for the noble national strains, "Ye Mariners of England," and the "Battle of the Baltic."

In 1809 he published "Gertrude of Wyoming, a Pennsylvania Tale." This was the second of his great poems, and it was exceedingly admired. Campbell was now settled at Sydenham, in England, and his circumstances were materially improved. His home was a happy one. The society in which he moved was of the most refined and intellectual character, and he enjoyed the personal friendship of many of his distinguished contemporaries. In 1820 he accepted the editorship of the "New Monthly Magazine," and acted in that capacity until he resigned it to take charge of the "Metropolitan." Many of his minor poems appeared in the "Magazine;" and one of these, "The Last Man," may be ranked among his greatest conceptions.

In 1824 he published "Theodric and Other Poems;" and though busy in establishing the London University, he was, in 1827, elected lord rector of the university of his native city. He afterward made a voyage to Algiers, of which he published an account; and in 1842 appeared a slight narrative poem, unworthy of his fame, entitled "The Pilgrims of Glencoe." Among the literary engagements of his later years was a "Life of Mrs. Siddons," and a "Life of Petrarch."

In 1831, the year in which the gallant struggle of the Poles for their independence was terminated by entire defeat, Campbell, who in his earliest poem had referred in such beautiful language to the shameful partition of Poland, more than revived his youthful enthusiasm for her cause. He had watched with an anxiety almost bordering on fanaticism, the progress of the patriotic movement, and the news of the capture of Warsaw by the Russians, affected him as if it had been the deepest of personal calamities. He was the founder of the association in London of the Friends of Poland, which not only served to maintain the strong interest felt by the British people for the Polish cause, but was the means of providing assistance and giving employment to large numbers of the unfortunate exiles who were driven to seek refuge in England. Never, till his dying day, did he relax his efforts in their behalf; and many an unhappy wanderer, who, but for unexpected aid, might have perished in the streets of a foreign city, had reason to bless the name of Thomas Campbell.

Critics may dispute regarding the comparative merits of his longer works; and, as they incline toward didactic or narrative poetry, may prefer the one composition to the other. Both are entitled to praise and honor, but it is on his lyrics that the future reputation of Campbell must principally rest. They have taken their place, never to be disturbed, in the popular heart; and, until the language in which they are composed perishes, they are certain to endure.

GEOFFREY CHAUCER.

CHAUCER was born about 1340, and he died in 1400. There is some controversy about the exact date of his birth.

Chaucer is known as "The Father of English Poetry." The annals also show that he was more conspicuously connected with public affairs than any noted poet since his time.

In 1357 he was page to Elizabeth. In 1359 he was with the royal army in the invasion of France, where he was taken prisoner, but was released in 1360, by the king giving £16 towards his ransom.

Here a blank occurs till in 1366, when we find him in diplomatic service; in 1366 he married Philippa, one of the ladies of the chamber of the queen; 1367, received title of "our yeoman" from the king, together with an annuity of twenty marks; 1369 with second invasion of France; 1372 appointed envoy to Italy, and styled "esquire;" next appointed comptroller of customs and subsidies of wool, skins, etc., in the port of London; 1377, joint envoy on a secret mission to Flanders, afterwards sent to France to treat of peace with Charles V. Now passing other important missions and appointments filled by him with great ability, we will only note that in 1386 he sat in parliament as one of the knights of the shire for Kent.

We have no positive evidence of Chaucer's training in school, although it is claimed that he "studied both at Oxford and Cambridge." Successive investigators, however, have made quite a complete outline of biography, and his works give a knowledge of his ability. "They show that Chaucer was not merely a poet and a scholar, deeply read in what then passed for science and philosophy, as well as in the rich literature of his poetical predecessors, but a soldier, a courtier, a man of business, familiar from the circumstances of his birth and subsequent rise in position, with all sides of the life of his time."

But his literary life was one of toil. Depending almost entirely upon official patronage for support, he was obliged to labor all day, then study and write till nearly morning. While writing his "House of Fame" he refers to his work and says that he used to attend to the duties of his office, and make all the reckonings with his own hands, then go to his house and sit at his books till he seemed dazed or lost in his study. In spite of the want of literary patronage in his time, in spite of poverty and humble birth, Chaucer struggled on till he placed himself on record as "The Father of English Poetry." Upon the close of his busy life, "he was buried in Westminster Abbey, the first of the illustrious file of poets whose ashes rest in that great national sanctuary." The critic, Professor Bernard Ten Brink, records Chaucer's poems as follows: Before 1372, the "A, B, C," the "Romance of the Rose," and "Book of the Duchess;" before 1384, the "House of Fame," the "Life of St. Cecil," the "Parliament of Birds," "Troilus" and "Cressida," and the "Knight's Tale;" after 1384, "The Legend of Good Women," "Canterbury Tales," and other lesser poems. Some of the minor poems usually credited to Chaucer, including "The Court of Love," the "Flower and the Leaf," "Chaucer's Dream," and "Romance of the Rose," are rejected by critics as spurious. They are objected to on the ground that they do not conform to the laws of rhyme observed by the poet in his works known to be genuine. The "Canterbury Tales," however, form a durable monument of Chaucer's genius. This work consists of twenty-four stories supposed to have been told by a company of pilgrims on their way to Canterbury, with a "Prologue" and connecting narratives.

SAMUEL L. CLEMENS.

SAMUEL LANGHORNE CLEMENS, better known as Mark Twain, was born in Florida, Monroe County, Missouri, November 30, 1835, and is now living in Hartford City, Connecticut. His works have been immensely popular, and have brought him an ample fortune, thus enabling him to devote his entire time to literature.

He attended a common school until he was thirteen, when he entered the printing office of the "Courier" at Hannibal, Missouri, as an apprentice. Subsequently he pursued his trade in St. Louis, Cincinnati, Philadelphia and New York. "In 1855 he went to New Orleans intending to take passage for Para, to explore the Amazon, and to engage in the cacao trade; but the fact that there was no ship from New Orleans to Para prevented the fulfillment of his plans. On his way down the Mississippi, he had made friends with the pilots, and for the consideration of $500 they engaged to make him a St. Louis and New Orleans pilot. He went up and down the river steering and studying the 1,275 miles of the route, and after a time re-

ceived his license, and secured a situation as a pilot at $250 per month." The incidents of his career as a pilot form some of his happiest sketches.

In 1861 his brother received the appointment as secretary of the Territory of Nevada, and Samuel accompanied him as his private secretary. He worked in the mines for about a year, and says in his "Roughing It" that he was really worth a million dollars for just ten days, and lost it through his own heedlessness. He then shoveled quartz in a silver mill for ten dollars a week for one week only. All of these experiences are turned to account most admirably in his writings; and they formed an excellent schooling for him.

He commenced his literary labor by means of occasional letters to the Virginia City "Enterprise." In 1862 he became editor of "The Enterprise," a position he held for three years. Part of the time he reported legislative proceedings from Carson, summing up results in weekly letters to "The Enterprise," which he signed "Mark Twain." The name calls to mind his steamboat days on the Mississippi, where it indicated a depth of two fathoms of water. Mark Twain is now a name better known in literature than in steamboat vernacular. He next went to San Francisco, and for five months reported for the "Morning Call" newspaper. In pursuit of wealth, he next went to Calaveras County, where he dug for gold for about three months without result. Returning to San Francisco, he followed the newspaper business for a short time. In 1866 he spent about six months on the Hawaiian Islands. Returning again to California, with considerable reputation he entered the lecture field, and was more than successful. His peculiar vein of humor tickled the public ear, hence he decided to give his thoughts to the world in book form. In 1867 he went East and brought out his first book in New York. "The Jumping Frog and Other Sketches" was at once popular, and was immediately republished in England.

Finding that his style pleased the public exceedingly, he entered upon his career as author with systematic earnestness. In 1867 he crossed the Atlantic in the steamer Quaker City, and traveled through Spain, Italy, Greece, Egypt and the Holy Land. The account of his travels appeared in 1869, in that marvel of wit and humor, "The Innocents Abroad." Within three years, the work reached the enormous sale of 125,000 copies. Mark Twain edited a daily paper at Buffalo, for a short time, but soon entered the lecture field again and revisited England in 1872. In the same year, he published "Roughing It," which reached a sale of 91,000 in nine months. At this time, London publishers gathered all his sketches, many of which were never published in America, and many of which were not written by Mark Twain, and issued them in four volumes. From the pen of this American genius and humorist have proceeded the "New Pilgrim's Progress," "Tramp Abroad," "Burlesque Autobiography," "Eye-openers," "Good Things," "Screamers," "A Gathering of Scraps," "The Gilded Age," "Tom Sawyer," "Life on the Mississippi," and "Adventures of Huckleberry Finn." His works are published in the Old World at London and Leipsic, and are very popular on both sides of the Atlantic.

Without a doubt, he is the most popular of living humorists. His language is pure and elevated, except when it is necessary to use the language of classes to represent certain characters. The world is bound to laugh as long as Mark Twain lives, or as long as his works are kept in print.

SAMUEL TAYLOR COLERIDGE.

COLERIDGE was born at Ottery, St. Mary, Devonshire, England, October 21, 1772 (given 1773 by some of his biographers), and on July 25, 1834, he passed away, and was buried in the vault of Highgate Church on August 2.

His father was a clergyman, and was known for his scholarship, simplicity of character, and interest in the pupils of the grammar school where he taught before devoting his full time to the ministry. The poet's mother was Anne Bowden, a woman noted for the interest which she took in the training of her children.

SAMUEL TAYLOR COLERIDGE.

Upon the death of his father young Coleridge was taken to Christ's Hospital, where he studied for eight years. While here he gave strong evidence of a powerful imagination. He was industrious, and possessing a rare memory, he retained everything he read. The youth attracted the special attention of one of the teachers, who reported him to the head master as a boy who read Virgil for amusement. Some verses written by him at sixteen show strong marks of genius.

In February, 1791, he was entered at Jesus College, Cambridge. It was the custom of the students to lay aside their school books occasionally to discuss the pamphlets of the day. Ever and anon a pamphlet came from the pen of Burke, and one of Coleridge's fellow-students declared that there was no use of having the book before them, for Mr. C. had read it in the morning, and in the evening he could repeat it verbatim. But growing tired of university life, and being hard pressed by debts, he enlisted as a soldier.

His military record was thus described by the Rev. Mr. Bowles, who received the facts from Coleridge's own mouth:

"The regiment was the 15th, Elliot's light dragoons; the officer was Nathaniel Ogle, eldest son of Dr. Newton Ogle, and brother of the late Mrs. Sheridan; he was a scholar, and leaving Merton College, he entered this regiment a cornet. Some years afterward (I believe he was then captain of Coleridge's troop), going into the stable at Reading, he remarked, written on the white wall, under one of the saddles, in large pencil characters, the following sentence in Latin:

"'*Eheu! quam infortunii miserrimum est fuisse felicem!*'

"Being struck with the circumstance, and himself a scholar, Captain Ogle inquired of a soldier, whether he knew to whom the saddle belonged. 'Please your honor, to Comberback,' answered the dragoon. 'Comberback!' said the captain, 'send him to me.' Comberback presented himself, with the inside of his hand in front of his cap. His officer mildly said, 'Comberback, did you write that Latin sentence which I have just read under your saddle?' 'Please, your honor,' answered the soldier, 'I wrote it.' 'Then, my lad, you are not what you appear to be. I shall speak to the commanding officer, and you may depend upon my speaking as a friend.' The commanding officer was, I think, General Churchill. Comberback (the name he gave when he enlisted) was examined, and it was found out, that having left Jesus College, Cambridge, and being in London without resources, he had enlisted in this regiment. He was soon discharged—not from his democratic feelings, for whatever those feelings might be, as a soldier he was remarkably orderly and obedient, though he could not rub down his own horse. He was discharged from respect to his friends and his station. His friends having been informed of his situation, a chaise was soon at the door of the Bear Inn, Reading, and the officers of the 15th cordially shaking his hands, particularly the officer who had been the means of his discharge, he drove off, not without a tear in his eye, whilst his old companions gave him three hearty cheers as the wheels rapidly rolled away along the Bath road to London and Cambridge."

While in the tap-room at Reading, he wrote one of his finest poems, "Religious Musings," which furnished a fine subject for a painting by Wilkie.

The youth returned to Cambridge for a short time, but left the university without a degree in 1794. In the same year he visited Oxford and formed the acquaintance of Southey. The two formed a friendship that continued through life. The two friends commenced to build up a plan for founding a brotherly community on the banks of the Susquehanna, where selfishness was to be extinguished, and the virtues were to reign supreme. Failing to get funds, the scheme was abandoned in 1795, much to Coleridge's chagrin. In the same year he married Sarah Frickes, and settled at Clevedon on the Bristol Channel. Within a few weeks Southey married a sister of Mrs. Coleridge and started for Portugal.

As a means of support the poet began to lecture. He selected politics and religion as subjects, but the Bristol public did not support him well, hence he published his lectures in book form. In the course of the summer excursions of this year Coleridge formed the acquaintance of Wordsworth and his gifted sister. As in the case of Southey, a life-long friendship followed. Wordsworth's sister describes Coleridge as "thin and pale, the lower part of his face not good, wide mouth, thick lips, not very good teeth, longish, loose, half-curling, rough, black hair,"—but all was forgotten in the magic charm of his utterance. Wordsworth declared that Coleridge was the only wonderful man that he ever knew. Wordsworth soon settled near Coleridge, and Southey afterward joined them, thus making the trio known in literature as the Lake Poets. The Lake Poets was a term first used by critics in making light of the writings of the three friends, but it was soon made famous by the masterly spirits it included. Coleridge projected a periodical known as "The Watchman," but it lived only two months. In 1796 he published a volume of "Juvenile Poems," for which he received thirty guineas. The volume was successful, and at once made the author famous. In 1798 the Wedgwood brothers granted him an annuity, whereupon he, in company with Wordsworth and his sister, started for Hamburg with the intention of making a tour of the continent. In the same year the two friends published jointly the "Lyric Ballads."

The annuity granted him opened a new period in his life. Thus provided with means, he attended lectures at Gottingen, Germany, where he mastered the German language. Upon his return home he wrote some of the principal papers for the "Morning Post," and also translated some dramas of Schiller. Soon after, Coleridge accompanied Sir Alexander Ball to Malta, as his secretary. Returning from Malta, he wrote "Remorse," a tragedy in blank verse, equal in some respects to the masterly productions of Shakespeare. Its forcible thought and excellent expression greatly enhanced the author's reputation.

In 1801 Coleridge left London for the Lakes, making his home for some time with Southey. As a result of what may be called his opium period, the next fifteen years of his life were far from pleasant. He accomplished but little. Occasionally, however, he appeared in London, and he was then always the delight of admiring circles. The "Ode to Dejection" and the poem of "Youth and Age," show the evidences of his sad prostration of spirit. In 1809 he published "The Friend," and for about three years lectured upon Shakespeare. In 1813 appeared the tragedy of "Remorse," which was very successful. "Three years after this the evil habit against which he had struggled bravely but ineffectually, determined him to enter the family of

Mr. Gillem, who lived at Highgate. The letter in which he discloses his misery to this kind and thoughtful man gives a real insight into his character. Under kind and judicious treatment the hour of mastery at last arrived. The shore was reached, but the vessel had been miserably shattered in its passage through the rocks. He hardly, for the rest of his life, ever left his home at Highgate." It was there that "Christabel," written some time before, was first published. In 1816 appeared his "Lay Sermons" and the "Biographia Literaria," and a revised edition of "The Friend" soon followed.

Seven years later, his most mature and his best prose work, entitled "Aids to Reflection," was given to the world. In 1830 his last effort, being a work on "Church and State," appeared. He died in 1834. Four volumes of "Literary Remains" were published after his death. His prose works are the chief source of his fame, although the "Rime of the Ancient Mariner" and "Christabel" are among the best poems in the English language.

"He lacked continuity of thought," and that, perhaps, is his principal fault. His conversational powers were scarcely less than those of Samuel Johnson. So great was his fame that the most remarkable young men of the period resorted to Highgate as to the shrine of an oracle. As a poet, Coleridge's own place is safe. His niche in the great gallery of English poets is secure. The exquisite perfection of his metre and the subtle alliance of his thought and expression must always secure for him the warmest admiration of true lovers of poetic art.

JAMES FENIMORE COOPER.

J. F. Cooper was born at Burlington, New Jersey, September 15, 1789, and he died of dropsy, at Cooperstown, New York, in 1851.

His father was a person of ability, who served the public as judge and as member of Congress. The boy was reared on his father's estate near Lake Otsego. In that then wild region Cooper may have received impressions which were valuable in his delineations of border life and character.

His school life began at Albany and New Haven. At the age of thirteen he entered Yale College, where he studied for three years. The youngest student on the rolls, he yet sustained himself in his classes and gained a good education. In his sixteenth year he entered the United States navy, where he served for six years. Cooper made a few voyages to perfect himself in seamanship. Having obtained a commission as lieutenant, he married, and resigning his commission in 1811, entered upon a life of literary labor. He settled at Westchester, where, in 1819, he produced "Precaution," a novel of the fashionable school. The book was published anonymously and attracted but little attention. It was taken for granted that a new writer was skirmishing under an assumed name to test his ability. The little attention given to the first book, encouraged the author to try again, hence, in 1821, appeared "The Spy," a powerful and interesting romance, founded upon incidents connected with the American Revolution. The great success of "The Spy" at once established the author's popularity; and, in 1823, his fame was still more increased by "The Pioneers," the first of the Leatherstocking series, and "The Pilot," a bold and dashing sea story. The above works placed Cooper in a very favorable light before the public. He at once became popular both in the New and Old World. Thus encouraged he entered in earnest upon a very fruitful literary career.

In 1825 he published "Lionel Lincoln," a feeble work; 1826, "Last of the Mohicans," a book often quoted as his masterpiece; and in the same year he went to France, where he published "The Prairie," and in the succeeding year, "The Red Rover." These are among his very best works. In nearly all respects "The Prairie" is his best effort. In 1826 Cooper seemed to be the most popular living novelist.

"The Wept of the Wish-ton Wish," appeared in 1827; "The Notions of a Traveling Bachelor," 1828; "The Water Witch," 1830, the poorest of his sea stories; "The Bravo," 1831; "The Heidenmauer," 1832; "The Headman of Berne," 1833. These works were all widely read on both sides of the Atlantic. The object of most of his writings while abroad was to exalt the masses at the expense of the aristocracy. While abroad he also wrote a series of letters for the "National," a journal of Paris, in which he defended his country against certain charges that had been made by the "Revue Britannique."

Upon returning to the United States in 1833, he published "A Letter to my Countrymen," explaining the controversy in which he had engaged through the Paris papers. For the rest of his life he continued to skirmish occasionally upon national topics through the public journals. His publications continued by the appearance of "Monikins," and "The American Democrat," 1835; "Notes" on his travels and experiences in Europe, in three volumes, published in 1837. These three volumes are estimated by foreigners as "a burst of vanity and ill-temper." "Homeward Bound," and "Home as Found," were published in 1838. For these several works he was criticised most severely by the public press. Cooper retaliated by commencing a series of libel suits. In all of these he was successful, after which he returned to his book work with unusual vigor. In 1839 he published a "Naval History of the United States;" 1840, "The Pathfinder," an excellent Leatherstocking novel, and "Mercedes of Castile;" 1841, "The Deerslayer;" 1842, "The Two Admirals," and "Wing and Wing;" 1843, "Wyandotte," "The History of a Pocket Handkerchief," and "Ned Myers;" 1844, "Afloat and Ashore,"

and "Miles Wallingford;" 1845, "The Chainbearer," and "Satanstoe;" 1846 "The Redskins." In 1846 he published, also, a set of "Lives of Distinguished American Officers," being supplemental to "Naval History," etc. Taking up his line of novels again in 1847, he published "The Crater, or Vulcan's Peak;" 1848. "Oak Openings," and "Jack Tier;" 1849, "The Sea Lions;" 1850, the final work, "The Ways of the Hour." It must appear from the above that Cooper's pen was never idle. In his novels he appears to be at home, but in his numerous notes on travels, and in his many treatises on the institutions of America, he subjected himself to severe censure.

In the realm of fiction he has but few equals. "He emphatically belongs to the American nation," as Washington Irving has said, "while his painting of nature under new and striking aspects, has given him a European fame that can never wholly die." The last statement may be strengthened by our quoting Cooper's description of "Lake Otsego," in its surroundings, while the wilderness remained unbroken:

"On all sides, wherever the eye turned, nothing met it but the mirror-like surface of the lake, the placid view of heaven, and the dense setting of woods. So rich and fleecy were the outlines of the forest, that scarce an opening could be seen; the whole visible earth, from the rounded mountain-top to the water's edge, presenting one unvaried line of unbroken verdure. As if vegetation were not satisfied with a triumph so complete, the trees overhung the lake itself, shooting out toward the light; and there were miles along its eastern shore where a boat might have pulled beneath the branches of dark Rembrandt-looking hemlocks, quivering aspens, and melancholy pines. In a word the hand of man had never yet defaced or deformed any part of this native scene, which lay bathed in the sunlight, a glorious picture of the affluent forest grandeur, softened by the balminess of June, and relieved by the beautiful variety afforded by the presence of so broad an expanse of water."

His stories have been translated into nearly all the languages of Europe, and into some of those of Asia, and are even now found worthy of a reprint. Balzac admired him greatly; while Victor Hugo pronounced him greater than the great master of modern romance, and this verdict was echoed by a multitude of readers, who were satisfied with no title for their favorite less than that of "the American Scott."

WILLIAM COWPER.

WILLIAM COWPER was born November 26, 1731, at Great Berkhamstead, Hertfordshire, England, and after being reduced to the last stage of feebleness, he died peacefully, April 25, 1800.

His father, the Rev. Dr. Cowper, belonged to the aristocracy, and his mother was allied to some of the noblest families of England. He counted among his ancestors kings and earls, and persons who had filled the most prominent places in the English government. His mother died when he was only in his sixth year.

Cowper's health was very delicate, hence his school life was not altogether pleasant. He was sent to Dr. Pitman's school in Market street, Bedfordshire, as soon as he was six years old. There he was subjected to the ridicule of his rude companions. Cowper thus wrote of one of his schoolmates—"His savage treatment of me impressed such a dread of his figure on my mind, that I well remember being afraid to lift my eyes upon him higher than his knees, and that I knew him better by his shoe-buckle than by any other part of his dress." Without doubt, the mental anguish which he suffered in school had a decided influence upon the rest of his life, which lay under the clouds of despondency. At the age of ten he was sent to the Westminster school. There Churchill, Lloyd and Warren Hastings were his fellow students. There, also, he served a seven years' apprenticeship to the classics. Being surrounded by strangers, and naturally very shy, his fits of despondency grew darker, and his mind became greatly depressed. Inflammation of the eyes threatened to make him blind, and he soon showed signs of consumptive tendency. In this condition, at the age of thirteen, he had the small-pox, which completely restored his eyesight. Under all of these unfavorable circumstances Cowper distinguished himself in his studies.

At the age of eighteen he was taken from Westminster, and placed under the instruction of Mr. Chapman, an attorney in London. The duties of this new position were in direct opposition to the literary tendencies of the poet's mind. Thurlow, who afterward became lord chancellor of England, was in the same office, and Cowper bears witness that they spent their leisure hours in "giggling, and making giggle," instead of studying law. When his three years had expired with Mr. Chapman, he went to the Middle Temple in 1752. There the solitary hours passed heavily, and his spirits sank into a deep gloom. Finally, while sitting with a few friends by the sea, the shadows passed away, and life presented itself in a new light. He returned to London and entered the gayest society, and, for a time, gave himself up wholly to pleasure. In 1752 he was admitted to the bar, but the allurements of literature and social life kept him from following his profession. His father soon died, leaving but a small fortune. In 1759 Cowper removed to the Inner Temple, where, instead of studying law, he continued to give most of his time to literary study. He studied Homer, and, with his brother, translated part of "Henriade." There, also, he formed the acquaintance of prominent men, and met many of his old school fellows. He joined the Nonsense Club, and commenced to write prose and poetry for the press.

Cowper had become quite fond of dress and of gay society. At the same time his little fortune was about exhausted. Circumstances led him to seek some suitable employment. His friend and kinsman, Major Cowper, gave him the lucrative office of clerk to the committees of the House of Lords. In order to test Cowper's fitness for the office an examination was called for at the bar of the House. He immediately undertook to prepare himself for the examination. The result is described by himself as follows—"The journal books were thrown open to me—a thing which could not be refused, and from which, perhaps, a man in health and with a head turned to business might have gained all the information he wanted; but it was not so with me: I read without perception, and was so distressed that had every clerk in the office been my friend, it could have availed me little, for I was not in condition to receive instruction, much less to elicit it out of manuscripts without direction." The dread of appearing before the House of Lords for a public examination so affected his mind that it reappeared to him in dreams. In order to escape the ordeal he attempted suicide. The effort proved a failure, but Cowper was removed to a private asylum at St. Albans. There he remained for two years, when he removed to Huntington, to be near his brother. An intimacy grew up between Cowper and the family of the Rev. Morley Unwin, a minister living in the place. The poet having given up all ambition for public trust and abandoned many of the hopes of his youth, wished only to pass into some quiet retreat. The home of the Unwins was offered to him, and he soon became as one of the family. In 1767, Mr. Unwin died, and the family, including the poet, removed to Olney.

In 1773 his insanity returned. Mrs. Unwin, with all possible care, attended him in his long illness. At length his mind commenced to gain strength, and he busied himself with gardening and other light work. For a time his only serious thoughts were upon religious subjects. Mrs. Newton, wife of the local minister, and a lady of excellent qualities, became a constant visitor. Up till about 1775, Cowper had only written a few hymns, but by Mrs. Unwin's suggestion, he commenced a poem on the "Progress of Error." His writing progressed rapidly, and in a few months, he brought out a volume including "Progress of Error," "Table Talk," "Conversation," "Truth," "Expostulation," "Hope," "Charity," "Retirement." This work attracted but little attention.

The turning point in Cowper's life occurred in 1781, when he formed the acquaintance of Lady Austen. Her sparkling wit, genial nature and lively conversation, soon drove away his melancholy. He wrote songs which she set to music and sang to the harpsichord. Observing him to be rather depressed, Lady Austen related the story of John Gilpin. The poet was so delighted with the story, that upon retiring, he turned it into verse, and at the breakfast table repeated it to her.

His new friend next suggested "The Task." This he commenced in 1783, and published in 1785. Its succeess was complete, and Cowper's name was rendered immortal, and placed at the head of living English poets.

He printed his translation of Homer in 1791, then engaged to edit an edition of Milton, but his mental condition prevented him from doing the work. In 1794 the crown gave him a pension of £300. His last poem was the "Castaway."

His friend, Mrs. Unwin, died in 1796, and Cowper sank into a mental gloom which continued till his death in 1800.

Cowper was the most popular poet and letter writer of his age. "His muse does not sit apart in sublime seclusion—she comes down into the ways of men, mingles in their every day concerns, and is interested in crops and rural affairs. * * * He brought back nature to poetry, and his influence has been extensive and lasting. Shakespeare, Spenser and Milton are spirits of an ethereal kind. Cowper is a steady and valuable friend, whose society we may sometimes neglect for that of more splendid and attractive associates, but whose unwavering principle and purity of character, joined to rich intellectual powers, overflow upon us in secret, and bind us to him forever."

ALIGHIERI DANTE.

Dante was born at Florence, Italy, in May, 1265; and banished from the sunny home of his nativity, he died September 14, 1321, in Ravenna, where his remains still repose.

Dante descended from an ancient and honorable family, though not one of the highest rank. Certain of his biographers attempt to prove his origin from one of the oldest senatorial families of Rome. It is given as authentic, however, that he was connected with the Elisei who took part in the building of Florence, under Charles the Great. Dante traces his ancestry back to the warrior Cacciaguida, but it would not be of special interest to trace the descent here, except to note that the poet's father was a second

Aldighiero, a lawyer of some reputation. The father was married twice; and by his second wife, Donna Bella, whose family name is not known, he had Dante and a daughter. Dante was born under the sign of the twins, " the glorious stars pregnant with virtue, to whom he owes his genius, such as it is." Astrologers considered this constellation as favorable to literature and science, and Brunetto Latini, his instructor, tells him in the " Inferno" that, if he follows its guidance, he cannot fail to reach the harbor of fame.

But little is known of his boyhood, except that he was a hard student and a pupil of Brunetto Latini. Boccaccio tells us that he became very familiar with Virgil, Horace, Ovid, Statius, and all other famous poets; and that, " taken by the sweetness of knowing the truth of the things concealed in heaven, and finding no other pleasure dearer to him in life, he left all other worldly care and gave himself to this alone, and, that no part of philosophy might remain unseen by him, he plunged with acute intellect into the deepest recesses of theology, and so far succeeded in his design that, caring nothing for heat or cold, or watchings or fastings, or any other bodily discomforts, by assiduous study he came to know of the divine essence and of the other separate intelligences all that the human intellect can comprehend." Leonardo Bruni says that " by study of philosophy, of theology, astrology, arithmetic, and geometry, by reading history, by turning over many curious books, watching and sweating in his studies, he acquired the science which he was to adorn and explain in his verses." He became master of all the sciences of his age at a time when it was not impossible to know all that could be known. Like Milton, he was trained in the most strict academical education which the age afforded. He was also skilled in drawing, for he tells us that on the anniversary of the death of Beatrice, he drew an angel on a tablet.

Dante's misfortunes grew out of his political relations and the unstable condition of the government of Florence. In 1215 Florence was enjoying peace. A private feud between families of opposing parties introduced into the city the horrors of civil war. Out of these feuds grew the parties of Guelphs and Ghibellines in Florence. These factions were at constant war with each other, each at times victorious, and the victors always banishing the vanquished. The defeated party gaining aid, returned with redoubled fury. The historian tells us that Dante fought with distinction at Campaldino and at the battle of Caprona. His party being victorious, he returned to his studies in 1289.

The archives of Florence show that Dante took part in the several councils of the city from 1295 to 1301. In 1299 he was engaged in an embassy to the town of San Gemignano, and in 1300 he held the office of prior. This office was the cause of all his miseries. Factions again arose, and it became the duty of the six priors to protect the city. Dante and his colleagues banished the heads of the rival parties in different directions to a distance from the capital. The banished parties returned in force, and by foreign aid conquered the city, destroyed all the effects of their adversaries and doomed 600 families to exile. In 1302 Dante with three others was condemned to pay a heavy fine, to be exiled from Tuscany for two years, and never again to hold office in the republic. In the same year Dante with fourteen others, was condemned to be burned alive if they should ever come into the hands of the republic. The sentences were repeated in 1311 and 1315, but were finally reversed in 1494, long years after the poet's death. After his banishment he made one desperate effort to defeat his rivals, but failing in the attempt, his wanderings commenced.

We cannot trace this great man in all his wanderings, but many cities claim the honor of giving him shelter, or of being for a time the home of his inspired muse. He visited the University of Bologna, and also of Paris. Having studied in the Rue Fouarre, it is claimed that he went to Oxford. At various times, circumstances and the prospect of returning to his home caused him to build up strong hopes, which were in turn destroyed. Finally, weary and in great poverty, he retired to Ravenna, where he ended his life, and where his bones still repose, while cities are contending for the honor of having furnished him a home. In 1316 Dante might have returned to Florence by paying a fine and walking in the dress of humiliation to the church of St. John to do penance for his offenses, but he refused to tolerate the shame. The letter is still extant in which he declines to enter Florence except with honor, secure that the means of life will not fail him, and that in any corner of the world he will be able to gaze at the sun and stars, and meditate on the sweetest truths of philosophy.

The story of his social life may be stated briefly. At the age of nine he met Beatrice Portinari at the house of her father on May-day, 1274. She became at once the idol of his affections, although he never declared his love to her. He saw her only twice when she married another. The worship of her lover, however, was stronger than ever for the remoteness of the object. The story of his passion is told in the last chapter of the "Vita Nuova." She died in 1290, and he wrote most affectionately of her. In 1292 Dante married Gemma, daughter of Manetto Donati, a connection of the celebrated Corso Donati, afterward his bitter foe. By this lady he had seven children. His son Piero, who wrote a commentary on the "Divina Commedia," settled in Verona. His daughter Beatrice lived a nun in Ravenna. His direct line became extinct in 1509; but the blood still runs in the veins of the Marchesi Serego Alighieri, a noble family of the city of the Scaligers.

It now remains to sketch his literary life. In 1307 he completed "Vita Nuova," or "Young Life," of Dante. This contains the history of his love for Beatrice. The "Convito," or "Banquet" is the work of his manhood. This was probably intended for a handbook of universal knowledge, but the date of its completion is unknown. His minor poems were entitled "Rime di Dante." Such minor poems as are known to be genuine secure Dante a place among lyric poets scarcely if at all inferior to that of Petrarch. The Latin treatise "De Monarchia" in three books, was written between 1310 and 1313; and, as the title indicates, contains his governmental creed. "De Vulgari Eloquio," in two books, seeks to establish the Italian language as a literary tongue, and to lay down rules for poetical composition. "De Aqua et Terra" was completed about 1321. This discusses the question, then in dispute, whether in any place on the earth's surface water is higher than the earth. It gives an insight into Dante's studies and modes of thought. His wonderful poem, the "Divina Commedia," was probably not completed till just before his death, but it bears the date of 1318. It is a literary masterpiece. The letters of Dante form an important part of his works, but we will not take the space to describe them here. We close this

sketch by quoting a critical opinion concerning the "Character of Dante's Genius:" "Dante may be said to have concentrated in himself the spirit of the middle age. Whatever there was of piety, of philosophy, of poetry, of love of nature, and of love of knowledge in those times is drawn to a focus in his writings. His is the first great name in literature after the night of the dark ages. The Italian language in all its purity and sweetness, in its aptitude for the tenderness of love and the violence of passion, or the clearness of philosophical argument, sprang fully grown and fully armed from his brain. The 'Vita Nuova' is still the best introduction to the study of the Tuscan tongue; the astronomy and science of the 'Divine Comedy' are obscure only in a translation. Dante's reputation has passed through many vicissitudes, and much trouble has been spent by critics in comparing him with other poets of established fame. Read and commented upon in the Italian universities in the generation immediately succeeding his death, his name became obscured as the sun of the renaissance rose higher toward its meridian. In the 17th century he was less read than Petrarch, Tasso, or Ariosti; in the 18th he was almost universally neglected. His fame is now fully vindicated. Translations and commentaries issue from every press in Europe and America. Dante societies are formed to investigate the difficulties of his works. He occupies in the lecture-rooms of regenerated Italy a place by the side of those great masters whose humble disciple he avowed himself to be. The 'Divine Comedy' is indeed as true an epic as the 'Æneid,' and Dante is as real a classic as Virgil. His metre is as pliable and flexible to every mood of emotion, his diction as plaintive as sonorous. Like him he can immortalize by a simple expression, a person, a place, or a phase of nature. Dante is even truer in description than Virgil, whether he paints the snow falling in the Alps, or the homeward flight of birds, or the swelling of an angry torrent. But under this gorgeous pageantry of poetry there lies a unity of conception, a power of philosophic grasp, an earnestness of religion which to the Roman poet were entirely unknown. Still more striking is the similarity between Dante and Milton. This may be said to lie rather in the kindred nature of their subjects, and in the parallel development of their minds, than in any mere external resemblance. In both the man was greater than the poet; the souls of both were 'like a star and dwelt apart.' Both were academically trained in the deepest studies of their age; the labor which made Dante lean made Milton blind. The 'Doricke sweetness' of the English poet is not absent from the tender pages of the 'Vita Nuova.' The middle life of each was spent in active controversy; each lent his services to the state; each felt the quarrels of his age to be the "business of posterity," and left his warnings to ring in the ears of a later time. The lives of both were failures. 'On evil days though fallen and evil tongues,' they gathered the concentrated experience of their lives into one immortal work, the quintessence of their hopes, their knowledge and their sufferings. But Dante is something more than this. Milton's voice is grown faint to us—we have passed into other modes of expression and of thought. But if we had to select two names in literature who are still exercising their full influence on mankind, and whose teaching is still developing new sides to the coming generations, we should choose the names of Dante and Goethe."

DE QUINCEY.

THOMAS DE QUINCEY was born at Greenham, near Manchester, England, August 15, 1785, and he died in Edinburgh, December 8, 1859, aged seventy-four, and was buried in the West Churchyard.

His father, an opulent merchant, came from a Norman family. He lived abroad much of his time to look after his interests, and for the benefit of his health. He died in his thirty-ninth year, leaving a wife and six children, with an ample fortune yielding an income of £1,600 per annum. Mrs. De Quincey was a lady of excellent qualities and fine culture, and she secured for her children the thorough education and good social advantages which her position and wealth afforded. "From boyhood he was more or less in contact with a polished circle; his education, easy to one of such native aptitude, was sedulously attended to. When he was in his twelfth year, the family removed to Bath, where he was sent to the grammar school, at which he remained for about two years; and for a year more he attended another public school at Winkfield, Wiltshire. At both his proficiency was the marvel of his masters. At thirteen he wrote Greek with ease, and at fifteen he not only composed Greek verses in lyric measures, but could converse fluently in Greek and without embarrassment. One of his masters said of him, "That boy could harangue an Athenian mob better than you or I could an English one." Toward the close of his fifteenth year, he visited Ireland, with a companion of his own age, Lord Westport, the son of Lord Altamont, an Irish peer, and spent there in residence and travel some months of the summer and autumn of 1800,—being a spectator at Dublin of the final ratification of the bill which united Ireland to Great Britain. On his return to England, his mother having now settled at St. John's Priory, a residence near Chester, De Quincey was sent to the Manchester grammar school, mainly that it might be easier for him to get thence to Oxford through his obtaining one of the school exhibitions.

He became discontented because he thought his guardians were not letting him advance fast enough, hence he ran away from school. The matter was arranged for him to reside in Wales and have a weekly allowance, that he might prepare himself for college as soon as he wished. Not finding books to suit him, he again ran off and hid himself in London. There he remained for about one year. Becoming reconciled to his guardians, he was sent to Oxford in 1803, at the age of nineteen. In the second year of his college life he commenced the use of opium to allay neuralgic pains. The habit once formed held terrible sway over a part of his life. In 1808 he graduated from college, and in 1812 settled on the borders of Grasmere, where he might be near Wordsworth. De Quincey is said to have been the first man in all Europe to appreciate Wordsworth's genius. Here, also, he had the society of Coleridge, Wilson and Southey. He continued his classical and German studies. In 1816 he married, and resided at Grasmere until 1820. Later he lived in London and Lasswade near Edinburgh. In a suburb of Edinburgh he spent the closing years of his life. He edited the "Westmoreland Gazette" for one year.

De Quincey's literary life covered a period of about fifty years, during which time he maintained himself by his pen. But a part of his life was so given over to the influence of opium, that his literary labors were not as extensive or as valuable as they otherwise might have been. He projected works that he could never arouse energy to complete. Finally driven to desperate circumstances, he commenced to write for magazines, and the success of his articles, combined with his need, induced him to place a partial control over his dreadful habit. Making a desperate effort to reform, he contributed his famous "Confessions of an English Opium Eater" to "The London Magazine." In 1820 "The Confessions" were published in book form, and at once attracted a remarkable degree of attention. They were remarkable for their disclosure of his excessive use of opium, and for the marvelous beauty of the style, its romantic episodes, and extraordinary power of dream painting.

"All De Quincey's other writings appeared in periodicals—'Blackwood's Magazine,' 'Tait's Magazine,' 'Hogg's Instructor,' etc. No other literary man of his time, it has been remarked, achieved so high and universal a reputation from merely fugitive efforts. Since his works were brought together, that reputation has not been merely maintained, but extended. The American edition of twelve volumes was reprinted in England in 1853, under the author's own supervision, and extended to fourteen volumes; upon his death two more volumes were made up of previously uncollected material. For range of thought and topic, within the limits of pure literature, no like amount of material of such quality of merit has proceeded from an eminent writer of his day. However profuse and discursive, De Quincey is always polished, and generally exact—a scholar, a wit, a man of the world, and a philosopher as well as a genius."

De Quincey's power of sustaining a fascinating and elevated strain of "impassioned prose" is allowed to be entirely his own. In this his genius most emphatically asserts itself; if it be not admitted that in that dread circle *none* durst walk but he, it will be conceded without hesitation that there he moves supreme. Another obvious quality of all his genius is its overflowing fullness of allusion and illustration, recalling his own description of a great philosopher or scholar. "Not one who depends simply on an infinite memory, but also on an infinite and electrical power of combination, bringing together from the four winds, like the angel of the resurrection, what else were dust from dead men's bones, into the unity of breathing life."

He was a born critic and dreamer, a logician by instinct and culture, a student by choice, a scholar by right of conquest of the stores of many minds, a writer of English of the first quality by dint of native command of language and long study and practice. A short and fragile, but well proportioned frame, a shapely and compact head, a face beaming with intellectual light, with rare, almost feminine beauty of feature and complexion, a fascinating courtesy of manner, and a fullness, swiftness, and elegance of silvery speech,—such was the irresistible "mortal mixture of earth's mould" that men named De Quincey. He possessed in a high degree what the American poet Lowell calls "the grace of perfect breeding, everywhere persuasive, and nowhere emphatic;" and his whole aspect and manner exercised an undefinable attraction over every one, gentle or simple, who came within his influence.

CHARLES DICKENS.

CHARLES DICKENS was born at Landport, in Portsea, England, February 7, 1812, and on the 9th of June, 1870, he passed away. His remains repose in Westminster Abbey.

His father was a clerk in the Navy Pay Office, stationed at Portsmouth, when Charles was born, but subsequently served in the same capacity at Chatham and London. The father was industrious, but failed to accumulate money very rapidly. Mrs. Dickens was a lady of energy and culture, and from her the boy received the rudiments of Latin. The father became embarrassed and was imprisoned in Marshalsea for debt. Charles was set to work in a blacking warehouse, for six shillings per week. In that establishment, it was the boy's duty to tie blue covers on pots of paste blacking. This uncongenial work he followed for about two years. In after life Dickens never complained of unkind treatment while thus employed, but he looked back over that period as the dark hour in his life. It was dark because uncongenial both in work and associates. The lad was quick to learn, sensitive, and ambitious to be "a learned and distinguished man." Thus constituted, the chains of his bondage must have been very galling to him. "And perhaps he was right in after-life to wonder at the thoughtlessness of his parents in subjecting him to such a humiliation. His sufferings were so acute, and made such an impression on him, that years afterward he could not think of them without crying; and there were certain quarters of the town through which he used to pass to his daily work, and where he used to loiter with less than enough to eat, that he habitually shunned for their painful memories." In his wretched condition there were numerous chances for him to become a rogue or a vagabond, but he survived these dangers and became a great novelist. Instead of sinking into the depth of the thronging atoms, he arose above them, or kept apart from them, observed them, and became their describer. It is difficult to tell how much of his success in after life was due to his severe schooling in the blacking warehouse. He did not learn the classics, but he did learn of the many varieties of life, odd and sad, laughter-moving and pitiful, that swarmed in the streets and inhabited the poorer houses of London. In this respect it was an instructive school. It was the true road to the knowledge which he used in his writings. Before his father's misfortunes, the boy had devoured the contents of the paternal library, which consisted of "Roderick Random," "Peregrine Pickle," "Humphrey Clinker," "Tom Jones," "The Vicar of Wakefield," "Don Quixote," "Gil Blas," "Robinson Crusoe," "The Arabian Knights," "Mrs. Inchbald's Farces," and "Tales of the Genii." He was an attentive student and so far absorbed what he read as to live the life of his favorite characters. In that early period of his life, he tried to imitate what he read, wrote a tragedy founded upon one of the "Tales of the Genii," and acquired great fame among his associates as a story teller.

A new period soon commenced in the life of Charles. His father's affairs improved so far as to enable him to send the lad to school. At the age of fifteen, he was placed in an attorney's office among the younger clerks, but poor chances for advancement induced him to abandon the office and take to shorthand as a business for life. In the law office he was a close observer, as may be seen in "Pickwick" and "Nickleby." In the meantime, the father had become a newspaper parliamentary reporter; and the boy, after having mastered the difficulties of shorthand, "spent two years in reporting law cases, practicing in Doctors' Commons and other law courts." It would be difficult to conceive a more perfect way of completing the education of the future novelist, giving him an insight into the strange by-paths of that higher stratum of which he had before had but little experience. At the age of nineteen he entered the parliamentary gallery to enlarge his knowledge still further. He was a reporter of political speeches in and out of parliament for five years, from 1831 to 1836. First he reported for the "True Sun," then for the "Mirror of Parliament," and finally for the "Morning Chronicle." In his excursions into the country and back again with his "copy," he saw the last of the old coach days and of the old inns that were a part of them; but it will be long, as Mr. Forster remarks, "before the readers of his living page see the last of the life of either." As a newspaper reporter Dickens distinguished himself; out of eighty or ninety he was acknowledged as the best.

Dickens' life as an author commenced in 1834. He sent to the "Old Monthly Magazine" a series of nine sketches under the title of "A Dinner at Poplar;" and later he was engaged to write some for an evening off-shoot of the "Morning Chronicle." In the above he wrote under the *nom de plume* of "Boz," a name which he adopted from the nickname of one of his brothers. In 1836 the first series of "Sketches by Boz" was collected and published in two volumes. So popular did the "Sketches" at once become, that the first edition was exhausted in a few months and another called for. "No wonder, for in them we find already in full swing the unflagging delight in pursuing the humorous side of a character, and the inexhaustible fertility in inventing ludicrous incidents, which had only to be displayed on a large scale to place him at once on a pinnacle of fame. There are many of them, such as 'The Parish,' 'The Boarding House,' 'Mr. Minns and his Cousin,' and 'The Misplaced Attachment of Mr. John Donnee,' which show Dickens' humor at its very richest. He had formed, too, by this time, his characteristic likes and dislikes, and plays them off upon his butts and favorites with the utmost frankness. The delight in homely sociability and cheerfulness, in the innocent efforts of simple people to make merry, the kindly satire of their little vanities and ambitions, the hearty ridicule of dry fogies who shut themselves up in selfish cares and reserves, and of sour mischief-makers who take pleasure in conspiring against the enjoyments of their neighbors,—these tendencies, which remained with Dickens to the last, are strongly marked in the 'Sketches,' though lighter-hearted in their expression than in his later works. The mark and indispensable condition of all great work is there, that which Mr. Carlyle calls veracity—the description of what the writer has himself seen, heard, felt, the fearless utterance of his own sentiments in his own way."

In 1836 also appeared the first number of "The Posthumous Papers of the Pickwick Club." These "Papers" were the outgrowth of a suggestion from the publishers, Messrs. Chapman & Hall. These gentlemen, together with the artist, Mr. Seymour, had agreed to issue a monthly serial to be illustrated. Dickens' "Sketches" having attracted their attention, they proposed to him that he should furnish a series of articles descriptive of the adventures of a Nimrod Club, the members of which should go out shooting, fishing, and so forth, and get themselves into difficulties through their want of dexterity. Dickens undertook the work, but he obtained the diverting incidents for the artist through different machinery, namely, the Pickwick Club. The "Pickwick Papers" went off slowly till the fifth number, when Sam Weller was introduced. With this number the sales improved. Seeing the merit of Dickens' writings Mr. Bentley contracted with him to edit a monthly magazine and to write a serial story for it, and also to write two other tales at an early date. But the "Pickwick Papers" were progressing and in a very few weeks the author stood at the very pinnacle of fame. One writer refers to him as standing beyond the reach of critics. The monthly sales

CHARLES DICKENS.

reached 40,000 copies. Sam Weller's sayings were catchwords in the streets and the household wherever the English language was spoken. In 1837, while the "Pickwick Papers" were appearing in monthly installments, he doubled his work by commencing "Oliver Twist." The two progressed steadily side by side. In addition to the above, the "Life and Adventures of Nicholas Nickleby" appeared between April, 1838, and October, 1839.

He resigned his editorship of "Bentley's Miscellany," and started a new publication entitled "Master Humphrey's Clock," the first number of which appeared in April, 1840. This number reached a sale of 70,000 copies. "Master Humphrey" was soon expanded into "The Old Curiosity Shop," which appeared in weekly installments. The completion of "Barnaby Rudge," in 1841, also completed "Master Humphrey's Clock."

In January, 1842, he set out for America. In this country he was accorded a reception greater than Americans usually give to royal visitors. He returned in June to write "American Notes." The people of the United States complained, and justly too, of the treatment they received at his hands. In his "Notes," he was frequently unjust, but all was apparently forgotten before his second visit.

In 1843 he commenced "Martin Chuzzlewit," but this did not sell to meet his expectations. In the same year he wrote the "Christmas Carols." Quitting England again, he settled in Genoa, where he finished "Chuzzlewit," and wrote the "Chimes," his Christmas tale for 1844. He visited various parts of Italy, and then returned to England in 1845, by way of Switzerland. A fortnight's experience as editor of the "Daily News," convinced him that he was out of his place, hence he resigned and again started abroad and wrote a novel in shilling monthly numbers. "Dombey and Son" was the result. A series of letters published in the "Daily News," he afterward collected into a volume, entitled "Pictures from Italy." "David Copperfield" appeared in 1849 and 1850, perhaps the most perfect, natural and agreeable of his novels. "Bleak House" appeared in 1852-'53; "Hard Times," 1854; "Little Dorrit," 1855-'57; "A Tale of Two Cities," 1859; "Great Expectations," 1860-'61; "The Uncommercial Traveller," 1860; "Our Mutual Friend," 1864-'65. An interval of five years between this and the first number of "The Mystery of Edwin Drood," was broken only by contributions to three Christmas numbers of "All the Year Round," and "A Holiday Romance," and "George Silverman's Explanation," written for an American publisher.

For the purpose of establishing closer relations between himself and the people he had started a weekly publication, but in 1858 he decided to draw still closer to the people by a series of popular public readings from his works. Having visited various parts of the United Kingdom, he renewed his acquaintance with the Americans. In 1867-68 he crossed the ocean and visited some of the principal cities of the United States. The success of these readings was enormous from every point of view. Mr. Forster mentions that Dickens remitted from America £10,000 as the result of thirty-four readings. Returning to England, he commenced his work upon "Edwin Drood," but died before its completion. In his will he had desired that he should be buried in "an inexpensive, unostentatious, and strictly private manner, without any announcement of the time and place of his burial." These conditions were observed, but his executors did not consider them inconsistent with his receiving the honor of interment in Westminster Abbey, where he was buried on the 14th of June, 1870, by the side of the honored scholars, statesmen, and warriors of England.

The novels of Dickens will live because they take hold of the permanent and universal sentiments of the race,—sentiments which pervade all classes, and which no culture can ever eradicate. His fun may be too boisterous for the refined tastes of his own time, or for the matter of that, of posterity; his pathos may appear maudlin; but they carried everything before them when they first burst upon our literature, because, however much exaggerated, they were exaggerations of what our race feels in its inner heart; and unless culture in the future works a miracle, and carries its changes beneath the surface, we may be certain that Dickens will keep his hold. The best critics unite in ranking Dickens among the greatest novelists of all time.

BENJAMIN DISRAELI.

THE RIGHT HONORABLE BENJAMIN DISRAELI was born in London, England, December 21, 1804, and he died in London, April 19, 1881, at the age of seventy-six.

His father was Mr. Isaac D'Israeli, a man of great ability. The father belonged to a Jewish family that had been driven from Spain by the Inquisition. The family settled in Venice about the close of the fifteenth century, and assumed the now famous name of D'Israeli.

Benjamin Disraeli was most fortunate in his parentage. The son of a literary genius, he had all the opportunities for culture that books and teachers and paternal encouragement could give. Having secured an excellent education privately, he was placed in a solicitor's office that he might acquire a knowledge of business. As in the case of his father, Benjamin's inclinations were for literature, not business. Encouraged in his inclinations, he appeared as an author in 1826, in a novel entitled "Vivian Grey." The two volumes which appeared at first were increased by a second part the next year. "Vivian Grey" became at once the book of the season and the talk of the town. Referring so directly to public men, society and character in high life, it was read with eagerness by nearly all classes. In 1828 his vein of sarcasm was continued in "The Voyage of Captain Popanilla," an adaptation of Swift's "Gulliver" to modern times and circumstances. He next traveled through Italy, Greece, visited Constantinople, and explored Syria, Egypt and Nubia. Upon his return to England he commenced to take part in politics; but we will give an outline of his literary and political work separately. From 1830 to 1833 he produced "The Young Duke," "Contarini Fleming," "The Wondrous Tale of Alroy," "The

Rise of Iskander," "Ikion in Heaven," etc. In 1834 appeared in quarto "The Revolutionary Epick," a poem which is considered about the poorest of his writings. "Henrietta Temple," "A Love Story," and "Venetia" were published in 1836-37; "Alcaros," a tragedy, in 1839; 1844-45 two successful semi-political novels, "Coningsby, or the New Generation," and "Sybil, or the Two Nations;" 1847, "Tancred, or the New Crusade." This work closed Disraeli's career as a novelist for twenty-four years. His next work was a volume entitled "Lord George Pentinck, a Political Biography," published in 1851. In 1870 he again came forward with the novel "Lothair." His literary life closed with "Endymion."

It remains now for us to tell the story of his political life. Upon his return from the tour which we have already described, he commenced to mingle in politics. Desiring a seat in parliament, he made two unsuccessful attempts as an extreme Reformer, and one as a Conservative. Three times defeated, he finally became the leader of the party known as "Young England." This party proposed to look to the young men of England for national reform and prosperity. About 1837 Disraeli was sent to parliament from the borough of Maidstone, along with Mr. Wyndham Lewis, who died in 1838. In the following year, Disraeli married the widow of his late colleague, who, in 1868, was elevated to the peerage with the title of Viscountess Beaconsfield.

His first speech was looked for with much interest. Having become famous as a writer, and having made numerous threats against leaders of the opposition, which gave them to understand that they might expect a warm contest if ever he reached parliament, the members of that body expected he would make them considerable amusement, if he did not gain a complete triumph. At the appointed time he commenced his speech, which in style and delivery so resembled Disraeli's oriental magnificence as to excite shouts of derisive laughter. Fairly broken down, he took his seat with the prophetic statement: "I have begun several times many things, and have often succeeded at last. I shall sit down now, but the time will come when *you will hear me.*" He profited by the failure, and, determined to avenge the wrongs done him, he commenced a thorough discipline which finally enabled him to become the leader in that trying arena where he first failed. It was Jeffrey's assault on Byron which first woke to activity the powers of that great genius; so the derisive laughter that greeted Disraeli's first speech was the birth-pang of his statesmanship. "He came furious to life, ready-armed like Minerva, blazing in sudden light and deadly power, with a quiver full of poisoned arrows, an unsheathed sword which cut wherever it touched." He soon became conspicuous as a debater. His opponents were handled with great severity. Sir Robert Peel, because of his views on the question of handling the trade interests of England, "was assaulted night after night by Disraeli in speeches memorable for their bitterness, their concentrated sarcasm, and studied invective." In 1851 he was made Chancellor of the Exchequer, but retired with his party in less than a year. Upon Lord Derby's return to power in 1858, he also returned to his old position. At the close of a year the administration was overthrown, and Disraeli retired. In 1868, he was appointed first Lord of the Treasury, or Premier, a position he held till the administration was changed to that of Mr. Gladstone. In 1874 he was again restored to the high office of First Minister of the Crown, and in 1876 he was called to the House of Lords as Earl of Beaconsfield, a title conferred upon him after the death of his wife, the Viscountess of Beaconsfield.

His life as a man of letters, and his efforts as a politician and debater were crowned with brilliant success, and he takes his place in history as one of the most remarkable men of his time.

DRAKE.

JOSEPH RODMAN DRAKE was born in New York, August 7, 1795, and he died in his native town, September 21, 1820, at the age of twenty-five.

At an early age he and his three sisters were left in destitute circumstances by the death of their father. With true heroism he determined his course in life, and entered upon the study of medicine. Having taken his degree, he married in 1816. His wife's father, Mr. Henry Eckford, was a wealthy ship-builder, and he at once placed the young couple in possession of an ample fortune.

Among his most intimate associates may be mentioned James Fenimore Cooper, the eminent American novelist, and Fitz-Green Halleck, the accomplished poet. Drake's longest and perhaps best poem, "The Culprit Fay," written in 1816, was suggested by his conversations with Cooper and Halleck upon the poetical uses of American rivers. The poem became popular, and at once took rank as one of the finest imaginative poems of American origin. In 1818 Drake traveled in Europe, and while abroad wrote several very excellent, witty, poetical letters to Halleck.

Returning to his own country, he formed a literary partnership with Halleck. The two friends wrote together, and signed their names variously as follows: "Croaker," "Croaker, Jr.," and "Croaker & Co." Under the above signatures they carried on an interesting and amusing correspondence through the columns of the New York "Evening Post." The partnership was immensely popular, and the public looked with much interest for the Croaker verses in "The Post." But Drake's health failed before the close of the year, and he went to New Orleans, where he spent the winter. In the spring of 1820 he returned to New York, where he died with consumption within a few weeks of his arrival. He was buried at Hunter's Point, in Westchester County.

The young poet lived just long enough to capture the hearts of the people, and to write a few poems that have made his name immortal. The esteem in which he was held is beautifully expressed by Halleck:

> "Green be the turf above thee,
> Friend of my better days!
> None knew thee but to love thee,
> None named thee but to praise."

The "Croakers" were collected and included in an edition of Halleck's poems published in 1869. In 1835 his only daughter, Mrs. Janet Halleck DeKay, published Drake's poetry in one volume. This volume includes "The American Flag," a lively, patriotic, and beautiful poem, which alone would keep the author's name in the valued literature of his country. There is no more popular poem in the language. It will always stand by the side of "The Star Spangled Banner," by Francis S. Key; "Hail Columbia," by Joseph Hopkins; and will form a part of the popular current literature with Wordsworth's "Old Oaken Bucket," and J. H. Payne's "Home, Sweet Home."

JOHN DRYDEN.

John Dryden was born at Aldwinkle, in Northamptonshire, August 9, 1631, and died May 1, 1700.

Dryden's family came from Cumberland stock, although for three generations his ancestors had lived in Northamptonshire, where they had acquired estates and a baronetcy. The family had inter-married with other landed families in that county. The poet's great-grandfather carried the name south, and acquired the estate of Canons Ashby, by marriage. He is said to have been so proud of his acquaintance with Erasmus, that he named his eldest son Erasmus.

The name was also borne by the poet's father. The natural tendencies of the family were Puritan and anti-monarchical, and "Sir Erasmus Dryden chose rather to go to prison than to pay loan money to Charles I." Sir John Dryden, the poet's uncle, and Erasmus, his father, served on Government commissions during the Commonwealth.

Dryden's education was in keeping with the standing of the respectable families from which he came. The poet was the eldest of a family of fourteen. The father's fortune, although not great, procured the boy's admission to Westminster school as a King's scholar, under the famous Dr. Busby. In May, 1650, he passed from Westminster up to Cambridge. In the same year he was elected a scholar of Trinity, and he took his B. A. degree in 1654. His father died in 1654, leaving the young poet two-thirds of a small estate in Blakesley, worth about sixty pounds per annum. Dryden is said to have spent the next three years at Cambridge, where he laid the foundation of that habit of learned discussion of literary methods which is so remarkable a feature in the prefaces to his plays and poems. His first poems of any length showed strong marks of scholarly attainments, and a good command of verse.

In 1657 he left the university and took up his residence in London. Here it is claimed that Sir Gilbert Pickering, a favorite of Cromwell, made Dryden his clerk. The Protector died in 1658. Dryden emerged from obscurity in his "Heroic Stanzas," to the memory of Cromwell. This poem is a magnificent tribute to the greatness of the Protector. Each stanza in the poem contains one clear-cut, brilliant point, finely embellished by the grandeur of the massive whole. As it gives great pain to lose confidence in a friend, so are our finer sensibilities shocked at the moral propriety of Dryden's next appearance in verse. A hereditary Puritan and a panegyrist of Cromwell, we ought to expect that he would retire, like the great Milton, and remain true to the principles of his party; but upon the restoration of the king, Dryden deplores his long absence and the prosperity of the rebels, and hails the return of Charles in "Astræa Redux." His haste to welcome

JOHN DRYDEN.

Charles shows a shameful contrast to Milton, who was awaiting his fate in blindness. This poem is inferior to "Heroic Stanzas." The unfavorable contrast between these two poems is owing to the fact, no doubt, that "Heroic Stanzas" paid a tribute to liberty, while "Astræa Redux" welcomed the return of tyranny. Again Dryden shows a shamelessly accommodating spirit. The return of Charles revived the popularity of the stage, and Dryden turned his pen toward tragedy. His first effort in this direction proved a failure, whereupon he directed his attention to comedy. In doing this, he makes the following confession: "My chief endeavors are to delight the age in which I live." He acknowledged his inability to appear to advantage outside of verse, but he found it convenient to resort to the best paying branches of literature for a support. However, he does not expect to improve his reputation by his writings for the stage. "The Wild Gallant," taken from Spanish sources, and acted in 1663, was a failure. In the same year appeared "The Rival Ladies," which was described as "a very innocent and most pretty, witty play."

"The Assignation, or Love in a Nunnery," produced in 1673, followed the fate of his first play. After twenty years' experience to guide him in writing plays, his "Limberham, or the Kind Keeper," was considered too indecent for the stage. In verse Dryden was fortunate. He assisted Sir Robert Howard, in 1664, in composing "The Indian Queen," a tragedy in heroic verse. This was the greatest success since the re-opening of the stage. Dryden formed the acquaintance of Lady Elizabeth Howard, whom he married in 1663. The success of "The Indian Queen" led to "The Indian Emperor," which was acted in 1665.

While Dryden was residing in the country at the house of his father-in-law, the Earl of Berkshire, he prepared an "Essay of Dramatic Poetry." His brother-in-law, Sir Robert Howard, made some offensive comments on the essay. "Dryden at once replied to his brother-in-law in a masterpiece of sarcastic retort and vigorous reasoning." This reply appeared as his preface to "The Indian Emperor." Dryden wrote with varying success, till he had passed the middle life. From about 1666 till 1678 he wrote under contract for the stage. His contract came to light by his undertaking to w a play for a rival house. Finally, "Tyrannic Love, or the Royal Martyr," a tragedy, proved very popular. "All for Love," and "Antony and Cleopatra," are two excellent plays. Dryden declares that he put his whole energy into the play "All for Love," and wrote it for himself, not caring what the public might think of it. If Dryden had died before this date, we should not feel it our duty to rank him among the stars whose biographies fill this volume.

At last our author abandoned heroic couplets and attempted satire. Striking the new idea with his "majestic step and energy divine, he immediately took the lead." His first step was Mulgrave's "Essay on Satire," circulated in 1679, followed in the same year by Oldham's "Satire on the Jesuits." The immense success of these satires caused Dryden to take the field as a satirist in 1681. "Absalom and Achitophel" passed through nine editions in rapid succession. These satires secured his fame and made him supreme in English literature during the closing years of his life. He was also Poet Laureate.

GEORGE ELIOT.

MARY ANN EVANS was born at Griff House, England, near Nuneaton, November 22, 1820. Upon reaching womanhood, she married the eminent English author, George H. Lewes. By his suggestion, she commenced to write fiction. Her literary name was George Eliot, and by that name we shall know her in the world of letters. She died in London, December 22, 1880.

Her father, Mr. Robert Evans, was able to give his daughter an exceptionally good education. There were and are so many bad schools for girls that it was a piece of singular good fortune that Mrs. Wellington, at Nuneaton, and afterward Miss Franklin, at Coventry, undertook her educa-

GEORGE ELIOT.

tion. To Mrs. Wellington, the writer in the "Graphic" thinks that George Eliot owed some of the beauty of her intonation in reading English poetry. Besides the studies at school, she was fortunate in finding a willing instructor in the then head master of Coventry Grammar School, Mr. Sheepshanks; and motherless as she was, she possibly studied more deeply than a mother's care for a delicate daughter's health would have permitted. However this may be, the years that she spent in Coventry, on her father's removal to Foleshill, till his death in 1849, were years of excessive work, issuing in a riper culture than that attained by any other prominent English woman of our age, and only approached by that of Elizabeth Barrett Browning. Her first introduction to serious literary work was brought about by Mr. and Mrs. Bray, of Coventry. Mrs. Bray's brother, Mr. Charles Hennell, was interested in a translation of Strauss' "Leben Jesu," which had been intrusted to the lady he was about to marry, and who had performed about one-fourth of the work. When the lady was married, the work of completing the translation was turned over to our author, who performed her duty most acceptably.

On Mr. Evans' death, in 1849, his daughter went abroad with the Brays, and staid behind them at Geneva for purposes of study. Some time after her return to England she became a boarder in the house of Mr. — now Dr. — Chapman, who with his wife, was in the habit of receiving ladies into their family. She assisted Mr. Chapman in the editorship of the "Westminster Review," and her literary career in London was fairly begun. Her work on the "Westminster Review" was chiefly editorial. During the years in which she was connected with it she wrote far fewer articles than might have been supposed. The most important of them were the following, written between 1852 and 1859, inclusive: "Women in France," "Madame De Sable;" "Evangelical Teachings" (on Dr. Cumming); "The Natural History of German Life;" "German Wit" (on Heine); "Worldliness and Other Worldliness" (on Young and Cowper).

While in London she formed numerous valuable acquaintances among literary persons, among whom may be mentioned Herbert Spencer, Mr. Pigott, and George H. Lewes. Her acquaintance with Lewes resulted in her marriage to him. These two eminent scholars lived together most happily; and each profited by the companionship of the other.

Her own somewhat somber cast of thought was cheered, enlivened and diversified by the vivacity and versatility which characterized Mr. Lewes. Was the character of Ladislaw, to ourselves one of very great charm, in any degree drawn from George Henry Lewes, as his wife first remembered him? The suggestion that she should try her hand at fiction undoubtedly came from Mr. Lewes. Probably no great writers ever know their real vein. But for this outward stimulation, she might have remained through life the accurate translator, the brilliant reviewer, the thoughtful poet, to whom accuracy of poetic form was somewhat wanting, rather than as the writer of fiction who has swayed the hearts of men as no other writer but Walter Scott has done, or even attempted to do.

In the maturity of her life and intellectual powers she became known as a writer of fiction. There are those who regard the "Scenes of Clerical Life" as her best work. Beautiful as they are, that is not our opinion, and, at any rate, the "Scenes" failed to attract much notice at first. The publication of "Adam Bede," in 1859, however, took the world by storm. Five editions were sold within as many months. Considerable anxiety was manifested as to the authorship of the novel. In this matter, the actual author was greatly complimented, for the popularity of her work induced one Joseph Liggins to copy the entire book, and then, by exhibiting his manuscript, to claim the authorship. The impostor received some money by subscription before the authorship of "Adam Bede" was fully settled. In 1859 also appeared "The Mill on the Floss," a work fully up to the standard of her former production; and in 1861, "Silas Marner" sustained George Eliot's reputation as a powerful writer. In 1863 she published a more ambitious work than any before attempted. It was an historical novel of Italian life in the days of Savonarola, entitled "Romola." By many this is considered her greatest intellectual effort. She published "Felix Holt, the Radical," in 1866; "Middlemarch, a Study of English Provincial Life," 1871-'72; "Daniel Deronda," a story of modern English life, 1876; "The Gypsie Queen," an elaborate dramatic poem, 1868; "Agatha," a poem, 1869. In 1878 her husband died, thus leaving her alone. The loss was deeply felt by her, but she soon commenced to enter society again, when she married Mr. J. W. Cross. Although many of her friends were not favorable to the new union, yet it proved to be a happy one. In company with Mr. Cross, she visited Italy, and her health seemed greatly benefited by that sunny clime. Upon returning to England, however, the severe winter which followed was most unfavorable. She moved to her new home in Chelsea, but from the effects of a severe cold, died within two weeks of the change, and was laid to rest by the side of Mr. George Henry Lewes.

The complete works of George Eliot have been issued in this country, in eight volumes. While she has written some verses of considerable merit, yet her fame rests upon her prose works. There is probably no question but what she is the greatest female novelist England has produced, and a large class of critical writers deem her the greatest that ever lived.

R. W. EMERSON.

Ralph Waldo Emerson, the most original of American philosophers and essayists, was born in Boston, Massachusetts, May 25, 1803, and he died at Concord, in his native State, April 27, 1882.

His father was a Unitarian minister, and the boy was trained for the same profession. Emerson entered Harvard University at the age of fourteen and graduated at eighteen. He was ordained minister of a Boston Unitarian congregation in 1829, but changes in his religious views led to his resignation of his charge in 1832.

In 1833 he visited England, where he spent a year, then returned and lived a quiet, retired life at Concord, Massachusetts.

His pen first attracted attention in 1837, through two orations entitled

"Nature and Man Thinking," delivered before the Phi Beta Kappa Society at Cambridge. In 1838 appeared his "Address to the Senior Class in Divinity College, Cambridge," also "Literary Ethics," an oration. In 1841 he brought out "The Method of Nature," "Man the Reformer," the first series of his "Essays," and several lectures; 1844, "Young America," and the second series of "Essays."

For four years, from 1840 to 1844, Mr. Emerson was associated with Margaret Fuller, Countess d'Ossoli, in conducting a literary journal, entitled "The Dial;" and on the death of the Countess, he joined with Mr. W. H. Canning in writing a memoir of that learned and remarkable woman, which was published in 1852. In 1846 he brought out a volume of poetry. In 1848 he revisited England and delivered a course of lectures in Exeter Hall, London. "The logicians have an incessant triumph over him," said Harriet Martineau, "but their triumph is of no avail; he conquers minds as well as hearts." In the succeeding year he delivered another course of lectures upon "Representative Men." These lectures are considered among the greatest of his works. In 1856 appeared "English Traits;" 1860, "The Conduct of Life;" 1865, an "Oration on the Death of President Lincoln;" 1870, "Society and Solitude," twelve essays; 1875, "Parnassus," "Selected Poems," and a volume of "Essays." In 1866 Harvard College conferred upon Mr. Emerson the degree of LL. D.

For profound and original thought he has but few equals and perhaps no superiors. He is known as the American Carlyle. No man has made a greater or more lasting impression upon the literature of the age than has the great American essayist and poet.

It is impossible not to be refreshed and gratified by Emerson's prose; but perhaps his poetry more completely carries the reader with it, as being a higher and purer production of genius. The best passages of it are indeed as unmitigated poetry as ever was written; they are poetry down to the last syllable; they are verses which, as he himself expresses it, seem to be found not made. Their meaning is as intimately connected with their form as sound is with speech. The mystic obscurity of some of the poems, however, and the unfamiliar subjects treated, have discouraged or repelled many from the

RALPH WALDO EMERSON.

study of any of them. In reading poetry the mood and the point of view of the poet must be caught, otherwise all is in vain. Emerson's point of view is so far from being conventional or obvious, and is, besides, so lofty and abstract, that the careless and hasty glance of the general reader cannot be expected to apprehend it. Yet such lines as those which compose the poem called "Forerunners," (to select an instance) cannot be paralleled by any contemporary poet; they even recall, in elevation of motive and sustained beauty of symbolic expression, Shakespeare's matchless sonnet which begins, "Let me not to the marriage of true minds," etc. Every word tells, and there is a grand space and breathing room around every word. The movement of the verse is pliant and varied; the choice of words is felicitous and naive, and there are kindlings of imagination worthy of the greatest masters.

Emerson was a fearless critic, and such men as Longfellow, Lowell, Holmes and Whittier, were never offended at his apparent severity in reviewing their writings. He was rarely assailed for his criticisms. Speaking of the magical suggestiveness of Shakespeare's expression, he said: "The recitation begins; one golden word leaps out immortal from all this painted pedantry, *and sweetly torments us with invitations to its own inaccessible homes.*" The scholarly critic and essayist, E. P. Whipple, thus writes of Emerson: "After his return from his second visit to England, in 1847, I had a natural wish to learn his impressions of the distinguished men he had met. His judgment of Tennyson was this, that he was the most 'satisfying' of the men of letters he had seen. He witnessed one of Macaulay's brilliant feats in conversation at a dinner where Hallam was one of the guests. The talk was on the question whether the 'additional letters' of Oliver Cromwell, lately published by Carlyle, were spurious or genuine. 'For my part,' said Emerson, 'the suspicious fact about them was this, that they all seemed written to sustain Mr. Carlyle's view of Cromwell's character. But the discussion turned on the external evidences of their being forgeries. Macaulay overcame everybody at the table, including Hallam, by pouring out with victorious volubility instances of the use of words in a different meaning from that they bore in Cromwell's time, or by citing words which were not in use at all until half a century later. A question which might have been settled in a few minutes by the consent of a few men of insight opened a tiresome controversy which lasted during the whole dinner. Macaulay seemed to have the best of it; still I did not like the arrogance with which he paraded his minute information; but then there was a fire, a speed, fury, talent, and effrontery in the fellow which were very taking.'" When Emerson, on his return, made in his "English Traits" his short, contemptuous criticism on Macaulay as a writer, representing the material rather than the spiritual interests of England, it is evident that the verbal bullet hit the object at which it was aimed in the white. "The brilliant Macaulay, who expresses the tone of the English governing classes of the day, explicitly teaches that *good* means good to eat, good to wear, material commodity; that the glory of modern philosophy is its direction or 'fruit,' to yield economical inventions, and that its merit is to avoid ideas and to avoid morals. He thinks it the distinctive merit of the Baconian philosophy, in its triumph over the old Platonic, its disentangling the intellect from theories of the all-Fair, and the all-Good, and pinning it down to the making a better sick-chair and a better wine-whey for an invalid; this not ironically, but in good faith; that 'solid advantage,' as he calls it—meaning always sensual benefit—is the only good." This criticism, though keen, is undoubtedly one-sided. Macaulay felt it. In the height of his fame, in January, 1850, he writes in his diary: "Many readers give credit for profundity to whatever is obscure, and call all that is perspicuous shallow. But *coragio!* and think of A. D. 2850. Where will your Emersons be then?" Well, it may be confidently predicted, they will at least march abreast of the Macaulays.

His works are translated into all the languages of Europe, and are read by thinkers and scholars all over the world. The thinking portion of society will always treasure up the memory and the works of "the sage of Concord."

EDWARD EVERETT.

EDWARD EVERETT was born in Dorchester, near Boston, Massachusetts, November 11, 1794, and he died January 15, 1865.

His father was the Reverend Oliver Everett, for some time a Congregational minister in Boston, and afterward judge of probate for Norfolk County. The father died when Edward was a child, and the mother removed to Boston after her husband's death.

Everett entered Harvard College, Cambridge, when he was only thirteen years of age, and took his degree of bachelor of arts at the age of seventeen. He was a thorough student, and took the first honors of his class. While at college he was the chief editor of "The Lyceum," the earliest in the series of college journals published at the American Cambridge. His verses and prose essays then show some of the facility and grace which appear in his later writings, and much of the humor which in later times he was always trying to repress. The advice of a distinguished preacher in Boston led him to prepare for the pulpit, and in this calling he at once distinguished himself. He was called to the ministry of one of the largest Boston churches before he was twenty years old. His sermons and his theological writings attracted wide attention in that community. But his tastes were then, as always, those of a scholar; and in 1814, after a service of little more than a year in the pulpit, he resigned his charge to accept a professorship of Greek literature in Harvard College. After nearly five years spent in Europe in preparation, he entered with alacrity on his duties, and, for five more years, gave a vigorous impulse, not simply to the study of Greek, but to all the work of the college. About the same time he assumed the charge of the "North American Review," which now became a quarterly;

and he was indefatigable in contributing on a great variety of subjects. The success of his lectures in Cambridge, and the enthusiasm aroused by the rebellion in Greece led him to deliver a series of popular lectures in Boston, on Greek antiquities. They were the first lectures on purely literary or historical subjects ever delivered in America, and were the first steps toward a system of popular entertainment and education which now has very wide sweep in the United States. He was eagerly engaged in this country in the measures taken for the relief of Greece in her struggle.

Edward Everett's life is almost equally distinguished in statesmanship, authorship, public lectures, and the interest he took in public enterprises. For convenience in considering his life we will keep these items separate. Briefly, then, the following is his public record: In 1824 he entered Congress, where he remained for ten years. He was on the committee of foreign affairs during the whole ten years, and he served, also, on numerous other important committees. In 1835 he was nominated for governor of Massachusetts, and elected. He brought to the duties of the office the untiring diligence which is the characteristic of his public life. We can only allude to a few of the measures which received his efficient support,—the establishment of the board of education, the first of such boards in the United States; the scientific surveys of the States, the first of such public surveys; the criminal law commission, and the preservation of a sound currency under the panic of 1837. Everett filled the office of governor for four years.

Everett availed himself of the opportunity, the following spring, to make a visit with his family to Europe. In 1841, while residing in Florence, he was named United States minister to England, and arrived in London to enter upon the duties of his mission at the close of that year.

Polk's elevation to the presidency led to Everett's recall in 1845. He was immediately appointed to the presidency of Harvard College, but at the end of three years his failing health compelled him, under the advice of his physician, to resign. His retirement was of short duration. Upon the death of Daniel Webster, Everett was made Secretary of State and served during the closing part of President Fillmore's administration. As soon as he was

EDWARD EVERETT.

relieved from this office, he was chosen to represent Massachusetts in the United States Senate. He entered upon the duties of this new position with his usual zeal and intelligence, but before the close of his term of office, he was obliged to resign on account of his poor health.

Everett's literary record may be given in connection with his public lectures. He was perhaps the most finished orator on this continent. The ten years of his life after he had retired from public office most widely established his reputation and extended his influence throughout America. He was frequently invited to deliver an oration on one or another public topic of historical or other interest. With him, these orations, instead of being the ephemeral entertainments of an hour, became careful studies of some important theme, so that the collected editions of them is now one of the standard books of reference in an American's library. Eager to avert, if possible, the impending conflict of arms, Everett prepared an oration on Washington, which he delivered in every part of America. The eagerness to hear him was so great that, from the first, his hosts arranged, almost always, that tickets should be sold to all auditors; and as he traveled wholly at his own expense, the audiences thus contributed more than one hundred thousand dollars for the purchase of the old home of Washington at Mount Vernon, and the securing it as a shrine for American patriotism.

He also prepared the article on Washington for the "Encyclopædia Britannica," which was printed in book form in 1860. In 1858 he entered into a contract with Robert Bonner, editor of the "New York Ledger," to write one article a week for one year, in consideration of $10,000 to be paid into the Mount Vernon fund. These articles were republished as the "Mount Vernon Papers" in 1861. In 1857 he delivered an address upon charities and charitable associations. The address was first given in Boston, then repeated in different places fifteen times, thus raising $13,500 for charitable purposes. In 1859 his address in Boston upon the "Early Days of Franklin" yielded about $4,000 for charitable purposes. In 1858 he pronounced the eulogy on Thomas Dowse, before the Dowse institute, at Cambridge, Massachusetts. At the consecration of the National Cemetery, at Gettysburg, Pennsylvania, November 19, 1863, he delivered the address. When Savannah was taken by General Sherman, Everett addressed a large meeting in Boston to raise funds for the Southern poor in Savannah. He caught cold at the meeting, which was followed by sudden illness and death. He was the subject of eulogies in public meetings throughout the entire country.

Everett wrote "The Dirge of Alaric," "The Visgoth," "Santa Croce," and other poems, besides a life of "General Stark" for "Spark's American Biography." His "Orations and Speeches on Various Occasions" fill four volumes, published in 1869. He also superintended the publication of the works of Daniel Webster, at his special request. A statue of Everett has been placed in the Boston public library, and one in the public gardens.

In Everett's life and career was a combination of the results of diligent training, unflinching industry, delicate literary tastes and unequaled acquaintance with modern politics. This combination made him in America an entirely exceptional person. He was never loved by the political managers; he was always enthusiastically received by the assemblies of the people. He would have said himself that the most eager wish of his life had been for the higher education of his countrymen. A work on public law, on which he was engaged at his death, was never finished.

BENJAMIN FRANKLIN.

Benjamin Franklin was born in Boston, in the colony of Massachusetts, January 17, 1706; and, full of honors as of years, he died in Philadelphia, April 17, 1790, at the age of eighty-five.

His father was born in Northamptonshire, England, where the family line can be traced back about four centuries. In 1682 the father, together with his wife and three children, moved to America.

At the age of eight he was sent to school, but after two years of school life, he was called home to assist his father in the business of a tallow-chandler and soap-boiler. This employment the boy followed for two years, when he was apprenticed to his elder brother James, who, in 1720-'21, established "The New England Courant," the second paper that was published in America. Benjamin made himself proficient in the printer's art, but his tastes inclined him toward intellectual rather than mechanical work, hence he surrounded himself with excellent books. He became familiar with the "Pilgrim's Progress," "Locke on the Understanding," and odd numbers of the "Spectator," then with a large number of the literary novels of the day. In 1723 he sold a few of his books and started in search of employment. He reached Philadelphia, four hundred miles from home, without money and without friends, at the age of seventeen. A printer by the name of Keimer gave him employment. Keimer was not well acquainted with his trade, hence Franklin, being a rapid composer and a person of careful thought and ingenuity, came to be the most important person in the office. Sir William Keith, the governor of the province, assured Franklin that he would assist him to start in business for himself. Accordingly it was arranged for the young printer to go to England and purchase an outfit for an office. Having reached London, he found that Keith had broken his pledge and left him to depend upon finding employment to secure his daily bread. In July, 1726, he again set sail for Philadelphia. While in London, he had been engaged in setting type for an edition of Wollaston's "Religion of Nature;" and this work led him to print a pamphlet, entitled "A Dissertation on Liberty and Necessity, Pleasure and Pain." Forming the acquaintance of Mr. Meredith, a person of some means, Franklin accepted a proposition to direct the business if Meredith would furnish the means for the purchase of a printing office. The money was furnished, the outfit purchased, and Franklin, for the first time in his life, was in business for himself. About the same time, September, 1729, he purchased, for a small price, the "Pennsylvania Gazette." Some spirited remarks on a controversy then waging between the Massachusetts assembly and Governor Burnett attracted considerable attention, and at once assured the success of the young journalist. For the next seventeen years he stood at the head of American journalism.

Franklin's work as a public benefactor and as a literary man commenced in 1731, when he established the first circulating library on this continent. In 1732 he began "Poor Richard's Almanac," a work that continued for twenty-five years, and attained a marvelous popularity. He also became familiar with the French, Italian, Spanish and Latin languages. In 1736 he was chosen clerk of the general assembly, and the succeeding year, Colonel Spotswood, then Postmaster General, appointed Franklin deputy postmaster at Philadelphia. He was also elected a member of the general assembly, and re-elected for ten successive years. About 1737 he organized the first police force and fire companies in the colonies. Shortly after this, he set in operation movements which resulted in the founding of the University of Pennsylvania, the American Philosophical Society, in the organization of the state militia force, in paving the streets, and in founding a hospital. The records show that Franklin was the moving spirit in everything done for the benefit of the city in which he lived.

While thus engaged he made his discoveries in electricity that placed him in the front rank as one of the most eminent of natural philosophers. The experiment was made as follows: a kite was constructed from a silk handkerchief and sent up into the air just before a thunderstorm. To the hempen string he fastened a key. At length the flashes of lightning came, the cord seemed agitated, and the key emitted sparks that gave quite an electrical shock. Thus the discovery was made that lightning and electricity are identical. A friend of Franklin presented the report to the "Gentleman's Magazine," where it was published. A copy fell into the hands of Buffon, who had the article translated into French. There, as in England, it became popular. The "Philadelphia Experiments" were performed in the presence of the royal family of Paris, and became the sensation of the period. The Royal Society of London elected Franklin a member of the Society, and for the rest of his life sent him a copy of the "Transactions." This important discovery carried Franklin's name and fame into every enlightened community on the face of the whole earth.

In 1754 he was sent to a congress of commissioners from different colonies, ordered by the Lords of Trade to convene at Albany, to confer with the chief of the Six Nations for their common defense. Franklin reported a plan for colonial organization that would save England the necessity of sending troops to assist the colonies in their defense. The plan provided that the crown should appoint a presiding general, and that the colonies should elect representatives. Thus organized into a government, the colonies could defend themselves and save England all expense. Fearing that such a union would reveal to the colonies their strength, the Lords of Trade took advantage of Franklin's casual absence from the hall to reject his plan. In place of permitting the colonies to unite and defend themselves, England sent General Braddock over with two regiments of regulars, with instructions to the colonists to maintain them. The assembly sent Franklin to carry a petition to the king. "He arrived in London on the 27th of July, 1757, not this time as a poor printer's boy, but as a messenger to the most powerful sovereign in the world from a corporate body of some of his most loyal subjects."

Lord Grenville was then president of the council, and Franklin, in an interview with that gentleman, learned the opinions of the British Government in regard to the rights and the government of the colonies. Franklin frankly told his lordship that this was new doctrine, and admits that he was alarmed by this conversation, but he was not as much alarmed as he had reason to be, for it distinctly raised the issue between the king and a faction of his people which was to require a seven years' war to decide. Franklin next sought an interview with the brothers Penn, to lay before them the grievances of the assembly. Finding them entirely inaccessible to his reasonings, he supplied the material for an historical review of the controversy between the assembly and the proprietaries, which made an octavo volume of 500 pages. After considerable discussion, the subject of the right of the colonists to tax all estates was settled. Franklin made a report to the effect that the tax be levied. King George II signed the report but a few weeks before his death. Thus he was successful in his first foreign mission.

In the five years that he remained in England, Franklin formed some valuable acquaintances, among whom may be named Hume, Robertson,

Adam Smith and young Edmund Burke. He also wrote numerous powerful pamphlets and articles.

Upon the death of George II in 1760, and his grandson's accession to the throne, there was a general clamor for peace, but Franklin was in favor of a vigorous prosecution of the war. He wrote a pamphlet entitled "On the Means of Disposing the Enemy to Peace." Upon the capture of Quebec, he prepared another paper, "The Interests of Great Britain Considered with Regard to her Colonies and the Acquisitions of Canada and Gaudeloupe," which had a strong influence with the ministry.

In 1762 he returned to America. The peace with the proprietary government was only temporary. Franklin was deprived of his seat in the assembly, after he had been chosen for fourteen successive years; but the assembly sent him back to England to try to secure a change in the government of the colony. He again crossed the Atlantic in 1764, but failed to secure the desired result. The war with France had just closed, and the British Government was considering the best way of paying the "war debt," which amounted to £73,000,000 sterling. Lord Grenville proposed to the American agents in London that the colonists should pay part of the debt by means of a stamp duty. Franklin and the other American agents resident in England wrote to their respective colonies, stating the demands of the British ministry. The colonists objected to the tax on the ground that they were already taxed beyond their strength, that they were surrounded by the Indians, making it necessary to be at constant expense for defense, and lastly that the tax was an indignity because levied by a parliament in which they were not represented. While such was the feeling, the colonists passed resolutions to the effect that if the king would let them know the amount needed they would do their best to raise it for him. The British government objected to the colonists having anything to say about the method of raising the money; hence the "Stamp Act" was presented to the Commons and promptly passed with only fifty dissenting votes, and to the Lords, where it received every vote.

The offensive Act was received with a storm of indignation. Parliament again called up the American affairs, whereupon Edmund Burke made his famous speech for the repeal of the "Stamp Act." Franklin was examined most carefully, and the historian tells us that he was the only witness who lifted a voice that could be heard by posterity. Burke declared that the scene reminded him of a master examined by a parcel of school boys. The celebrated field preacher, George Whitefield, wrote: "Our trusty friend, Dr. Franklin, has gained immortal honor by his behavior at the bar of the House. The answer was always found equal to the questioner. He stood unappalled, gave pleasure to his friends and did honor to his country." The "Stamp Act" was repealed by a majority of 108 almost immediately upon the conclusion of Franklin's examination.

Franklin remained in London from 1764 till 1775, trying to settle the matter in some way, but all his efforts were in vain. He took the position that the Houses of Commons and Lords had nothing whatever to do with the colonies, but that the king and the colonial assemblies constituted the sole law-making authority over them. Then, according to good English authority, the solemn petitions of the colonists to the throne were treated with neglect or derision, and their agents with contumely, and Franklin was openly insulted in the House of Lords, was deprived of his office of deputy postmaster, and was scarcely safe from personal outrage. Satisfied that his usefulness in England was at an end, he placed his agency in the hands of Arthur Lee, an American lawyer practicing at the London bar, and, on the 21st of March, 1775, started for Philadelphia.

Upon reaching home, he found the smoke of battle had scarcely rolled away from Concord and Lexington, and the colonists were in open rebellion. From a peace-maker he became a war-maker. On the morning that he landed at home, the assembly of Pennsylvania elected him a member of the Continental Congress then sitting at Philadelphia. This Congress united the armies of the colonies, and appointed George Washington commander, issued the first continental currency, and resisted the imperial government. Franklin served on not less than ten committees. A postal system was organized, and Franklin was made first Postmaster General. He also planned an appeal to the King of France for aid, and wrote the instructions of Silas Dean, who was to present the appeal. He was one of three commissioners sent to Canada to get the Canadians to join the colonial union. Franklin was next elected a member of the conference which met June 18, 1776, and renounced all allegiance to King George, and called a convention to form a constitutional government for the United Colonies. He was one of the committee of five to draft the "Declaration of Independence." Hancock made the remark when about to sign the document: "We must be unanimous; there must be no pulling different ways; we must hang together." "Yes," replied Franklin, "we must hang together, or we will be pretty sure to hang separately." He was made president of the Pennsylvania constitutional convention in 1776, and in the same year was selected by Congress to treat with Admiral Lord Howe concerning terms of peace, and unanimously chosen to be one of three to repair to the court of Louis XVI to secure his aid.

"At the time of Franklin's arrival in Paris, he was already one of the most talked about men in the world. He was a member of every important learned society in Europe; he was a member and one of the managers of the Royal Society, and one of eight foreign members of the Royal Academy of Sciences in Paris. Three editions of his scientific works had already appeared in Paris, and a new edition, much enlarged, had recently appeared in London. To all these advantages he added a political purpose—the dismemberment of the British empire—which was entirely congenial to every citizen of France."

Franklin secured a treaty with France by which that government introduced the United Colonies into the family of independent nations. He also secured help in money at different times, in all amounting to 26,000,000 francs. His career has scarcely a parallel in the literature of diplomacy. Finally, in 1783, he was one of the commissioners to sign the treaty of peace between England and America. Before this, Congress had refused to accept his resignation as minister to France, but on the close of the war his request was granted.

After numerous attentions from prominent Frenchmen, Franklin set sail for home. On September 13, 1785, he disembarked again at the very wharf where sixty-two years before he had landed a houseless, homeless, friendless and penniless runaway apprentice of seventeen. Note the change.

This time he was received with every mark of distinction. The assembly of Pennsylvania voted him a congratulatory address, public bodies waited upon him, Washington congratulated him by letter upon his safe arrival and eminent services rendered his country. Within a month he was elected member and chairman of the municipal council of Philadelphia, and in a short time was elected president of Pennsylvania with but one dissenting vote. He said in a letter to a friend, "I have not firmness enough to resist the unanimous desire of my country folks, and I find myself harnessed again to their service another year. They engrossed the prime of my life. They have eaten my flesh and seem resolved now to pick my bones." He was unanimously re-elected in 1786 and 1787. In the latter year he was chosen a member of the convention that met to frame a constitution for the United States.

Shortly after his first return from England he married Miss Read, by whom he had two children, a boy and a girl. The boy died young, but the daughter married Richard Bache, of Yorkshire, England. The descendants of this union are the only persons left who inherit any of the blood of Franklin. He left a property valued at about $150,000.

"Though rendering to his country as a diplomatist and statesman, and to the world as a philosopher, incalculable services, he never sought nor received from either of these sources any pecuniary advantage. Wherever he lived he was the inevitable center of a system of influences always important and constantly enlarging; and dying, he perpetuated it by an autobiography which to this day not only remains one of the most widely read and readable books in our language, but has had the distinction of enriching the literature of nearly every other. No man has ever lived whose life has been more universally studied by his countrymen, or is more familiar to them."

GIBBON.

EDWARD GIBBON was born at Putney, England, April 27, 1737, and died in London, January 16, 1794. The date of birth is given in "Old Style."

Gibbon was descended, he tells us, from a Kentish family of considerable antiquity; among his remote ancestry he reckons the Lord High Treasurer Finnes, Lord Say and Seal, whom Shakespeare has immortalized in his "Henry VI." His father was educated at Westminster and Cambridge, but never took a degree, traveled, became member of parliament. His mother was the daughter of a London merchant, and Edward was the eldest of a family of six sons and a daughter. He was the only one of the children who survived childhood; his own life in youth hung by a mere thread. His mother did but little for him. A maiden aunt had the main care of young Edward.

Under the kind care of this aunt his education was commenced. As circumstances allowed, she appears to have taught him reading, writing and arithmetic—acquisitions made with so little of remembered pain that "were not the error corrected by analogy," he says, "I should be tempted to conceive them as innate." At seven, he was committed for eighteen months to the care of a private tutor, from whom he learned the rudiments of English and Latin grammar.

In his ninth year, he was sent to school at Kingston-upon-Thames, but poor health prevented his rapid advancement. He declares that he purchased his knowledge of Latin syntax at the expense of many tears and much suffering. Upon his mother's death, in 1747, he was taken home, but lived chiefly under the care of his devoted aunt, and became passionately fond of reading.

In 1749, in his twelfth year, he was sent to Westminster, still residing, however, with his aunt, who, rendered destitute by her father's bankruptcy, but unwilling to live a life of dependence, had opened a boarding-house for Westminster school. Here in the course of two years, 1749-'50, interrupted by danger and debility, he "painfully climbed into the third form;" but it was left to his riper age to "acquire the beauties of the Latin and the rudiments of the Greek tongue." The continual attacks of sickness which had retarded his progress induced his aunt, by medical advice, to take him to Bath; but the mineral waters had no effect. He then resided for a time in the house of a physician at Winchester; the physician did as little as the mineral water; and, after a further trial of Bath, he once more returned to Putney and made a last futile attempt to study at Westminster. Finally it was concluded that he would never be able to encounter the discipline of a school, and casual instructors at various times and places were provided for him.

But his habit of reading proved of good service to him. He seemed delighted to get historical works. Echard's "History of Rome," and Ackley's book on the Saracens first charmed him and opened his eyes. He exhausted all that he could find in English upon the topics that interested him. Health returned when he was about sixteen; accordingly in 1752, he was again placed at his studies under the care of Dr. Francis, translator of Horace. Before the close of the year, however, he was sent to Oxford, where he was matriculated as a gentleman commoner of Magdalen College. His habits of reading had worked to the detriment of his systematic school studies, hence he was not a favorite at Oxford. His work at the college was soon relinquished. In the meantime he had resolved to write a book. The father, not yet contented with the son's accomplishments, and partly to overcome a class of religious influences that had been thrown around him, placed Edward under the instructions of M. Pavilliard, a Calvinist minister at Lausane. In as far as regards the instructor and guide thus selected, a more fortunate choice could scarcely have been made. From the testimony of his pupil, and the still more conclusive evidence of his own correspondence with the father, Pavilliard seems to have been a man of singular good sense, temper and tact. At the outset, indeed, there was one considerable obstacle to the free intercourse of tutor and pupil. M. Pavilliard appears to have known little of English, and young Gibbon knew practically nothing of French. But this difficulty was soon removed by the pupil's diligence; the very exigencies of his situation were of service to him in calling forth his powers, and he studied the language with such success that at the close of his five years' exile he declares that he "spontaneously thought" in French rather than in English, and that it had become more familiar to his ear, tongue and pen.

His new teacher marked out a systematic course of study, and Gibbon improved very rapidly. In 1758 he returned to England, and for a time remained at home. His father's library was used to good advantage in gathering material. He also used a large part of his quarterly allowance to secure such books as seemed suited to his life work.

In 1761 he published his first work, entitled "Essai sur l' Etude de la Litterature." Though criticised by some, and most of all by himself in later years, yet the essay was well received. But before its publication, Gibbon in May, 1759, became captain in the Hampshire militia, and for two years led a military life. He complains of "busy idleness" in the time spent in military service.

When the militia was disbanded in 1762 Gibbon went to Paris, and in 1764 entered upon his Italian tour. He thus describes his visit to Rome: "My temper is not very susceptible of enthusiasm, and the enthusiasm which I do not feel I have ever scorned to affect. But, at the distance of twenty-five years, I can neither forget nor express the stormy emotions which agitated my mind as I first approached and entered the Eternal City. After a sleepless night, I trod with a lofty step the ruins of the forum; each memorable spot where Romulus stood, or Tully spoke, or Cæsar fell, was at once present to my eye; and several days of intoxication were lost or enjoyed before I could descend to a cool and minute investigation." Here at last his long yearning for some great theme worthy of his historic genius was gratified. The first conception of the "Decline and Fall of the Roman Empire" arose as he lingered one evening amid the vestiges of ancient glory. "It was at Rome, on the 15th of October, 1764, as I sat down musing amidst the ruins of the capitol, while the barefooted friars were singing vespers in the temple of Jupiter, that the idea of writing the decline and fall of the city first started to my mind."

Returning from this tour in 1765, he remained at home till his father's death in 1770. This period seems to have been the most unhappy portion of his life. At the age of thirty he still found himself a dependent. He expressed regrets that he had not "embraced the lucrative pursuits of law or of trade, the chances of civil office or Indian adventure, or even the fat slumbers of the church." But the "Decline and Fall of the Roman Empire" continued to haunt his mind. In 1767 he executed a book in French upon the revolutions of Switzerland; but it was condemned, and never got beyond the rehearsal of a literary society of foreigners in London. In the same year, in company with a friend, he started a literary journal, but the enterprise failed. In a work entitled "Critical Observations," published in 1770, he made his first deep impression. A critic declares it the first distinct print of the lion's foot. It appeared in a style, and with a profusion of learning, which called forth the warmest commendations both at home and abroad.

In 1768 he commenced in earnest upon his great historical work. He exhausted all the references he could find upon the subject. Finally in February, 1776, the first volume of the "Decline and Fall" appeared in print. The success was instant, and, for a quarto, probably unprecedented. The entire impression was exhausted in a few days; a second and third editions were scarcely adequate to the demand. In addition to public applause he was gratified by the more select praises of the highest living authorities in that branch of literature: "the candor of Dr. Robertson embraced his disciple;" Hume's letter of congratulation "overpaid the labor of ten years." The latter, however, with his usual sagacity, anticipated the objections which he saw could be urged against the famous fifteenth and sixteenth chapters. "I think you have observed a very prudent temperament; but it was impossible to treat the subject so as not to give grounds of suspicion against you, and you may expect that a clamor will arise."

The "clamor" thus predicted was not slow to make itself heard. Within two years the famous chapters had elicited what might almost be called a library of controversy. The only attack, however, to which Gibbon deigned to make any reply was that of Davies, who had impugned his accuracy or good faith. His "Vindication" appeared in February, 1779; and, as Milman remarks, "this single discharge from the ponderous artillery of learning and sarcasm laid prostrate the whole disorderly squadron" of his rash and feeble assailants.

In 1781 the second and third quartos of his "History" were published. They were received quietly, but bought and read with considerable interest. Before the appearance of these two volumes he had been elected to parliament in 1774. In 1779 he performed an important work on behalf of the ministry. The French government had issued a manifesto preparatory to a declaration of war, and Gibbon was solicited by Chancellor Thurlow and Lord Weymouth, Secretary of State, to answer it. In compliance with this request, he produced the able "Memoire Justificatif," composed in French, and delivered to the courts of Europe; and shortly afterward he received a seat at the Board of Trade and Plantations,—little more than a sinecure in itself, but with a very substantial salary of nearly £800 per annum.

Gibbon was thirty-eight when he entered parliament. His political career was not satisfactory to himself or his constituency, and he was not returned at the next election. That he might enjoy quiet and devote his life to literature, he sold all his effects but his library and removed to Lausanne, in September, 1783. Again taking up his literary work, the fourth volume, partly written in 1782, was completed in June, 1784. The preparation of the fifth volume occupied less than two years; while the sixth and last, begun May 18, 1786, was finished in thirteen months. The feelings with which he brought his labors to a close must be described in his own inimitable words: "It was on the day, or night, rather, of the 27th of June, 1787, between the hours of eleven and twelve, that I wrote the last lines of the last page in a summer house in my garden. After laying down my pen I took several turns in a *berceau*, or covered walk of acacias, which commands a prospect of the country, the lake, and the mountains. The air was temperate, the sky was serene, the silver of the moon was reflected from the waters and all nature was silent. I will not dissemble the first emotions of joy on the recovery of my freedom, and, perhaps, the establishment of my fame. But my pride was soon humbled, and a sober melancholy was spread over my mind by the idea that I had taken an everlasting leave of an old and agreeable companion, and that whatsoever might be the future fate of my 'History,' the life of the historian must be short and precarious." Taking the manuscript with him, Gibbon, after an absence of four years, once more visited London; and the fifty-first anniversary of the author's birthday, April 27, 1788, witnessed the publication of the last three volumes of "The Decline and Fall." They met with quick and easy sale, and were greatly praised.

Returning again to Switzerland, he entered upon the writing of his "Autobiography" in 1789, from which we gain our knowledge of his personal history. In 1793 he was called to England by the death of Lady Sheffield, and he never returned to his adopted home. Sickness seized him and he died in 1794.

M. Guizot, the distinguished philosopher and statesman, has translated Gibbon's works into French. He reviews the great "History" carefully, criticising its errors and praising its excellencies, then concludes as follows: "I then felt that this book, in spite of its faults, will always be a noble work; and that we may correct its errors and combat its prejudices without ceasing to admit that few men have combined, if we are not to say in so high a degree, at least in a manner so complete and so well regulated, the necessary qualifications for a writer of history."

GOETHE.

JOHANN WOLFGANG VON GOETHE was born August 28, 1749, in Frankfort, and on the 22d day of March, 1832, while sitting in his arm-chair, he went so peacefully to sleep that it was long before the watchers knew that his spirit was really gone. He was buried near his friend Schiller, in the grand-ducal vault.

His parents lived in Frankfort, a free town of the German empire, where they were considered among the valuable families. The house in which Goethe was born is still pointed out to the traveler, in the Hirschgraben. His education was irregular, as he went to no regular school. His father's social standing encouraged the boy to select the profession of an advocate, and to desire to pass the regular course of civil offices in his native town. The elder Goethe, being fond of art and of the German poetry then in fashion, gave his boy the advantages of a cultivated home, and stimulated him to improvement. At that time French influences gave direction to the literary tone of Europe, and young Goethe was greatly influenced by it. In 1765, at the age of sixteen, he went to Leipsic where he was admitted to the university as a student of law. He studied for three years, but the charms of literature drew him away from legal studies. While in school he attended Gellert's lectures on literature. This distinguished man advised Goethe to abandon poetry for prose, and to make authorship an employment subordinate to the serious occupations of life. He also attended the lectures of Clodius, another literary professor. This young teacher corrected Goethe's writing and showed him how to mend his faults. In 1766 Goethe wrote a poem of congratulation on the marriage of his uncle. Following the fashion of the day, this poem was full of gods and goddesses and mythological appa-

ratus. Clodius criticised the production very severely, whereupon Goethe satirized the young teacher in a poem in praise of the confectioner Handel, and by a parody of his drama "Medon." His conduct toward his teacher placed him in bad standing at the university. But his associates were his real school, for they gave direction to his talents. J. G. Schlosser, private secretary to the duke of Wurtemberg, and who afterward married Goethe's sister, had great influence in introducing him into a wider circle of German, French, English, and Italian poetry. Behrisch, tutor of the young Count Lindenau, became Goethe's friend, and his friendly criticisms had a strong effect in producing the simplicity and naturalness of the poet's style.

While at Leipsic he wrote a drama, "Die Laune des Verleibten, or Lovers' Quarrels," and "Die Mitschuldigen, or The Fellow Sinners." The plays possessed ordinary merit.

In 1770 he went to Strasburg, where he attended lectures upon anatomy and chemistry.

Taking his degree as doctor of laws, Goethe returned to Frankfort. He was disgusted with the idea of practicing law. Finally he determined his career in life by adopting literature as a profession. Frankfort was not a literary town, hence Goethe removed to the neighboring town of Darmstadt, where there was a literary circle. These months were full of literary activity. To them belong an oration on Shakespeare, delivered at Frankfort, an essay on Erwin Von Steinbach, the builder of the Strasburg cathedral, two theological treatises of a neologistical character on the commandments of Moses, and the miraculous tongues of Pentecost, and a number of reviews written for the "Frankfurter Gelehrte Anzeiger," which had been founded by Merck. But the work into which he threw all his genius, was the dramatization of the history of the imperial knight of the Middle Ages, Gottfried or Gotz von Berlichingen. The immediate cause of this enterprise was his enthusiasm for Shakespeare. After reading him he felt, he said, like a blind man who suddenly receives his sight. The study of a dull and dry biography of Gotz, published in 1731, supplied the subject for his awakened powers. From this miserable sketch he conceived within his mind a complete picture of Germany in the 16th century. The chief characters of his play are creatures of his imagination, representing the principal types which made up the history of the time. Every personage is made to live; they speak in short, sharp sentences like the powerful lines of a great master's drawing. The first sketch of "Gotz" was finished in six weeks, in the autumn of 1771. Cornelia was consulted at every stage in the work. Herder saw it, and gave his approval. On his return from Wetzlar in 1773, Goethe wrote the piece over again, and published it, with the help of Merck, in the form in which we now possess it. It ran like wildfire through the whole of Germany. It was the progenitor, not only of the "Sturm und Drang" period to which it gave the tone, but of the romantic knightly literature which teemed from the German press.

His "Werther" was printed about 1774, and was immediately translated into every language in Europe. The work was suggested by the following circumstances: A young man belonging to the Brunswick legation, was with Goethe at the university. Being of a moody temperament, having failed in his profession, and being soured by a hopeless passion for the wife of another, young Jerusalem borrowed a pair of pistols from Kestner under pretense of a journey, and shot himself on the night of October 29th. As "Werther," interweaving, as it did, the above circumstances, spread over Germany and made the round of the world, penetrating even to China, the "fever wrung the hearts of men and women with imaginary sorrows; floods of tears were shed; young men dressed in blue coats and yellow breeches shot themselves with 'Werther' in their hands."

"Werther" represents the languid sentimentalism, the passionate despair, which possessed an age vexed by evils which nothing but the knife could cure, and tortured by the presence of a high ideal which revealed to it at once the depth of its misery and the hopelessness of a better lot. "Gotz" was the first manly appeal to the chivalry of German spirit, which, caught up by other voices, sounded throughout the fatherland like the call of a warder's trumpet, till it produced a national courage founded on the recollection of an illustrious past, which overthrew the might of the conqueror at the moment when he seemed about to dominate the world. "Werther" is the echo of Rousseau, the lamentation of a suffering world; "Gotz," in its short, sharp dialogue, recalls the pregnant terseness of mediæval German before it was spoiled by the imitators of Ciceronian Latinity. "Werther," as soft and melodious as Plato, was the first revelation to the world of that marvelous style which, in the hands of a master, compels a language which is as rich as Greek to be also as musical."

He translated Goldsmith's "Deserted Village," and wrote numerous satires and small poems, while engaged upon his great works. His satires were chiefly aimed at the prevailing follies of the day. "Gods," "Heroes," and "Wieland," are the most important of these writings. At the same time, in 1773, he was actively engaged as an advocate. In 1774 "Memoires" or "Pleadings" were published, and the play of "Clavigo" arranged.

"Attracted to Weimar in the strength and beauty of his youth, Goethe rose upon the society like a star. From the moment of his arrival he became the inseparable and indispensable companion of the grand duke." Here he was finally ennobled by the emperor and he took for his arms a silver star set in an azure field. For the purpose of enriching his works he took long journeys to places laden with historic associations. He studied science and art and literature wherever he went, and the fruits of his researches appear in his writings. Finally, meeting Schiller, an eternal friendship sprang up between them that was mutually beneficial. Each exerted a great influence over the other. The first effect of Schiller's influence was the completion of "Wilhelm Meister's Lehrjahre," which ranks among Goethe's best writings.

Schiller and Goethe have been inseparable in the minds of their countrymen and have reigned as twin stars in the literary firmament. If Schiller does not hold the first place it is at least true that he is more beloved, although Goethe may be more admired. It would be invidious to separate them. But it is evident that the best fruits of Schiller's muse were produced when he was most closely under Goethe's influence, and the foreign student of German culture has ground for believing that at some future time the glory of the lesser luminary will be absorbed in that of the greater, and the name of Goethe will represent alone and unrivaled the literature of his age and country. In 1808 an edition of Goethe's works in thirteen volumes was published. "Faust" is considered the best of all his works. A long list of ballads, lyrics, letters, dramas, stories and criticisms, came from his pen in almost endless variety and in masterly style and thought. For the last twelve years of his life he was the literary dictator of Germany and Europe. He took but little interest in the direction in which the younger German school was moving, and was driven to turn his eyes abroad. He conceived an intense admiration for Byron, which was increased by his early death. Byron appears as Euphorion in the second part of "Faust." He also recognized the greatness of Scott, and was one of the first to send a greeting to the Italian Mazzini. He conceived the idea of a world literature, transcending the narrow limits of race and country, which should unite all nations in harmony of feeling and aspiration. German writers claim that his design has been realized, and the literature of every age and country can be studied in a tongue which Goethe had made rich, flexible and serviceable for the purpose. The "Wanderjahre," although it contains some of Goethe's most beautiful conceptions, "The Flight into Egypt," "The Description of the Pedagogic Province," "The Parable of the Three Reverences," is yet an ill-assorted collection of all kinds of writings, old and new. Its author never succeeded in giving it form or coherency, and his later style, beautiful as it is, becomes in these years vague and abstract. Still, without this work, we should not be acquainted with the full richness and power of his mind.

Goethe differs from all other great writers, except perhaps Milton, in this respect, that his works cannot be understood without a knowledge of his life, and that his life is in itself a work of art, greater than any work which it created. This renders a long and circumstantial biography a necessity to all who would study the poet seriously. At the same time he is so great that we are even now scarcely sufficiently removed from him to be able to form a correct judgment of his place in literary history. He is not only the greatest poet of Germany, he is one of the greatest poets of all ages. Posterity must decide his exact precedence in that small and chosen company which contains the names of Homer, Dante and Shakespeare. He was the apostle of self-culture. Always striving after objective truth and sometimes attaining it, he exhibited to the world every phase of his plastic mind in turn, and taught both by precept and example the husbandry of the soul. The charge of selfishness so often brought against him can not be maintained. His nature responded to every influence of passing emotion. Like a delicate harp, it was silent if not touched, and yet gave its music to every wooing of the willful wind. The charge of unsympathetic coldness roused the deep indignation of those who knew him best. He learned by sad experience that the lesson of life is to renounce. Rather than cavil at his statuesque repose, we should learn to admire the self-conflict and self-command which moulded the exuberance of his impulsive nature into monumental symmetry and proportion. His autobiography has done him wrong. It is the story not of his life, but of his recollections. He needs no defense, nothing but sympathetic study. As Homer concentrated in himself the spirit of antiquity, Dante of the middle ages, and Shakespeare of the renaissance, so Goethe is the representative of the modern spirit, the prophet of mankind under new circumstances and new conditions, the appointed teacher of ages yet unborn.

OLIVER GOLDSMITH.

OLIVER GOLDSMITH was born at Pallas, Longford County, Ireland, November 10, 1728, and he died April 4, 1774.

His father, the Rev. Charles Goldsmith, belonged to a Protestant and Saxon family, which had long been settled in Ireland. The father was very poor, and as his profession would not support him, he was obliged to rent and till a small farm which, added to his professional labors, furnished a living for his family. Later, however, the father received a living worth £200 per year, in the county of West Meath. The cottage in the wilderness was soon exchanged for a good dwelling-house on a public road, near the village of Lissoy. This better fortune enabled the father to educate his children.

Oliver, the fourth of seven children, was taught his letters by a maid-servant. In his seventh year he was sent to the village school taught by Byrne, an old soldier, who had been quarter master in the wars of Queen Anne. This old soldier on half-pay professed to teach nothing but reading, writing and arithmetic, but he had a fund of stories and adventures which he delighted to relate to his pupils. The youthful minds were regaled with stories about ghosts and fairies, about the great Rapparee chiefs, Baldearg O'Donnell and galloping Hogan, and about the exploits of Peterborough and Stanhope, the surprise of Monjuich, and the glorious disaster of Brihuega. This man was of the aboriginal race, and could speak Irish, and "pour forth unpremeditated Irish verses." Oliver thus became passionately fond of Irish music, and it may be that his wanderings in after life were the results of the stories and adventures related by his teacher.

In his ninth year Goldsmith was taken from the humble academy kept by the old soldier. In the grammar schools which he afterward attended he gained some knowledge of the ancient languages. Oliver's life in those schools was made miserable by the ridicule which he received from his fellow students. His features were harsh and ugly, and "the small-pox had set its mark on him with more than usual severity." This, added to his small stature, awkward limbs, and disposition to blunder, made him the common butt of boys and master. "He was pointed at as a fright in the playground and flogged as a dunce in the school-room." We might add here, by way of remark, that when Oliver Goldsmith's name was seen attached to the "Vicar of Wakefield" and the "Deserted Village," those who had once derided him ransacked their memories for the events of his early years, and took great pride in the fact that they had been associated with him in school.

In his seventeenth year Oliver went to Trinity College, Dublin, as a sizar. The sizars paid nothing for board and tuition, and the lodging cost but little. All of Oliver's necessary expenses were paid by his uncle. The poet was lodged in a room in a garret, and his name scrawled on the window, by himself, is still read with interest. Goldsmith did not seem to appreciate his opportunities. He suffered all the humiliations, but threw away all the advantages of his situation. In this, as in former schools, "he neglected

OLIVER GOLDSMITH.

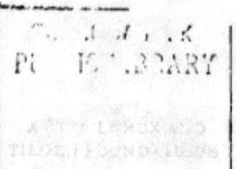

the studies, stood low at the examinations, was turned down to the bottom of his class for playing the buffoon in the lecture room, was severely reprimanded for pumping on a constable, and was caned by a brutal tutor for giving a ball in the attic story of the college to some gay youths and damsels from the city." The tutor's cruelty finally caused Goldsmith to leave college. He wandered about Dublin, leading a life of distress and dissipation, till his brother Henry gave him clothes and carried him back to college. In the meantime his father died, leaving but a mere pittance. On the 27th of February, 1749, he obtained his degree of B. A. and left the university. The next two years were idled away among relatives. Finally, deeming it necessary to do something, Goldsmith tried several professions in turn, without success. He became tutor in a wealthy family, but soon gave up the situation on account of a dispute about play. Having failed in everything else, he determined to seek for fame in the new world. His relatives gladly made up a purse of £30, and "with much satisfaction saw him set out for Cork on a good horse." In about six weeks, however, he returned, and informed his mother that the ship sailed while he was at a pleasure party. Goldsmith next determined to study law, and his relatives promptly gave him £50. This he lost in a gaming house in Dublin. Thinking next of medicine, he received a small purse from his friends and went to Edinburgh, in his twenty-fourth year. At Edinburgh, he spent eighteen months, picking up some superficial information. Next he appeared at Leyden, "still pretending to study physic." In his twenty-seventh year Goldsmith left that celebrated university without a degree, and with but a small amount of medical knowledge and no property but his clothes and his flute. " He rambled on foot through Flanders, France and Switzerland, playing tunes that everywhere set the peasantry dancing, and which often procured for him supper and bed." He went as far as Italy. In 1756 Goldsmith landed at Dover without money, friends or calling. He claimed, however, that the University of Padua gave him a doctor's degree. But we must pass over many more trials in his life, to record the last failures before the grandeur of his mind shone out through the darkness that enveloped him. He obtained a medical appointment in the service of the East India Company, but this was speedily revoked. He next "presented himself at Surgeon's Hall for examination as mate to a naval hospital," but was found unqualified for the position. "Nothing remained but for him to return to the lowest drudgery of literature." He rented a garret and settled down at the age of thirty to toil like a "galley slave." Perhaps it would be impossible to find a life filled with more uncertainties and failures than Goldsmith's up to that time. But from the dark clouds flashed a dazzling light that set the whole heavens ablaze.

He wrote for magazines, newspapers, etc., and published anonymously "An Inquiry into the State of Polite Learning in Europe," "Life of Beau Nash," "History of England," in a series of letters, "Sketches of London Society," also in a series of letters. As his popularity increased, he commenced to widen the circle of his acquaintance. Johnson, the greatest of living English writers, Reynolds, the first of English painters, and the eloquent Burke, were numbered among Goldsmith's intimate friends. In 1763 he was one of the nine who formed the celebrated Literary Club of England. He was enabled to quit his miserable dwelling in a garret, and take more comfortable rooms in a civilized region. However, his expensive habits continued to keep him in poverty. In 1764, being unable to pay his rents, an officer was called in. Goldsmith sent for his friend Johnson, who soon appeared on the scene. The unfortunate poet produced a manuscript. After a brief examination, Johnson pronounced it good, and sold it to a bookseller for £60. This amount relieved his wants, but the manuscript was the "Vicar of Wakefield." Just before this novel was printed Goldsmith reached the crisis in his literary life. In the latter part of 1764 he published his famous poem, the "Traveller." This work was the first to which he had put his own name, and it at once placed him in the ranks as a "legitimate English classic." When the "Traveller" had reached the fourth edition the "Vicar of Wakefield" appeared in print. This work immediately obtained a popularity that has lasted to the present, and must continue so long as the English language is spoken. Charles Fox and Dr. Johnson are unreserved in their praise of the "Traveller," and his two famous works were referred to most favorably by the critics.

Trying his skill as a dramatist, he produced "Good-natured Man," and

"She Stoops to Conquer," two good plays. As a historian, he prepared a "History of Rome," a "History of England," a "History of Greece," and a "Natural History." For the first three he received £1,150, and for the last 800 guineas. These works were designed for use in schools, and were merely compilations in abridged forms and presented in his "own clear, pure and flowing language." He makes some blunders, but the books are valuable for their arrangement and style.

Another celebrated poem, the "Deserted Village," remains to be noticed. In diction and versification, this celebrated poem is fully equal, perhaps superior, to the "Traveller."

"In the closing years of his life, Goldsmith's income was fully £400 per year, and yet he died in debt, in his forty-sixth year. He was buried in the churchyard of the Temple, but, the spot not being marked, is unknown. His friends have honored him with a cenotaph in Westminster Abbey, and Johnson wrote the inscription.

"There have been many greater writers; but perhaps no writer was ever more uniformly agreeable. His style was always pure and easy, and, on proper occasions, pointed and energetic. His narratives were always amusing, his descriptions always picturesque, his humor rich and joyous, yet not without an occasional tinge of amiable sadness."

THOMAS GRAY.

Thomas Gray was born in Cornhill, London, December 26, 1717, and he died on the 30th day of July, 1771.

His father, Philip Gray, was an exchange broker, a man of some wealth and respectability. The father was brutal, and he treated his family with neglect, so that his wife was forced to separate from him.

The poet's mother was an amiable lady, and it was to her affectionate care that he was indebted for an education. The mother and her maiden sister kept a millinery shop, and prospered by their occupation. Mrs. Gray's brother was assistant to the master of Eton, and also a fellow of Pembroke College, Cambridge. "Under his protection, the poet was educated at Eton, and thence went to Peterhouse, Cambridge, attending college from 1734 to September, 1738."

His contemporaries at Eton were Richard West, son of the lord chancellor of Ireland, and Horace Walpole, son of the Whig minister, Sir Robert Walpole. In the spring of 1739, Gray, by invitation, started with Horace Walpole for a tour through France and Italy. Gray wrote remarks on all that he saw of interest. His sketches show admirable taste and deep learning. "Since Milton, no such accomplished English traveler had visited those shores." The galleries of Rome, Florence, Naples, etc., furnished ample opportunity for observations on art, in which department, also, he proved to be at home.

The poet returned to England in 1741. His father died in November following, leaving but a small fortune. Thus left without the means to study, he fixed his residence at Cambridge for the purpose of following literature as a profession. There "he had the range of noble libraries," and "he pursued with critical attention the Greek and Roman poets, philosophers, historians, and orators." He was well versed in every department of human learning, excepting mathematics. He was too studious and critical to be a voluminous writer.

In 1765 the poet journeyed into Scotland and Wales, also to Cumberland and Westmoreland, to view the scenery of the lakes. His letters descriptive of these excursions are "remarkable for elegance and precision, for correct and extensive observation, and for a dry, scholastic humor peculiar to the poet." Returning from these holidays, Gray settled down in his college retreat for close application to study.

A few poems include all the original compositions of Gray—the quintessence, as it were, of thirty years of ceaseless study and contemplation, irradiated by bright and fitful gleams of inspiration.

The following are his finest productions: "Ode to Spring," "Ode on a Distant Prospect of Eton College," and "Ode to Adversity," all composed in 1742. He commenced a didactic poem, "On the Alliance of Education and Government," but wrote only about one hundred lines. In 1751 Gray completed and published his "Elegy Written in a Country Churchyard." The Elegy at once gained a popularity that surprised the poet. "Its musical harmony, originality and pathetic train of sentiment and feeling render it one of the most perfect of English poems." The original manuscript was sold in 1854 for the almost incredible sum of £131. "The Progress of Poetry" and "The Bard" were published in 1757. On the death of Cibber, in 1757, Gray was offered the laureateship. This honor he declined. In 1768 he was appointed professor of modern history in the University of Cambridge at a salary of £400 per annum. But his health failed as his circumstances improved. While at dinner one day in college hall he was seized with an attack of gout in his stomach, which resisted all the powers of medicine, and proved fatal in less than a week. He died on the 30th of July, 1771, and was buried, according to his own desire, beside the remains of his mother at Stoke Pogis, near Slough in Buckinghamshire, in a beautiful sequestered village churchyard that is supposed to have furnished the scene of his "Elegy."

Gray wrote but little, but the uniform excellence of his productions entitle him to rank among the leading literary characters of the world. "He has always something to learn or communicate, some sally of humor or quiet stroke of satire for his friends and correspondents, some note on natural history to enter in his journal, some passage of Plato to unfold and illustrate, some golden thought of classic inspiration to inlay on his page, some bold image to tone down, some verse to retouch and harmonize. His life is, on the whole, innocent and happy, and a feeling of thankfulness to the Great Giver is breathed over all."

FITZ-GREENE HALLECK.

FITZ-GREENE HALLECK was born at Guilford, Connecticut, July 8, 1795, and died in his native town, November 19, 1867.

On his mother's side he was descended from John Elliot, who will be remembered as the great apostle of the Indians.

Halleck was a self-made man, not having enjoyed the advantages of extended training in schools. At an early age he became clerk in a store at Guilford, which position he held till he was eighteen. In 1823 he became connected with a banking house in New York, and for the greater part of his life he was connected with mercantile or banking business. John Jacob Astor recognized Halleck's eminent business ability in 1824 by making him his confidential agent for five years. That great merchant named him one of the trustees of the famous Astor Library, and settled upon him an annuity of two hundred dollars. This amount, added to the profits of his literary labor, enabled him to retire to his native town, where he lived with his sister.

In 1819 he met Joseph Rodman Drake, and a warm and mutual friendship sprang up almost at the first meeting. The young friends were of the same age, both having been born in 1795. Both possessed strong literary tastes and fine poetical sensibilities. Their lives blended so perfectly that upon the death of his friend in 1820 Halleck became a life-long mourner. In 1819 Halleck assisted Drake, under the assumed name of Croaker Junior, in a series of articles contributed to the "New York Evening Post," and known as the humorous series of "Croaker Papers." In 1821, "Fanny," his longest poem, was published. This poem, a good satire on local politics and fashions, was written in the measure of Byron's "Don Juan." In

1822-'23 he visited Europe, where the beauty and finish of his verses soon attracted attention and secured for him many marks of distinction. But very few of his poems, however, were printed till in 1827, when his "Poems" in one volume appeared. The book contained many pieces of great beauty written in England. Notable among these are "Alnwick Castle" and "Burns." The following, which appears in his history of the Scottish poet, will serve to illustrate Halleck's charming style:

> Strong sense, deep feeling, passions strong,
>   A hate of tyrant and of knave,
> A love of right, a scorn of wrong,
>   Of coward and of slave;
>
> A kind true heart, a spirit high,
>   That could not fear, and would not bow,
> Were written in his manly eye,
>   And on his manly brow.
>
> Praise to the bard! —his words are driven,
>   Like flower-seeds by the far winds sown,
> Where'er beneath the sky of heaven
>   The birds of Fame are flown!

"Young America," a poem of three hundred lines, was published in 1864, in the "New York Ledger." He is also author of an edition of Byron with notes and a memoir, and of two volumes of "Selections from the British Poets."

"Halleck's Life and Letters," edited by James Grant Wilson, appeared in 1869, in one volume. His poetical works were published by Wilson in 1871.

Our poet is not distinguished so much by the extent of his literary work as by the quality. His fame was won before he had attained the age of thirty-five; and, although he lived till 1867, he added nothing to the celebrity of his early manhood. Although purely a self-made man, he yet acquired all the polish of a finished scholar. His writings are noted for their care and finish and they show the author to have been possessed of a fine sense of harmony and of genial and elevated sentiments. His martial lyric, "Marco Bozzaris," is known almost in every English home; in fact, the English language contains no finer poem of its kind. Our only regret is that he wrote so little.

A handsome obelisk has been erected over his grave at Guilford, and a full-length bronze statue is to be erected in Central Park New York.

HAWTHORNE.

NATHANIEL HAWTHORNE was born at Salem, Massachusetts, July 4, 1804, and he died at Plymouth, New Hampshire, May 19, 1864.

Hawthorne's ancestors spelled their name "Hathorne;" but in early manhood our author changed the spelling to the first form given above. William Hathorne, of Wilton, Wiltshire, England, who came to this country with Winthrop and his company, in 1630, stands at the head of the American branch of the family. Having grants of land at Dorchester, Massachusetts, he settled at that place. In about six years from his first settlement, he was offered grants of land at Salem, as an inducement for him to remove to that place. Salem offered the inducement, thinking that his presence in the town would be a public benefit. In his new home he soon became a leading man. He represented his town in the legislature, and as captain of the first regular troops organized in Salem, he led his company in a campaign against the Indians in Maine, gaining a victory. Later he became a magistrate, in which capacity he took an active part in the Quaker persecutions. William Hathorne died in old age, well respected, and leaving an ample fortune to his son John. Inheriting the capacity as well as the fortune of his father, John became a legislator, a magistrate, a soldier, and a persecutor of witches. Before the death of Justice Hathorne in 1717, the destiny of the family suffered a sea-change, and they began to be noted as mariners. One of these seafaring Hathornes figured in the Revolution as a privateer, who had the

NATHANIEL HAWTHORNE.

good fortune to escape from a British prison-ship; and another, Captain Daniel Hathorne, has left his mark on early American ballad-lore. He, too, was a privateer, commanding the brig "Fair American," which, cruising off the coast of Portugal, fell in with a British scow laden with troops for General Howe. Hathorne and his valiant crew at once engaged the scow, and fought for over an hour, until the vanquished enemy was glad to cut the Yankee grapplings and quickly bear away. The last of the Hathornes with whom we are concerned, was a son of this sturdy old privateer, Nathaniel Hathorne. He was born in 1776, and about the beginning of the present century married Miss Elizabeth Clark Manning, a daughter of Richard Manning, of Salem, whose ancestors emigrated to America about fifty years after the arrival of William Hathorne. Young Nathaniel took his hereditary place before the mast, passed from the forecastle to the cabin, made voyages to the East and West Indies, Brazil, and Africa, and finally died of fever at Sarinam, in the spring of 1808. He was the father of three children, the second of whom, Nathaniel Hawthorne, is the subject of this sketch.

The above outline shows the characteristics of the family to which our author belongs. We know but little of Nathaniel's boyhood except that he was fond of taking long walks alone. Among the books which he is known to have studied while a child are Shakespeare, Milton, Pope, and Thomson, "The Castle of Indolence" being a special favorite. In his fifteenth year his mother removed to Raymond, Cambridge County, Maine, to live with an uncle, Richard Manning. In his new home he retained his old custom of taking long and solitary walks, but they were along beautiful streams in the primeval wilderness, in exchange for the narrow streets of Salem. In the summertime he visited the woods and streams with gun and rod; and in the moonlight nights of winter he skated alone till past midnight. While thus alone he acquired some skill in writing by recording in a blank book an account of his wanderings and adventures. After a year's residence with his uncle he returned to Salem to prepare for college. At this period the vision of his life work seems to have been presented to him. He edited a manuscript paper called the "Spectator," in which his lively style and unusual talents were clearly manifested. In a letter to his mother he said: "I do not want to be a doctor and live by men's diseases, nor a minister to live by their sins, nor a lawyer and live by their quarrels. So I do not see that there is anything left for me but to be an author. How would you like some day to see a whole shelf full of books, written by your son, with 'Hawthorne's Works' printed on the backs?"

In 1821 he entered Bowdoin College, Brunswick, Maine, where he graduated three years later. He distinguished himself in the classics, especially in Latin. His translations from the Roman poets were excellent, and he wrote several creditable English poems. In college he became acquainted with Henry W. Longfellow, and Franklin Pierce, afterward president of the United States. The college friendship formed by the three young friends, held them together for life. Longfellow was among the first to point out the beauty of Hawthorne's style, and Pierce gave him a public office.

Having graduated, he returned to Salem and withdrew entirely from society. The forenoons he set aside for studying, the afternoons for writing and the evenings for long walks along the rocky coast. So completely isolated was he that at times his meals were left by his locked door. In this early period he wrote extensively but destroyed most of his manuscript. In 1824 he published a melodramatic story entitled "Fanshawe." For want of merit it was speedily forgotten. His reputation was partially made by his writings in "The Token," a holiday annual published for fourteen years by S. G. Goodrich, or "Peter Parley." Nearly all of the greatest American writers contributed to "The Token," but Hawthorne seems to have been the only one who gained any reputation through its columns. In 1835 Henry F. Chorley, one of the editors of the "Athenæum," an English journal, reprinted from "The Token" one of our author's best sketches, and gave a very favorable recognition of his genius. About the same time Mr. Goodrich engaged him to edit an "American Magazine of Useful and Entertaining Knowledge," but paid him very poorly for his work. In 1837 his publishers brought out a collection of Hawthorne's writings under the title of "Twice-Told Tales." The book did not sell well although Henry W. Longfellow reviewed it in the "North American Review," declaring that it came from the hand of a man of genius, and possessed a beauty of style which was as clear as running water.

His authorship, however, was not a pecuniary success, hence he was obliged to look for other means of support. Mr. George Bancroft, the historian, holding an appointment under President Van Buren, as collector of the port of Boston, offered Hawthorne an appointment as weigher in the custom house, at a salary of $1,200 per annum. The position was accepted but its duties were distasteful to him. A change in the national administration left him free again, after two years of faithful public service. He immediately returned to Salem, where, in 1841, he wrote a collection of children's stories, entitled "Grandfather's Chair." In order that he might have leisure for study he united with several others in forming a social Utopia. The Brook Farm, as it was called, was an industrial association located at West Roxbury, Massachusetts, in which labor was to be distributed equally among the members and each was to have a certain number of hours a day for study. The scheme appeared well on paper but Hawthorne soon returned to the ordinary mode of living.

A new period in his life commenced in 1842, when he married Miss Sophia Peabody, and made a new home in an old manse at Concord, Massachusetts. His home was on historical ground, in sight of an old revolutionary battle-field, where he commenced his literary life in earnest. Contributions to the "Democratic Review" had given him a wide acquaintance, and gained for him the support of his entire party. In 1842 appeared a second portion of "Grandfather's Chair," and in 1845 a second volume of "Twice-told Tales." In the latter year he edited the "African Journals" of his college friend, Horatio Bridge, an officer of the navy. "Mosses from an Old Manse" appeared in 1846. Another change in the national administration secured for him the appointment as surveyor of the custom house of Salem, a position he held with distinction till the success of the Whigs retired him. While in office he wrote but little, having spent most of his time in studying. His next work, "The Scarlet Letter," appeared in 1850. This powerful romance at once settled forever all doubts as to Hawthorne's rank in the literary world; it placed him among the masters.

Removing his home to Lenox, Berkshire, Massachusetts, he wrote "The House of the Seven Gables," and "The Wonder-Book" in 1851. Changing his home again to West Newton, near Boston, he produced "The Blithedale Romance," "The Snow Image and other Twice-told Tales," in 1852. Again taking up his home in Concord, he wrote a "Life of Franklin Pierce," his college friend, in 1852; and "Tanglewood Tales" in 1853. A reference to history shows that Pierce was the Democratic candidate for the presidency at the time Hawthorne became his biographer. Our author undertook the work upon the positive assurance that he would not accept an appointment under his friend if he were successful, lest it might compromise him. President Pierce, however, offered Hawthorne the consulate at Liverpool, one of the best gifts at the president's disposal, and our author's friends finally prevailed upon him to accept.

In the summer of 1853 he departed for Europe to enter upon the duties of his office. He remained abroad for seven years, and within that time visited Scotland, the Lakes, and various other places, spending two years in France and Italy. As a result of his journey he produced "The Marble Faun" in 1860.

Returning to the United States he took up his abode at "The Wayside," his home at Concord, and sat down to his desk to write. This time he resumed his pen with a heavy heart. Indeed there were many sad hearts in 1860, for the black clouds of a civil strife were settling over our fair land. The fever of excitement was raging, and the pulse of the nation had quickened into a sharp, wiry throb. He was poor, and the attention of the public was so absorbed by other matters that ordinary literary labor was not likely to be rewarded. In the midst of the strife, in 1863, he published a volume of English impressions, entitled "Our Old Home." This was his last completed work. He commenced "Septimus Felton," but it was not published till after his death, when, in 1872, it was published by his daughter, together with a fragment of "Dolliver Romance." His health failed, his hair grew white as snow, and he sauntered idly on the hill behind his house. Starting on a Southern tour for his health, he reached Philadelphia, where he was shocked by the sudden death of his publisher, William D. Ticknor, who was accompanying him. He returned to The Wayside, and shortly afterward joined his friend, ex-President Pierce. His pen, however, was laid aside forever; for he died in May, and was buried at Sleepy Hollow, a beautiful cemetery at Concord, where he used to walk under the pines when he was living at the Old Manse, and where his ashes moulder under a simple stone, inscribed with the single word, "Hawthorne."

Henry A. Page has published an interesting volume of "Memorials of Hawthorne." His widow edited and published "Passages from the American Note-book of Nathaniel Hawthorne" in two volumes in 1868, and "Passages from the English Note-book" in two volumes in 1870. While the "Scarlet Letter" may be regarded as his masterpiece, yet "Seven Gables" and "Blithedale" are among the best works of the kind in print.

"The writings of Hawthorne are marked by subtle imagination, curious power of analysis, and exquisite purity of diction. He studied exceptional developments of character and was fond of exploring secret crypts of emotion. His shorter stories are remarkable for originality and suggestiveness, and his longer ones are as absolute creations as 'Hamlet' or 'Undine.' Lacking the accomplishment of verse, he was in the highest sense a poet. His work is pervaded by a manly personality, and by an almost feminine delicacy and gentleness. He inherited the gravity of his Puritan ancestors without their superstitions, and learned in his solitary meditations a knowledge of the night-side of life which would have filled them with suspicion. A profound anatomist of the heart, he was singularly free from morbidness, and in his darkest speculations concerning evil, was robustly right-minded. He worshiped conscience with his intellectual as well as his moral nature; it is supreme in all he wrote. Besides these mental traits he possessed the literary quality of style—a grace, a charm, a perfection of language, which no other American writer ever possessed in the same degree, and which places him among the great masters of English prose."

FRANCIS BRET HARTE.

BRET HARTE was born in Albany, New York, August 25, 1839, and at present, at the age of forty-five, he is enjoying the fruits of labor well rewarded, and a world-wide reputation.

When but seventeen years old, young Harte went to California and led a roving life for three years, sometimes among the miners digging for gold, sometimes teaching school, and finally acting as an "express messenger." In 1857 he worked as a compositor on the "Golden Era" in San Francisco. He contributed graphic and interesting sketches of California to this paper without making their authorship known to the editor. In a short time he was given a place on the editorial staff. Later he edited a weekly called "The Californian." For six years he was secretary of the United States branch mint in San Francisco. At the starting of the "Overland Monthly," in 1868, Hart became its editor, but resigned in 1871 and located in New York City.

His style is purely American. His poems are both grave and humorous, something after the style of J. R. Lowell, and his prose works give varied pictures of wild life in the West. Harte's excellent character sketches and original humor lifted him suddenly from obscurity to literary prominence, and carried his fame across the Atlantic. So popular did he become in England, that in 1871 and 1872 two London book-sellers republished his works and placed them on sale.

His most popular writings are "East and West," "That Heathen Chinee," "Truthful James," "Luck of Roaring Camp," and a prose work, "Condensed Novels," being a travesty of some popular works of fiction. Later, in 1876, appeared "Gabriel Conroy," his first complete novel, in the regular

BRET HARTE.

three-volume shape. Critics find greater faults in this than in his earlier sketches. His great reputation was won by his poems and sketches descriptive of his life among the California miners. These are mostly in the peculiar dialect of the miners, and they show the romance and the roughness, the crime and the tenderness, of the peculiar phase of American life in the mines of the West.

His sketches command universal admiration, and by common consent he is ranked among the most popular of living writers. At present he resides in New York.

MRS. HEMANS.

FELICIA DOROTHEA HEMANS was born in Duke Street, Liverpool, September 25, 1793, and she died on the evening of May 16, 1835, and was buried in a vault under St. Anne's Church, Dublin.

George Brown, her father, of Irish descent, was, at the time of Felicia's birth, a merchant at Liverpool. Her mother, a daughter of Mr. Wagner, Austrian and Tuscan consul at Liverpool, was of united Austrian and German descent. When Felicia was but seven years old, her father failed in business, and retired to Gwrych, near Abergele. There the young poetess and her brothers and sisters grew up in the wildest seclusion, in a romantic old house by the sea-shore, and in the very midst of the mountains and myths of Wales, the monotony of her young life being varied only by two visits to London, which she never revisited in after years. The little Felicia was a lovely, precocious child. Her education was desultory; and she may, indeed, be said to have educated herself, the only subjects in which she ever received regular instruction being French, English grammar and the rudiments of Latin. Books of chronicle and romance, and every kind of poetry, she read with avidity; and she studied Italian, Spanish, Portuguese and

German sufficiently to be able to read them with ease and enjoyment. She was also fond of music and played on the harp and piano, her preference being for simple national and pathetic melodies, especially those of Wales and Spain. In 1808, when she was only fourteen, a quarto volume of the "Juvenile Poems" was published by subscription. These poems show considerable ability from one so young, but they were harshly criticised in the "Monthly Review." Her sensitiveness is seen in the fact that she spent several days in tears over the criticisms she had received. Her strength is also shown in the fact that she soon returned to her task with redoubled energy.

A new theme presented itself in the war in Spain. One of her brothers was fighting under the celebrated Sir John Moore. Fired with military enthusiasm, she wrote an elaborate poem, entitled "England and Spain, or Valor and Patriotism." The poem was well received and even translated into Spanish. In 1812 appeared her second volume under the title of "The Domestic Affections and Other Poems." In the same year she married Captain Hemans. For a short time the young couple resided at Daventry, where her husband was appointed adjutant of the Northamptonshire militia; but about this time her father went on some commercial enterprise to Quebec and died there; and after the birth of her eldest son she and her husband took up their abode with her widowed mother at Bronwylfa. Here in the next six years four more children—all boys—were born; but in spite of domestic cares and uncertain health she still read and wrote indefatigably. Her poem entitled "The Restoration of Works of Art to Italy" was published in 1816; her "Modern Greece" in 1817, and in the following year appeared her volume of "Translations from Camoens and other Poets."

Mrs. Hemans' married life seems not to have been altogether fortunate. Captain Hemans went to Rome in 1818 and never returned. It was claimed that he went on account of his health, but it was mutually agreed that they should live apart for a time, on account of their limited means. For a little while a correspondence was kept up, and he was consulted concerning the interests of the children, but that soon ceased and they never again met. Thus left alone to care for her five little boys she commenced her literary work with great earnestness and unusual success. She continued to reside with her mother at Bronwylfa, where numerous and influential friends clustered around her.

In 1819 she published "Tales and Historic Scenes in Verse," and secured a prize of £50 offered for the best poem on "The Meeting of Wallace and Bruce on the Banks of the Carron." The poem appeared in "Blackwood's Magazine." In 1820 appeared "The Sceptic" and "Stanzas to the Memory of the Late King." She won a prize in 1821, which was accorded by the Royal Society of Literature for the best poem on the subject of "Dartmoor," and commenced in the same year her play entitled "The Vespers of Palermo." The play was not acted till in 1823, when she received £200 for the copyright, but it was considered a failure, and withdrawn. Later it was acted successfully in Edinburgh, when Sir Walter Scott wrote an epilogue for it which was spoken by Mrs. Henry Siddons. The subject led to a correspondence between Mrs. Hemans and the great novelist, which resulted in a lasting friendship. In 1821 she commenced the study of the German language, and wrote some on the grave of Korner, in which she paid a fine tribute to the genius of the young soldier-poet. In 1823 appeared "The Voices of Spring," one of her finest lyrics, contributed to the "New Monthly Magazine;" a volume of her poems containing "The Siege of Valencia," "The Last Constantine" and "Belshazzar's Feast;" also "De Chatillon, or the Crusaders." The manuscript of "De Chatillon" was lost, and the poem was not published till after her death, and then from a rough copy. In 1824 she began "The Forest Sanctuary," which, with "The Lays of Many Lands" and other pieces collected from her contributions to periodicals, was published in 1825.

In 1825 Mrs. Hemans with her family, an unmarried sister, and her mother, removed to Rhyllon, on the heights across the Clwyd River. The contrast between the new home and the old one suggested her "Dramatic Scene between Bronwylfa and Rhyllon." The poor house with its beautiful surroundings she celebrated in "The Hour of Romance," "To the River Clwyd in North Wales," "Our Lady's Well," and "To a Distant Scene." This seems to have been the most pleasant time of her life. Her children were growing up in her home; her fame was at its height; not England alone, but America as well had acknowledged her genius; and Professor Norton, of Harvard University, was bringing out a complete edition of her works in the New World, for her benefit. Her mother's death in 1827 was a great breaking-point in her life, and from that date she was an acknowledged invalid. In the summer of 1828 the "Records of Women" appeared; in 1830, "The Songs of the Affections;" in 1834, "Hymns of Children," which had previously appeared in America; in the same year, "National Lyrics," and "Scenes and Hymns of Life," also a translation of Goethe's "Tasso," with introduction and explanatory notes. While enduring great suffering, she wrote the lyric, "Despondency and Aspiration," "Thoughts during Sickness;" and when she seemed to be recovering, she wrote "Recovering." Her last poem, "The Sabbath Sonnet," was dedicated to her brother on April 26, and on May 16, following, she died. It will be seen that Mrs. Hemans wrote extensively for one in her delicate health, and charged with the sole care of a family.

In the later years of her life she visited Scotland, and was cordially received at Edinburgh. She formed numerous and valuable acquaintances, chief among whom were Jeffrey, who praised her in the "Edinburgh Review," and Sir Walter Scott. She enjoyed constant, almost daily intercourse, with Scott, who said to her at parting: "There are some whom we meet, and should like ever after to claim as kith and kin; and you are one of those." In 1830 she visited Wordsworth and the Lake country, and paid a second visit to Scotland. She seems to have been very greatly impressed with Wordsworth's beautiful home by Rydal Lake and Grasmere.

> O vale and lake, within your mountain urn
>   Smiling so tranquilly, and set so deep!
> Oft doth your dreamy loveliness return,
>   Coloring the tender shadows of my sleep
> With light Elysian; for the hues that steep
>   Your shores in melting lustre, seem to float
> On golden clouds from spirit-lands remote—
>   Isles of the blest—and in our memory keep
> Their place with holiest harmonies.

"Mrs. Hemans' poetry is the production of a fine imagination and enthusiastic temperament, but not of a commanding intellect or very complex or subtle nature. It is the outcome of a beautiful but singularly circumstanced life, a life spent in romantic seclusion, without much worldly experience, and warped and saddened by domestic unhappiness and real physical suffering. Perhaps from these circumstances, aided by a course of self-instruction at best desultory and unguided, the emotional in a sensitive and intensely feminine nature was unduly cultivated: and this undue preponderance of the emotional is a prevailing characteristic in Mrs. Hemans' poetry, and one to which Scott alluded when he complained that it was 'too poetical,' that it contained 'too many flowers,' and 'too little fruit.' But it is as a lyrist that Felicia Hemans has earned so high a place among our poets. In her lyrics she could concentrate her strength on the perfect expression of simple themes. Her skill in versification, her delicate ear for rhythm, and the few ruling sentiments of her nature found ample scope. In her lyrics, Mrs. Hemans is uniformly graceful, tender, delicately refined,—sometimes perhaps, even here, too fervent, too emotional,—but always pure and spiritual in tone; and in these, too, she occasionally displays those rare qualities which belong only to the finest lyric genius. Many of her poems, such as 'The Treasures of the Deep,' 'The Better Land,' 'The Homes of England,' 'Casabianca,' 'The Palm Tree,' 'The Graves of a Household,' 'The Wreck,' 'The Dying Improvisator,' and 'The Lost Pleiad,' have become standard English lyrics, and on the strength of these, and others such as these, Felicia Hemans is ranked among our chief British lyrical poets."

OLIVER WENDELL HOLMES.

HOLMES was born at Cambridge, Massachusetts, August 29, 1809, and is still young in spirits at the age of seventy-six.

At the age of twenty he graduated at Harvard University, then took up the study of law. This study, however, was soon abandoned for medicine. He studied in Europe for a short time, and took his degree as doctor of medicine, at Cambridge, in 1836. Two years later he was appointed to the chair of Anatomy and Physiology in Dartmouth College. This position he held till 1847, when he accepted a similar position at Harvard, where he still remains. All of his literary work has been performed in addition to the labors of a continuous professorship in college of about forty-seven years.

Holmes' literary tastes were early indicated by his comic and satiric verse contributed to "The Collegian." These were excellent of their kind. In his early works, the mirth so often outweighed the sentiment as to lessen the promise and the self-prediction of his being a poet indeed. While many of his youthful stanzas are serious and elegant, those which approach the feeling of true poetry are in celebration of companionship and good cheer. He seems to exemplify what Emerson was wont to preach, that there is honest wisdom in song and joy. He contributed numerous pieces to American periodicals, and in 1836 collected his poems into a volume. His life has not been marked by any noted events, but it has been like the steady movement of a great river. It has grown broader and deeper in each mile of its progress. "Holmes is a shining instance of one who has done solid work as a teacher and practitioner, in spite of his success in literature." "Poetry," a metrical essay, was followed by "Terpsichore," a poem; in 1846, "Urania;"

in 1850, "Astræa," "The Balance of Allusions," a poem. These poems were first delivered before college and literary societies.

"Though the most direct and obvious of the Cambridge group, the least given to subtleties, he is our typical university poet; the minstrel of the college that bred him, and within whose liberties he has taught, jested, sung, and toasted, from boyhood to what in common folk would be old age. Alma Mater has been more to him than to Lowell or Longfellow, and not until he came into her estate could Harvard boast a natural songster as her laureate. Two centuries of acclimation, and some experience of liberty, probably were needed to germinate the fancy that riots in his measures. Before his day, moreover, the sons of the Puritans hardly were ripe for the doctrine that there is a time to laugh, that humor is quite as helpful a constituent of life as gravity or gloom. Provincial-wise, they at first had to receive this in its cruder form, and relished heartily the broad fun of Holmes' youthful verse. Their mirth-maker soon perceived that both fun and feeling are heightened when combined. The poet of 'The Last Leaf' was among the first to teach his countrymen that pathos is an equal part of true humor; that sorrow is lightened by jest, and jest redeemed from coarseness by emotion, under most conditions of this our evanescent human life."

Turning his attention to prose, he published, in 1858, "The Autocrat of the Breakfast Table," a series of light and genial essays full of fancy and humor, which has been successful both in the New and Old World. It appears that this work was planned in his youth; but we owe to his maturity the experience, drollery, proverbial humor, and suggestion that flow at ease through its pages. Little is too high or too low for the comment of this down-east philosopher. A kind of attenuated Franklin, he views things and folks with the less robustness, but with keener distinction and insight. His pertinent maxims are so frequent that it seems, as was said of Emerson, as if he had jotted them down from time to time and here first brought them to application; they are apothegms of common life and action, often of mental experience, strung together by a device so original as to make the work quite a novelty in literature. The Autocrat holds an intellectual tourney at a boarding-house table; there jousts against humbug and stupidity, gives light touches of knowledge, sentiment, illustration, coins here and there a phrase destined to be long current, nor forgets the poetic duty of providing a little idyl of human love and interest.

This was followed by "The Professor at the Breakfast Table," and later by "The Poet at the Breakfast Table." "The Professor" is written somewhat in the manner of Sterne, yet without much artifice. The story of Iris is an interwoven thread of gold. The poems in this book are inferior to those of the Autocrat, but its author here and there shows a gift of drawing real characters; the episode of the Little Gentleman is itself a poem,—its close very touching, though imitated from the death scene in Tristram Shandy. "The Poet at the Breakfast Table," written some years after, is of a more serious cast than its predecessors, chiefly devoted to Holmes' peculiar mental speculations and his fluent gossip on books and learning. He makes his rare old pundit a liberal thinker, clearly of the notion that a high scholarship leads to broader views.

Between the second and third of the "Autocrat" series, appeared, in 1861, "Elsie Venner," and in 1868, "The Guardian Angel," two excellent novels. Then, in 1872, he published "Mechanism in Thought and Morals." He is also author of a valuable medical work, and of numerous essays and poems of value.

When the civil war broke out, this conservative poet, who had taken little part in the agitation that preceded it, shared in every way the spirit and duties of the time. None of our poets wrote more stirring war lyrics during the conflict; none has been more national so far as loyalty, in a Websterian sense, to our country and her emblem is concerned. He always has displayed the simple, instinctive patriotism of the American minute-man. He may or may not side with his neighbors, but he is for the nation. His pride is not of English, but of long American descent.

Than Holmes, no one has written a greater number of short beautiful poems, that are on every tongue. When a noted American ship was declared unseaworthy, and about to be abandoned, our poet came forward with a magnificent poem, entitled "Old Ironsides," that gave that fine old ship a half century of preservation.

"The Last Leaf," "My Aunt," "The Pilgrim's Vision," "The One Hoss Shay," "Union and Liberty," "Welcome to the Nations," "The Boys," and "Bill and Joe," are as good selections of the serious, grand, comic and humorous, as one could wish. E. C. Stedman tells us that with respect to style, there is no one more free from structural whims and vagaries. He has an ear for the "classical" forms of English verse, the academic measures which still bid fair to hold their own—those confirmed by Pope and Goldsmith, and here in vogue long after German dreams, Italian languors, and the French rataplan had their effect upon the poets of our motherland across the sea. His way of thought, like his style, is straightforward and sententious; both are the reverse of what is called transcendental. When he has sustained work to do, and braces himself for a great occasion, nothing will suit but the rhymed pentameter; his heaviest roadster, sixteen hands high, for a long journey. It has served him well, is his by use and possession, and he sturdily will trust it to the end:

> "Friends of the Muse, to you of right belong
> The first staid footsteps of my square-toed song;
> Full well I know the strong heroic line
> Has lost its fashion since I made it mine;
> But there are tricks old singers will not learn,
> And this grave measure still must serve my turn.
>
> * * * * * * *
>
> Nor let the rhymester of the hour deride
> The straight-backed measure with its stately stride;
> It gave the mighty voice of Dryden scope;
> It sheathed the steel-bright epigrams of Pope;
> In Goldsmith's verse it learned a sweeter strain;
> Byron and Campbell wore its clanking chain;
> I smile to listen while the critic's scorn
> Flouts the proud purple kings have nobly worn;
> Bid each new rhymer try his dainty skill
> And mould his frozen phrases as he will;
> We thank the artist for his neat device,—
> The shape is pleasing, though the stuff is ice."

In the later years of his life, he has not written as extensively as before, but he has given us some of the best thoughts. Many of his sayings must stand among the finest specimens of American wit and humor; and his writings, as a whole, will always be classed among the best of their kind. In his prose works we are constantly delighted by the frequent occurrence of the most brilliant and original thoughts. He will always stand in the temple of American literature, among the most brilliant and popular writers.

THOMAS HOOD.

THOMAS HOOD was born on May 23, 1789, and died May 3, 1845.

His father was a man of considerable ability, having written two successful novels. He was also a bookseller, of the firm of Vernor & Hood.

The teacher of Thomas Hood was a person who appreciated the boy's ability, and made him feel it impossible not to take an interest in his studies. This is considered one of the most fortunate incidents of his boyhood. Under the guidance of his teacher, Hood earned a few shillings by revising for the press a new edition of "Paul and Virginia." He was educated for the counting-house, and was given employment by a friend of the family, but he soon found that the work was not suited to his tastes. By close confinement in the room and at a distasteful occupation, his health, never vigorous, soon gave way, which led to his retirement from the merchant's desk. He was sent to reside with relatives at Dundee. "He has graphically described his unconditional rejection by this inhospitable personage, and the circumstances under which he found himself in a strange town without an acquaintance, with the most sympathetic nature, anxious for intellectual and moral culture, but without guidance, instruction or control. This self-dependence, however, suited the originality of his character; he became a large and indiscriminate reader, and before long contributed humorous and

poetical articles to the provincial newspapers and magazines. As a proof of the seriousness with which he regarded the literary vocation, it may be mentioned that he used to write out his poems in printed characters, believing that that process best enabled him to understand his own peculiarities and faults, and probably unconscious that Coleridge had recommended some such method of criticism when he said he thought 'print settles it.'"

While living at Dundee, Mr. Hood showed most clearly his taste for literature. He contributed to the local newspapers, and also to the "Dundee Magazine," a periodical of considerable merit. On the re-establishment of his health, he returned to London, and was put apprentice to a relation, an engraver. At this employment he remained just long enough to acquire a taste for drawing, which was afterward of essential service to him in illustrating his poetical productions. In 1821, Mr. John Scott, the editor of the "London Magazine," was killed in a duel, and that periodical passed into the hands of some friends of Hood, who proposed to him to take a part in its publication. His installation into this congenial post at once introduced him to the best literary society of the time; and in becoming the associate of such men as Charles Lamb, Cary, De Quincey, Allan Cunningham, Proctor, Talfourd, Hartley Coleridge, the peasant poet Clare, and other contributors to that remarkable miscellany, he gradually developed his own intellectual powers, and enjoyed that happy intercourse with superior minds for which his cordial and genial character was so well adapted, and which he has described in his best manner in several chapters of "Hood's Own." "Odes and Addresses"—his first work—was written about this time, in conjunction with his brother-in-law, Mr. J. H. Reynolds, the friend of Keats; and it is agreeable to find Sir Walter Scott acknowledging the gift of the work with no formal expressions of gratification, but "wishing the unknown author good health, good fortune, and whatever other good things can best support and encourage his lively vein of inoffensive and humorous satire." "Whims and Oddities," "National Tales," "Tylney Hall," a novel, and "The Plea of the Midsummer Fairies" followed. In these works the humorous faculty not only predominated, but expressed itself with a freshness, originality and power which the poetical element could not claim. There was much true poetry in the verse, and much sound sense and keen observation in the prose of these works; but the poetical feeling and lyrical facility of the one, and the more solid qualities of the other, seemed best employed when they were subservient to his rapid wit, and to the ingenious coruscations of his fancy. This impression was confirmed by the series of the "Comic Annual," a kind of publication at that time popular, which Hood undertook and continued, almost unassisted, for several years. Under that somewhat frivolous title he treated all the leading events of the day in a fine spirit of caricature, entirely free from grossness and vulgarity, without a trait of personal malice, and with an undercurrent of true sympathy and honest purpose that will preserve these papers, like the sketches of Hogarth, long after the events and manners they illustrate have passed from the minds of men.

"Up the Rhine" is a satire upon the absurdities of English travelers. In 1843 he published "Whimsicalities, a Periodical Gathering," in two volumes. These volumes were made up chiefly from his articles formerly published in the "New Monthly Magazine."

In another annual called the "Gem," appeared the poem on the story of "Eugene Aram," which first manifested the full extent of that poetical vigor which seemed to advance just in proportion as his physical health declined. He started a magazine in his own name, for which he secured the assistance of many literary men of reputation and authority, but which was mainly sustained by his own intellectual activity. From a sick-bed, from which he never rose, he conducted this work with surprising energy, and there composed those poems, too few in number, but immortal in the English language, such as the "Song of the Shirt," the "Bridge of Sighs," and the "Song of the Labourer," which seized the deep human interests of the time, and transported them from the ground of social philosophy into the loftier domain of the imagination. They are no clamorous expressions of anger at the discrepancies and contrasts of humanity, but plain, solemn pictures of conditions of life which neither the politician nor the moralist can deny to exist, and which they are imperatively called upon to remedy. Woman, in her wasted life, in her hurried death, here stands appealing to the society that degrades her, with a combination of eloquence and poetry, of forms of art at once instantaneous and permanent, and with a metrical energy and variety of which perhaps our language alone is capable. Prolonged illness brought on straightened circumstances, and application was made to Sir Robert Peel to place Hood's name on the pension list with which the British state so moderately rewards the national services of literary men. This was done readily and without delay, and the pension was continued to his wife and family after his death, which occurred on the 3d of May, 1845. Nine years after, a monument, raised by public subscription in the cemetery of Kensal Green, was inaugurated by Mr. Monckton Milnes (Lord Houghton) with a concourse of spectators that showed how well the memory of the poet stood the test of time. Artisans came from a great distance to view and honor the image of the popular writer whose best efforts had been dedicated to the cause and the sufferings of the workers of the world; and literary men of all opinions gathered around the grave of one of their brethren whose writings were at once the delight of every boy and the instruction of every man who read them. Happy the humorist whose works and life are an illustration of the great moral truth that the sense of humor is the just balance of all the faculties of man, the best security against the pride of knowledge and the conceits of the imagination, the strongest inducement to submit with a wise and pious patience to the vicissitudes of human existence. This was the lesson that Thomas Hood left behind him, and which his countrymen will not easily forget.

But a few days before his death, he wrote the following beautiful but melancholy lines:

> Farewell, Life! my senses swim,
> And the world is growing dim:
> Thronging shadows cloud the light,
> Like the advent of the night—
> Colder, colder, colder still,
> Upwards steals a vapour chill;
> Strong the earthy odour grows—
> I smell the mould above the rose!
>
> Welcome, Life! the spirit strives:
> Strength returns, and hope revives;

> Cloudy fears and shapes forlorn
> Fly like shadows at the morn—
> O'er the earth there comes a bloom;
> Sunny light for sullen gloom,
> Warm perfume for vapour cold—
> I smell the rose above the mould!
>
> April, 1845.

In his serious poems he develops a lofty and sustained style, and exhibits true poetic imagination, as may be seen by the rich and musical diction of his "Ode to the Moon:"

> Mother of light! how fairly dost thou go
> Over those hoary crests, divinely led!
> Art thou that huntress of the silver bow
> Fabled of old? Or rather dost thou tread
> Those cloudy summits thence to gaze below,
> Like the wild chamois on her Alpine snow,
> Where hunter never climbed—secure from dread?
> A thousand ancient fancies I have read
> Of that fair presence, and a thousand wrought,
>   Wondrous and bright,
>   Upon the silver light,
> Tracing fresh figures with the artist thought.
>
> What art thou like? Sometimes I see thee ride
> A far-bound galley on its perilous way;
> Whilst silvery waves toss up their silvery spray;
>   Sometimes behold thee glide,
> Clustered by all thy family of stars,
> Like a lone widow through the welkin wide,
> Whose pallid cheek the midnight sorrow mars;
> Sometimes I watch thee on from steep to steep,
> Timidly lighted by thy vestal torch.
> Till in some Latinian cave I see thee creep,
> To catch the young Endymion asleep,
> Leaving thy splendor at the jagged porch.
>
> Oh, thou art beautiful, howe'er it be!
> Huntress, or Dian, or whatever named—
> And he the veriest Pagan who first framed
> A silver idol, and ne'er worshiped thee:
> It is too late, or thou shouldst have my knee—

> Too late now for the old Ephesian vows,
> And not divine the crescent on thy brows,
> Yet call thee nothing but the mere mild moon,
>   Behind those chestnut boughs;
> Casting their dappled shadows at my feet;
> I will be grateful for that simple boon,
> In many a thoughtful verse and anthem sweet,
> And bless thy dainty face whene'er we meet.

Hood's works have been collected into four volumes: "Poems of Wit and Humor;" "Hood's Own, or Laughter from Year to Year;" "Whims and Oddities in Prose and Verse."

JOSIAH GILBERT HOLLAND.

Dr. Holland was born in 1819, and died in New York, October 12, 1881.

His family was of the oldest Puritan stock; the original ancestors, John and Judith Holland, appear to have been members of that church which was organized before sailing from Plymouth, in England, and which emigrated, bodily and ecclesiastically, into the wilderness at Dorchester.

During a considerable part of his childhood the family, pursued by misfortune, led a sort of roving life. For some years they lived in Heath; then they returned to Belchertown; then we find them migrating to South Hadley, to Granby, and elsewhere, as the unprosperous father was able to find work. The promising son, Josiah, had little chance for learning, getting but a few months in the public schools in winter.

While the family lived at Northampton Josiah entered the Northampton High School, where he pursued his studies with great eagerness and ability. The older inhabitants of a certain little mountain village in Vermont will tell you to-day of a tall young man who, more than forty-five years ago, taught penmanship from town to town, and who used to recite his own poems to his intimate friends. He tried daguerreotypy and district school teaching.

Finding it impossible to obtain such an education as he desired, he decided to study medicine. In 1844 he was graduated at the Berkshire Medical College with honor. In 1845 Doctor Holland formed a partnership with his classmate, Doctor Bailey, and commenced his medical practice at Springfield, Massachusetts. In the same year he married Miss Elizabeth Chapin, of Springfield. His married life was one of unusual happiness.

The practice of medicine was distasteful, hence the time that ought to have been given to his professional study was given to correspondence for the old "Knickerbocker Magazine" and other periodicals. Attracted to journalism, he started the "Bay State Weekly Courier" at Springfield. The paper was started as "A New Family Newspaper," but it survived only for six months. Not finding success in his profession, and failing in journalism, he became a teacher in Richmond, Virginia.

In 1849 Holland returned to Springfield, where he became assistant editor of the "Republican." With tireless energy and unlimited researches, he gathered local and general matter for his paper. Proceeding upon the theory that people are interested in themselves and in their own locality, he published a "History of Western Massachusetts." In 1857, "Bay Path," a novel, came from his study of local history. Nine years after he entered the office of this paper he began the publication of the "Letters to Young People, Married and Single," in the columns of the "Republican." The playful signature of "Timothy Titcomb," and all the circumstances of their production, go to show that the author had no thought of winning his first decisive battle with these general epistles. But they were popular from the start, and Holland found out then what all the world knows now, that he was a great preacher.

The poem of "Bittersweet" appeared in the same year, 1858, and was yet more successful. Its sale has run up to seventy-five thousand copies, beside its circulation in the collected poems. "Gold Foil," which appeared serially as "Preachings from Popular Proverbs," was put in covers in 1859;

JOSIAH GILBERT HOLLAND.

"Miss Gilbert's Career," a novel, was issued in the following year; "Lessons in Life" in 1861, and the "Letters to the Joneses" in 1863; a volume of lectures was published in 1865, and in the same year appeared Doctor Holland's "Life of Abraham Lincoln," which was sold by subscription, and brought him more money than he probably ever dreamed of possessing in his early life. The climax of his fame and popular success as an author of books was attained in 1868, when the poem "Katrina" appeared. It has outstripped all its fellows in popular favor, and outsold all other American poems except Longfellow's "Hiawatha." The sales now aggregate over ninety-nine thousand. "The Marble Prophecy," a poem founded on the Laocoon, was issued in 1872, and then appeared in succession, in the pages of "Scribner's Monthly" first, and afterward in book form, the later group of novels, "Arthur Bonnicastle," "Sevenoaks," and "Nicholas Minturn." "The Mistress of the Manse" appeared in 1875.

In addition to his other literary labors he was one of the most popular of American lecturers. In 1868 he went to Europe, where he remained two years. It was a very important epoch in his life, and an important point in the history of American literature and art, for it was, as he has related, on a bridge in Geneva that he proposed to his friend, Mr. Roswell Smith, the founding of "Scribner's Monthly." This institution is of itself enough to make American literature forever Dr. Holland's debtor.

He had his home in New York and his beautiful country place in the Thousand Islands of the St. Lawrence, and he was able to pass the closing hours of life's day-time in thorough enjoyment of the world.

Dr. Holland died suddenly of heart disease. Without failure of faculty, in the midst of his daily work, with no pain of prolonged suffering, in his own chamber, amid tender and sacred affection, his eyes closed.

He had written no word that he would blot, but a thousand words that have been a cheer and an impulse to thousands of his fellow-men.

VICTOR HUGO.

VICTOR MARIE HUGO was born in Basancon, February 26, 1802.

His father was a military officer, hence in childhood Victor was not settled in any one locality, but was carried to Elba, Corsica, Switzerland, and Italy.

In his seventh year he was taken to Paris, where his mother and an old priest superintended his education, and where he commenced his classical studies in company with an elder brother, Eugene, and a young girl who afterward became his wife. In 1811, his father having been made general and appointed major-domo of Joseph Bonaparte, the new king of Spain, Victor went to Madrid, and entered the seminary of nobles with a view of becoming one of the pages of Joseph; but subsequent events defeated this design. In 1812 Mme. Hugo returned to Paris, where her sons continued their classical studies. When the empire fell, the general and his wife parted, and the former took charge of the education of Victor. He was placed in a private academy that he might prepare himself for the school of polytechnics. He showed considerable mathematical ability, but his strong inclinations were toward poetry. His first poem gave such excellent promise that his father decided to prepare him for a literary life.

In 1817 he presented to the French academy a poem upon "Les Avantages de l'Etude." Afterward he won three prizes in succession at Toulouse academy of floral games. In 1822 he published his first volume of "Odes et Ballades," which created a decided sensation. In 1823 he published a novel entitled "Han d'Islande," and in 1825, "Bug-Jargal." These two novels took rank among the best writings of the time, and at once presented Victor

VICTOR HUGO.

Hugo as an original and forcible prose writer. In 1826 he published a second volume of "Odes et Ballades."

He contemplated starting a new school of literature in France. For this purpose Hugo, in company with others, formed a literary circle called the "Cenacle," in which they were to discuss new artistic and literary doctrines. For the purpose of carrying into effect their plans, they started a literary periodical called "La Muse Francaise." This journal attracted no particular attention. In 1827 the drama of "Cromwell" was performed as a specimen of the literary reforms aimed at by the new school. From this date Victor Hugo was acknowledged as the leader of the French literary school known as the Romanticists, and he waged a relentless warfare against the opposite school known as the "Classicists." His victory was complete. At the age of twenty-five he was acknowledged as master in French poetry and prose.

In 1828 his fame was greatly enhanced by the publication of "Les Orientales." "Le jour d'un Condamne" which followed, fascinated the public by its vivid delineations of the mental tortures of a man doomed to execution. For the next twelve or thirteen years, Hugo produced a literary cyclone in France, that carried everything before it. Dramas, poems and miscellaneous writings poured from his pen in perfect torrents. The contest between the two schools of literature reached its climax in 1830, when the drama of "Hernani" was produced at the Theatre Francais. In 1831 appeared "Marion Delorme," another dramatical triumph, also lyrical poems, and a novel entitled "Notre Dame de Paris." His reputation had become so great that he was elected to the French academy in 1841, although the old classic school opposed him. Thus, having reached the highest distinction in literature, he turned his attention to politics. His political aspirations were gratified by his being made a member of the Legion of Honor, and created a peer of France in 1845.

On the revolution of 1848 he was elected a deputy to the constituent assembly, where he generally voted with the conservative party. On his re-election he showed greater democratic tendencies, and in strong speeches denounced the action of the majority. He also opposed the secret policy of

President Louis Napoleon. When Napoleon declared himself king of France, Hugo boldly asserted the rights of the assembly, and sought to preserve the constitution. This action led to his proscription. Taking refuge in the island of Jersey he resumed his pen. However, he kept up his opposition to Louis Napoleon. In 1852 Hugo made a bitter attack upon the ruler in his "Napoleon le Petit;" and in 1853 in a fierce satire entitled "Les Chatiments." Hostile movements caused him to remove to the island of Guernsey for two years. The general amnesty offered to political exiles in 1859 he refused to accept. In 1856 Hugo published "Les Contemplations," a collection of lyrical and personal poems; in 1859, "Les Legende des Siecles," two volumes, being a series of poems mainly of an epic character. In 1862 "Les Miserables" appeared in nine different languages. The success of this romance was fully equal to that of any of his former works. We think this work should be in every popular library.

Passing over some of his writings, which, by the way, were fully up to his standard of excellence, we will note that in 1869 he again refused to return to France upon the emperor's amnesty proclamation. When the empire fell, however, and the republic was proclaimed, that prince of French writers and staunch friend of the people, Victor M. Hugo, returned to his own country. In 1871 he was elected to the national assembly. He opposed the parliamentary treaty of peace between France and Germany with so much earnestness as to arouse the anger of the party of "the right." When he attempted to address the assembly the opposition was so violent that he left the tribune and resigned his seat. Leaving France, he went to Brussels, but his bold movements there soon led the Belgian government to order him to leave. He next went to London, where he remained till the condemnation of the commune leaders. In 1872 he published a volume of poetry entitled "L'Annee Terrible," depicting the misfortunes of France; and also, in company with his son, started a democratic journal. In 1874 his novel, "Quatre-vingt-treize," was published simultaneously in several different languages. Two of his sons, Charles and Victor, have become prominent in literature.

Victor Hugo was a tireless worker, having recently finished his one-hundredth publication. He is said to have kept two secretaries busy writing while he dictated. When the hour came for him to commence his literary task for the day, he commenced walking around in the room, his head slightly elevated, and his eyes looking upward in an angle of about forty-five degrees. Under these circumstances he dictated the matter and language of his works, while his secretaries wrote down the sentences as they fell from his lips.

He died August 22, 1885, and was given a public funeral and burial. He was 83 years old on his last birthday, the 26th of February.

LEIGH HUNT.

James Henry Leigh Hunt was born at Southgate, England, October 19, 1784, and his singularly eventful life closed at Putney, on August 28, 1859.

His father, from West India, settled at Philadelphia, and entered upon the practice of law. His mother was the daughter of a Philadelphia merchant. Leigh Hunt was educated at Christ's Hospital. He was prevented from entering the university on the account of an impediment in his speech. His school life was creditable, but not specially brilliant. He left college at the age of fifteen; and for some time after did nothing, as he himself said, but visit his school-fellows, haunt book stalls, and write verse. In 1802 his father collected Leigh's poems and published them under the title of "Juvenilia." As most of the poems were written by the youth at the age of sixteen, they were considered good.

In 1805 his brother started a paper called "The News," and Leigh Hunt went to live with him and write the theatrical criticisms for its columns. He also secured a position as clerk in the War Office. In 1808 he left the clerkship, and, jointly with his brother, established "The Examiner" and assumed the editorial management. This was a weekly journal, and it soon acquired a high reputation for its independence in political and literary criticisms. Finally, "The Examiner" made an attack upon the prince regent, terming him "a fat Adonis at fifty." The prince was offended, and the chief cause of the offense was the truthfulness of the personality. Hunt was arrested, tried, and sentenced to two years' imprisonment in the Surrey jail. " The effect was naturally to make Hunt a hero for the time being, and to give a political direction to the career of the man of letters. The position was an essentially false one, and led to an entire misunderstanding of Leigh Hunt's character and aptitudes alike on the part of his friends and his antagonists. For the time he was exceedingly popular; the cheerfulness and gaiety with which he bore his imprisonment, and his amusing devices to mitigate its severity, attracted general attention and sympathy, and brought him visits from Byron, Moore, Brougham, and others, whose acquaintance exerted much influence on his future destiny."

Hunt drew the following beautiful and lively picture of his prison life: " I papered the walls with a trellis of roses; I had the ceiling colored with clouds and sky; the barred windows were screened with Venetian blinds; and when my bookcases were set up, with their busts and flowers, and a pianoforte made its appearance, perhaps there was not a handsomer room on that side of the water."

In 1816 he published his "Story of Rimini," an Italian tale in verse, which gave him a place in the front rank of English literature. It possessed fine taste; and it completely modified the generally accepted standard of literary composition. It has been remarked that it does not contain one hackneyed or conventional rhyme. At Hampstead nearly all the rising young men of liberal sympathies, including Keats, Shelley, Lamb, and Reynolds, gathered around him.

Hunt had married Miss Kent, and, for want of proper means, had become greatly confused in his business affairs. Shelley came to his rescue and saved him, in return for which Hunt became a warm friend and a strong defender of his benefactor. In 1818, when Shelley departed for Italy, Hunt's affairs became still more embarrassed, his health and his wife's failed, thus leading to a lessening of his literary work. At this time he was printing a series of essays in a paper entitled "The Indicator," but which failing health forced him to discontinue. At the request of Byron and Shelley he repaired to Italy in 1821-22, to join them in a new journal to be called "The Liberal." The sudden death of Shelley and the disaffection of Byron led to the final failure of the new publication. Pleased with the sunny skies of Italy, the poet extended his visit till in 1825, in which time he brought out his matchless translation of Redis' "Bacco in Toscana," and "The Religion of the Heart." Returning to England, he published, in 1827, his "Lord Byron and his Contemporaries." This work was considered the mistake of Hunt's life. While this book was valuable in itself, yet the facts it contained were gained while the poet was under Byron's roof. It was deemed ungrateful to say the least. The withering satires of Moore, and the condemnation of most of the British people were heaped upon him. For several years his life was one continued struggle with poverty. Several efforts to re-instate himself in the public confidence failed. "The Tatler," the "London Journal," and the "Monthly Repository" failed on his hands. Finally, "Sir Ralph Esher," a romance of the period of Charles the Second, proved successful, and "Captain Sword and Captain Pen," one of his best poems, assisted in re-establishing him in popular favor. In 1840 he wrote some beautiful lines on the birth of the princess-royal; and in the same year appeared his "Legend of Florence," a play of great merit, which greatly improved his condition, both in popularity and wealth. He also wrote for the stage, "Lover's Amazements," a comedy, and other successful plays that were not printed. In 1842 Hunt published "The Palfrey," a beautiful narrative poem, and commenced to write for the "Edinburgh Review." His financial matters were greatly benefited in 1844 by an annuity of £120, which the generous Mrs. Shelley and her son settled upon him; and in 1847 by a civil pension of £200 per annum, secured through the influence of Lord John Russel. This magnificent support gave Leigh Hunt leisure hours to devote to literature; and, as a result, numerous charming volumes fell from his pen. These we must mention briefly. "Imagination and Fancy," and

"Wit and Humor," in which he shows himself one of the most refined, appreciative, and happy of critics; "A Jar of Honey from Mount Hybla," a companion volume on the pastoral poetry of Sicily; "The Town and Men, Women and Books"; "Old Court Suburb," an anecdotic sketch of one of his old homes; "Stories in Verse," a collection of his narrative poems, original and translated; and his "Autobiography." His collection of "Stories in Verse" was made in 1855, and it closed his literary work. He died in 1859.

Leigh Hunt "excelled especially in narrative poetry, of which, upon a small scale, there are probably no better examples in our language than 'Abou ben Adhem,' and 'Solomon's Ring.' As an appreciative critic, whether literary or dramatic, he is hardly equaled; and his guidance is as safe as it is genial. The no less important vocation of a censor was uncongenial to his gentle nature, and was rarely essayed by him."

JEAN INGELOW.

JEAN INGELOW was born in Boston, Lincolnshire, England, in 1830. She lives in London, where she is greatly admired, both for her fine literary ability, and for the sympathetic interest she takes in the poor of the city.

Miss Ingelow received a good education, but her timidity caused her to lead a quiet, reserved and uneventful life. She was called from her retirement, however, in 1863, when she published her "Poems." This volume at once gave her high rank in poetry, and commanded the respect and approval alike of critics and the generous public. This volume contained numerous poems that have taken rank among the universally popular writings and have passed into the current literature of the world. Among these we may mention "Divided," "High Tide on the Coast of Lincolnshire," and the "Songs of Seven." The last named consists of seven poems representing seven epochs in the life of woman, and has been published separately with fine illustrations.

In 1864 she published "Studies for Stories;" 1866, "Stories Told to a Child;" 1867, "A Story of Doom, and other Poems;" 1868, "A Sister's Bye-Hours;" 1869, "Mopsa, the Fairy," "The Monitions of the Unseen," and "Poems of Love and Childhood," published only in Boston, Massachusetts, 1872, "Off the Skelligs," a novel, also the second series of "Stories Told to a Child."

Miss Ingelow is very popular, both in America and in Europe. In this country alone her poems have reached a sale of 98,000 copies and her prose works, 35,000. A prominent American educator declares that, on the death of Mrs. Browning, Jean Ingelow became by divine right the queen of English song. Poetry flows from her pen easily and gracefully and naturally. Her songs burst from her heart like showers from the summer cloud, and fall, like the showers, with refreshing influence upon the universal mind.

A MOTHER SHOWING THE PORTRAIT OF HER CHILD.

Are there voices in the valley,
Lying near the heavenly gate?
When it opens, do the harp-strings,
Touched within, reverberate?
When, like shooting stars, the angels
To your couch at nightfall go,
Are there swift wings heard to rustle?
Tell me! for you know.

WASHINGTON IRVING.

WASHINGTON IRVING was born in New York, April 3, 1783, and died of heart disease, at Sunnyside, his country-seat on the banks of the Hudson, on November 28, 1859.

Both his parents came from Great Britain. His father had intended Washington for the legal profession, but sickness interfered with his studies, and caused him to take a voyage to Europe, proceeding as far as Rome. Returning to the United States, he was admitted to the bar; but preferring literature, he gave but little attention to the practice of law.

His first literary effort appeared in the form of a satirical miscellany, entitled "Salmagundi," published jointly with his brother, William Irving, and J. K. Paulding, in 1807-8. This publication gave ample proof of Irving's talent as a humorist, and prepared the public mind for a favorable reception of his next effort. "The Knickerbocker History of New York," published in 1809, greatly added to Irving's popularity. "Though far from the most finished of Irving's productions, Knickerbocker manifests the most original power, and is the most genuinely national in its quaintness and drollery. The very tardiness and prolixity of the story are skillfully made to heighten the humorous effect."

Upon his father's death Irving became a silent partner in his brother's commercial house, a branch of which was established at Liverpool. The firm struggled with fate for some time, then became bankrupt. Fortunately for American literature, his business failure compelled him to resume his pen as a means of support. His reputation had preceded him to England, and the curiosity naturally excited by the then unwonted apparition of a successful American author, procured him admission into the highest literary

WASHINGTON IRVING.

circles, where his popularity was insured by his amiable temper and polished manners. Campbell, Jeffrey, Moore, Scott, were counted among his friends, and the last named zealously recommended him to the publisher, Murray, who, after at first refusing, consented in 1820 to bring out "Geoffrey Crayon's Sketch Book," which was already appearing in America in a periodical form. Some stories and sketches on American themes contribute to give it variety; of these "Rip Van Winkle" is the most remarkable. It speedily obtained great success on both sides of the Atlantic. In 1822 appeared "Bracebridge Hall," an excellent work upon a purely English subject, hence the humor is more English than American. "Tales of a Traveler" came from his pen in 1824, and Irving started for a tour on the continent. His literary work had already brought him an ample fortune, and his continued income furnished means for him to travel and enlarge the sphere of his observations. After a long course of travel he settled down at Madrid, in the house of the American consul Rich. His intention at the time was to translate Navarrete's recently published work on Columbus; finding, however, that this was rather a collection of valuable materials than a systematic biography, he determined to compose a biography of his own by its assistance, supplemented by independent researches in the Spanish archives. His work appeared in 1828 and obtained a merited success. It is a finished representation of Columbus from the point of view of the nineteenth century. Continuing in Spain in connection with the United States embassy, he gathered the material for his excellent works, "The Companions of Columbus," "The Conquest of Granada," and "The Alhambra."

Having been appointed secretary to the embassy at London, Irving proceeded to England to enter upon his duties. About the same time Oxford University conferred upon him the legal degree as a compliment to his literary ability. In 1832 he returned to the United States, after seventeen years absence, and "found his name a household word, and himself universally honored as the first American who had won for his country a recognition on equal terms in the literary republic.

He next undertook a tour in the Western prairies, and returning to the neighborhood of New York, built for himself a delightful retreat on the Hudson, to which he gave the name of "Sunnyside." His acquaintance with the New York millionaire, John Jacob Astor, prompted his next important work, "Astor," a history of the fur-trading settlement founded by Astor in Oregon, deduced with singular literary ability from the dry commercial records, and, without labored attempts at word-painting, evincing a remarkable faculty for bringing scenes and incidents vividly before the eye. "Captain Bonneville," based upon the unpublished memoirs of a veteran hunter, was another work of the same class. He also wrote "A Tour on the Prairies," and "Abbotsford and Newstead Abbey."

In 1842 Irving was appointed United States ambassador to Spain. Repairing to that country, he spent the four years in attending to the duties of his office. His pen seems to have been idle until after his return to the States. Upon reading Forster's "Life of Goldsmith" Irving was reminded that his own essay on his favorite author was not good enough to leave as a part of his collected writings. Thus stimulated, he wrote an excellent "Life of Oliver Goldsmith." Two years later he published "The Lives of Mahomet and his Successors." His last work was a biography of Washington, and he just lived to complete the work.

"He was far more of the poet than any of the writers of the eighteenth century, and his moralizing, unlike theirs, is unconscious and indirect. The same poetic feeling is shown in his biographies; his subject is invariably chosen for its picturesqueness, and whatever is unessential to portraiture is thrown into the background. The result is that his biographies, however deficient in research, bear the stamp of genuine artistic intelligence, equally remote from compilation and disquisition. In execution they are almost faultless; the narrative is easy, the style pellucid, and the writer's judgment nearly always in accordance with the general verdict of history. They will not, therefore, be easily superseded, and indeed Irving's productions are in general impressed with that signet's classical finish which guarantees the permanency of literary work more surely than direct utility or intellectual power. This refinement is the more amiable for being in great part the reflection of his own moral nature. Without ostentation or affectation he was exquisite in all things, a mirror of loyalty, courtesy, and good taste in all his literary connections, and exemplary in all the relations of domestic life which he was called upon to assume. He never married, remaining true to the memory of an early attachment which was blighted by death."

As an illustration of the popularity of his writings abroad we call attention to the fact that Irving received about twenty-five thousand dollars for the copyright of four of his works in England.

BEN JONSON.

Ben Jonson was born in 1573, nine years after Shakespeare, and he died in 1637. His tomb in Westminster Abbey, where the body was disposed vertically, was marked by a square stone, inscribed "O Rare Ben Jonson!"

Jonson's father, a clergyman, was of a Scottish family. The father died before our poet was born. His mother soon married again to a bricklayer. Ben was taken from Westminster school and put to his stepfather's occupation. The work not being congenial Jonson soon after enlisted in the army and served in the Low Countries. His youthful bravery is recorded here by his killing an antagonist in a single combat, in sight of both armies. On his return it is claimed that he entered St. John's College, Cambridge. At about the age of twenty he was married, and in London as an actor. Jonson, like Shakespeare, demanded attention both as poet and dramatist. He wrote many poems that show excellent taste and fine poetical expression of noble sentiments and fine feelings. "In 1616 Jonson published a volume containing his epigrams and poems. This book he styled 'Jonson's Works.' Without doubt his fine poetic genius would have placed him in the front rank had he devoted his whole time to the muse. But writers of moderate means are apt to follow that line of work which pays best. The time of Elizabeth and James I was a harvest time for the stage, hence the 'mighty line of Marlowe's,' the living, breathing sentences of Shakespeare, the massive, ponderous hand of 'O Rare Ben Jonson!' the genius of Beaumont and Fletcher, and the rays of the other stars that composed the constellation of the 'Elizabethan Age,' were all turned to the stage."

In the dramatic world the name of Ben Jonson stands second. He failed in his first attempt as an actor. " Every Man in his Humor" was written in 1596. This production was well received at the Globe Theatre, where Shakespeare himself was one of the performers in the play. Queen Elizabeth patronized the new poet. In 1599 appeared " Every Man out of his Humor." These were soon followed by "Cynthia's Revels," and "Poetaster." He produced numerous comedies and serious plays, which were popular both in court entertainments and with the masses.

His private life was one of constant excitement and spirited action. In a duel with a fellow dramatist Jonson killed his antagonist and was thrown into prison for the act. He was released without punishment. At another time he with others was thrown into prison by King James for certain passages in his "Eastward Ho" that reflected on the Scottish nation. This time he was threatened with the loss of his ears and nose but he was soon released. His life was also clouded by a fierce rivalry provoked by uncalled-for attacks upon Marston and Dekker, two fellow-dramatists, in his "Poetaster." His works comprise about fifty dramatic pieces. In 1619 he was made poet-laureate of England, receiving one hundred marks per annum, but later this pension was fixed at one hundred pounds per annum. An attack of palsy and his poverty rendered the close of his life dark and painful. Jonson, however, continued to write till death took away his pen in 1637.

SAMUEL JOHNSON.

SAMUEL JOHNSON was born at Lichfield, England, September 18, 1709, and in a serene frame of mind his sad but powerful life closed on December 13, 1784.

His father, Michael Johnson, held the position of magistrate of Lichfield, about 1700, and later was a bookseller of considerable note. The child inherited all of the excellent qualities of the father in a hundred fold power. From his ancestors, also, he inherited a scrofulous taint which could not be removed by medicine. In his third year his parents took him to London that he might be examined by the court surgeon, and prayed over by the court chaplains. While in London he was taken before Queen Anne. The queen placed her hand upon the child's head and gave him a piece of gold, but to no avail. Johnson's distorted features, scarred cheeks and imperfect eyesight still remained.

In spite of his bodily defects, his mind overcame all obstacles. Indolent though he was, he acquired knowledge easily, and was acknowledged to be the best scholar in every school he attended.

From sixteen to eighteen he studied at home. Without a guide or plan he passed over the pages of his father's library, retaining what was interesting and omitting what was dull. He read but little Greek, for he was not proficient in that language. Johnson was a good Latinist, hence he made a special study of the Latin literature. Finally, in his nineteenth year, Johnson was sent to Pembroke College, Oxford. "When the young scholar presented himself to the rulers of that society, they were amazed not more by his ungainly figure and eccentric manners, than by the quantity of extensive and curious information which he had picked up during many months of desultory but not unprofitable study. On the first day of his residence he surprised his teacher by quoting Macrobius; and one of the most learned among them declared that he had never known a freshman of equal attainments."

His father's trade was declining, hence Johnson's clothes were necessarily poor, even to raggedness, and his appearance excited the mirth and pity of his associates. "The needy scholar was generally to be seen under the gate of Pembroke, a gate now adorned with his effigy, haranguing a circle of lads, over whom, in spite of his tattered gown and dirty linen, his wit and audacity gave him an undisputed ascendency. In every mutiny against the discipline of the college he was the ringleader. Much was pardoned, however, to a youth so highly distinguished by abilities and acquirements." While in college Johnson gained considerable reputation by translating Pope's "Messiah" into Latin verse. His father's failure in business, however, forced Johnson to leave college in 1731, without a degree. In the following winter his father died, leaving him only about £20.

The story of Johnson's life for the next thirty years is one of unusual sadness, combined with a constant struggle with poverty. Before leaving college he had become an incurable hypochondriac. The following picture is drawn of him by his biographer: "His grimaces, his gestures, his mutterings, sometimes diverted and sometimes terrified people who did not know him. He would conceive an unintelligible aversion to a particular alley, and perform a great circuit rather than see the hateful place. He would set his heart on touching every post in a street through which he walked. If by any chance he missed a post he would go back a hundred yards to repair the omission." Numerous other peculiarities are related, but the above are sufficient to illustrate the infirmities of body and mind with which this peculiar genius had to contend.

As a means of support he became usher of a grammar school in Leicestershire, but he soon abandoned the position and removed to Birmingham where he earned a small amount of money by literary drudgery. At the age of twenty-seven Johnson married Mrs. Porter, a widow, who was forty-eight. She was poor as himself, but the man whom we have described,

DR. SAMUEL JOHNSON.

and the short, fat, coarse, painted and gaudy Mrs. Porter lived happily together.

He at once took a house and advertised for pupils, but in eighteen months only three came to his academy. Resolving to make literature a profession he set out for London with but a few guineas and a manuscript copy of " Irene." One of the publishers to whom he applied for employment advised him to "get a porter's knot and carry trunks." Before gaining employment he was reduced to the extreme of poverty. While in this condition his sufferings were relieved by Mr. Hervey. In later years the philosopher wrote, " Harry Hervey was a vicious man, but he was very kind to me. If you call a dog Hervey I shall love him." The sufferings which he endured made him almost savage in manners, and he resented insults most fiercely. Osborne, a brutal bookseller, relates that he was knocked down by the huge fellow that he had hired to puff the Harleian Library.

Cave, the proprietor of the "Gentlemen's Magazine," finally gave Johnson permanent employment. The " Magazine" had a larger circulation than any other periodical in the kingdom, and our author enriched its columns with numerous essays and reviews. He also wrote monthly accounts of parliamentary proceedings. It was not considered safe to publish the proceedings of either house except under disguise, hence the articles were entitled "Reports of the Debates of the Senate of Lilliput." Johnson was furnished with meager notes of the speeches, and he filled them out, furnishing both argument and eloquence. In his reports he took care, as he afterward said, that the Whig dogs did not have the best of it. Being a Tory himself, it is natural to suppose that he would put the strongest arguments into the mouth of his political friends.

While thus laboring obscurely under an assumed name, Johnson in 1738 published " London," a work that at once placed him among the best writers of the age. Pope tried to find out the name of the author of " London," remarking that such a man could not long be concealed. The name was soon discovered and Pope exerted himself to get a degree for the poor young poet. The attempt failed. In 1744 he published the " Life of Savage." This was considered the finest specimen of biography in the language.

The author's name was not attached to the book, but it was generally known that Johnson was the writer. Thus the fame of his abilities and learning continued to grow, till, in 1747, his reputation was such that several eminent booksellers engaged him to prepare a "Dictionary of the English Language." For this work they agreed to pay him fifteen hundred guineas.

Johnson addressed the prospectus of his "Dictionary" to Lord Chesterfield, a man of politeness, and long celebrated for the brilliancy of his wit and the delicacy of his taste. Chesterfield acknowledged the compliment very politely and gave Johnson a few guineas. For some time our author continued to call on his patron, but Chesterfield, not wishing the annoyance of his visits, directed the porter to say to Johnson that his lordship was not at home. The awkward scholar soon took the hint and stayed at home. But as the "Dictionary" approached its completion it became evident that it was to be the greatest work of the age, and Chesterfield, desiring that it should be dedicated to him, wrote articles in commendation of it. He proposed that its author be made dictator over the English language. But Johnson remembered when "his lordship was not at home" to his visits and brought out his famous work without a dedication.

The publication of the "Dictionary" in 1755 settled the question of literary supremacy in England, and awarded the first place to Johnson. His other literary works we record briefly as follows: "The Vanity of Human Wishes," published in 1749. "Irene" was brought on the stage, for which the author realized about £300.

"The Rambler" appeared from 1750 to 1752, and "The Idler" from 1758 to 1760. In 1759 he wrote "Rasselas" to defray the expenses of his mother's funeral and certain other debts. The little book was written in one week and he received £100 for the manuscript. In 1762 George III settled upon Johnson a pension of £300. He took a journey to the Hebrides in 1773, and two years later he published an account of his travels. He prepared "Lives of the Poets" in 1779 and '81, for which he received 300 guineas. Johnson also edited an edition of Shakespeare, but it was not worthy of his great ability. In the Literary Club, "including Burke, Reynolds, Goldsmith, Gibbon, Garrick, Murphy, and others, Johnson reigned supreme, the most brilliant conversationalist of the age." His remains rest in Westminster Abbey among the eminent men of England.

KEATS.

JOHN KEATS was born in London, October 29, 1795, and he died of consumption, February 23, 1821, in Rome.

Born in the common walks of life, it was necessary for him to rely upon his own efforts for a support. He was educated at Enfield. Choosing medicine as a profession, he was apprenticed, at the age of fifteen, to a surgeon at Edmonton. Although he spent most of his time in literary study, yet he completed his apprenticeship creditably and repaired to London to complete his work in the hospital.

While an apprentice Keats wrote out a literal translation of Virgil's Æneid. The more difficult Latin poetry he never attempted, and never studied Greek. Even in early life his literary ability became conspicuous, although his volume of juvenile poems did not possess much general merit. This volume was considered worthy of a boy of ten. In 1818 he published "Endymion, a Poetic Romance." Whatever may have been thought of his former volume, this one displayed rich powers of imagination. "Endymion" raised him to the height of the middle minstrels of England, and nearly all critics were willing to give him a permanent and honorable place in literature. However, Mr. John Croker criticised the poem with such severity through the columns of the "Quarterly Review," as to embitter Keats' existence. Shelley affirms that the first effect of the criticism resembled insanity, and it required constant watching to keep him from committing suicide. Under his great sufferings, he ruptured a blood vessel in his lungs. Shelley informs us that consumption commenced from the above causes. The records show, however, that the disease was a family one. Keats' biographer, Lord Houghton, thinks that the criticism had no injurious effect, but, on the contrary, it led him to purify his style and enlarge his poetical studies. Byron had criticised him most shamefully, calling his juvenile poems "the driveling idiotism of the manikin." Jeffrey reviewed the young poet's work through the "Edinburgh Review," in a spirit of fairness, but the friendship availed Keats naught, for he was dying. In the meantime, while these unfavorable criticisms were being made, his few personal friends remained confident in their opinions that he would yet rise to the front rank in poetry. In 1820 he published "Lamia," "Isabella," "The Eve of St. Agnes, and other Poems," the volume upon which his fame chiefly rests. This volume raised Keats to the front rank, and silenced his former critics. Lord Byron eulogized "Hyperion," declaring that it "seems actually inspired by the Titans; it is as sublime as Æschylus." Thus he lived long enough to prove to the world that he was a poet born for nothing short of the front rank.

"The state of the poet's health now became so alarming that, as a last effort for life, he was advised to try the milder climate of Italy. A young friend, Mr. Severn, an artist, generously abandoned his professional prospects at home in order to accompany Keats, and they sailed in September, 1820. The invalid suffered severely during the voyage, and he had to endure a ten days' quarantine at Naples. The thoughts of a young lady to whom he was betrothed, and the too great probability that he would see her no more, added a deeper gloom to his mind, and he seems never to have rallied from this depression. At Rome Mr. Severn watched over him with affectionate care, but he daily got worse, and died on the 23d of February, 1821. Keats was buried in the Protestant cemetery at Rome, one of the most beautiful spots on which the eye and heart of man can rest. 'It is,' says Lord Houghton, 'a grassy slope amid verdurous ruins of the Honorian walls of the diminished city, and surrounded by the pyramidal tomb which Petrarch attributed to Remus, but which antiquarian truth has ascribed to the humbler name of Caius Cestius, a tribune of the people only remembered by his sepulchre.' In one of those mental voyages in the past, which often precede death, Keats had told Severn that 'he thought the most intense pleasure he had received in life was in watching the flowers grow;' and at another time, after lying awhile still and peaceful, he said: 'I feel the flowers growing over me.' And there they do grow even all the winter long—violets and daisies mingling with the fresh herbage, and, in the words of Shelley, 'making one in love with death to think that one should be buried in so sweet a place.'"

"The Life, Letters, and Literary Remains" of Keats were published in two volumes in 1848; and "The Letters of John Keats to Fanny Brown" appeared in 1879.

CHARLES LAMB.

CHARLES LAMB was born in Crown Office Row, Inner Temple, London, February 10, 1775. While taking his daily walk in December, 1834, he stumbled and fell, bruising his face. The hurt appeared trifling, but erysipelas in the face came on, which caused his death on the 27th of the same month.

His father, John Lamb, was in moderate circumstances. The father filled the position of clerk and servant companion to Mr. Salt, one of the benchers of the Inner Temple. Charles was the youngest of three children; and at the age of eight he secured a presentation to Christ's Hospital, where he remained till he was fifteen. Fortunately he had Samuel Taylor Coleridge for a schoolfellow; and a lifelong friendship sprang up between them, which had considerable influence upon Lamb's life. An impediment in his speech prevented him from entering college, where he could receive a regular university education. His school life was marked by earnest, thoughtful study. He was timid and nervous, and very seldom joined in sports or became excited. Cool, quiet, attentive, he displayed almost maturity in childhood.

Quitting school at the age of fifteen, he spent some time at home and at Mr. Salt's looking over old English authors in his library. Not being able to overcome the impediment in his speech, that he might enter college and take holy orders, he was compelled to toil at the desk. For a short time he clerked in the South Sea House under his brother John. In 1792 he entered the accountant's office in the East India House, where he remained for the next thirty-three years. He had resided with his parents till their death, when "he felt himself called upon by duty to repay to his sister the solicitude with which she had watched over his infancy, and well indeed he performed it. To her, from the age of twenty-one, he devoted his existence, seeking thenceforth no connection which could interfere with her supremacy in his affections, or impair his ability to sustain and to comfort her. A sad tragedy was connected with the early history of this devoted pair. There was a taint of hereditary madness in the family; Charles had himself, at the close of the year 1795, been six weeks confined in an asylum at Hoxton, and in September of the following year, Mary Lamb, in a paroxysm of insanity, stabbed her mother to death with a knife snatched from the dinner-table. A verdict of lunacy was returned by the jury who sat on the coroner's inquest, and the unhappy young lady was placed in a private asylum at Islington. Reason was speedily restored. 'My poor dear, dearest sister,' writes Charles Lamb to his bosom friend, Coleridge, 'the unhappy and unconscious instrument of the Almighty's judgments on our house, is restored to her senses; to a dreadful sense and recollection of what has passed, awful to her mind and impressive, as it must be, to the end of life, but tempered with religious resignation and the reasonings of a sound judgment, which in this early stage knows how to distinguish between a deed committed in a transient fit of frenzy and the terrible guilt of a mother's murder.' In confinement, however, Mary Lamb continued until the death of her father, an imbecile old man, and then Charles came to her deliverance. He satisfied all parties who had power to oppose her release, by his solemn engagement that he would take her under his care for life, and he kept his word. For her sake he abandoned all thoughts of love and marriage, and with an income of scarcely more than £100 a year derived from his clerkship, aided for a little while by the old aunt's small annuity, set out on the journey of life at twenty-two years of age, cheerfully, with his beloved companion, endeared to him the more by her strange calamity and the constant apprehension of the recurrence of the malady which caused it." It seems that his sister had been worn down to a state of extreme nervous misery by attention to needlework by day and to her mother by night. In that condition she was seized with acute mania, in which she committed the dreadful deed. Her malady did return again, but Charles never after had any symptoms of insanity.

His first appearance as an author was in 1796, when a volume by Coleridge contained four sonnets by his friend, "Mr. Charles Lamb, of the Indian House." In the succeeding year he and Charles Lloyd contributed some pieces to Coleridge's new volume of "Poems." These productions contained some merit and served to call public attention to him. He published a pathetic prose tale entitled "Rosamond Gray," in 1798, and in 1799 he joined Coleridge and Southey in publishing the "Annual Anthology," to which he had contributed a religious poem in blank verse entitled "Living without God in the World." At this point in his history he was unfortunate in turning his attention to the stage. "John Woodril," a dramatic piece written in the style of the Elizabethan age, was considered a failure. The "Edinburgh Review" handled him most severely. In 1806 he brought out a farce named "Mr. H.," the point of which lay in the hero's anxiety to conceal his name, "Hogsflesh." Although the play failed completely in England, yet it has been put upon the stage in America with excellent success.

The failure of the play was a surprise to Lamb's friends, but he seemed to consider it as so much schooling. Taking it for granted that writing plays was not his forte, he turned his attention to a new field in which he won renown. "Tales Founded on the Plays of Shakespeare," written by Charles and Mary Lamb, appeared in 1807, and "Specimens of English Dramatic Poets who Lived about the Time of Shakespeare," in 1808. These volumes contained short but excellent critical notes. In the same year Mary Lamb, assisted by her brother, brought out "Poetry for Children" and a collection of short school-girl tales entitled "Mrs. Leicester's School."

In the same date, also, Charles Lamb wrote the "Adventures of Ulysses," which he designed to be a companion to the "Adventures of Telemachus." In 1810 "The Reflector," a quarterly periodical, was begun by Leigh Hunt, and our author became one of its best writers. Two of his best essays, those on Shakespeare and Hogarth, appeared in this periodical. In 1818 his writings were collected into two large volumes which he gave to the world. The "London Magazine" was established in 1820, and Charles Lamb wrote for its columns some of the finest essays in the English language. These rose into instant popularity, and Elia, the name he signed to his essays, became one of the best known names in literature.

"'They are all,' said his biographer, Sergeant Talfourd, 'carefully elaborated; yet never were books written in a higher defiance to the conventional pomp of style. A sly hit, a happy pun, a humorous combination, lets the light into the intricacies of the subject, and supplies the place of ponderous sentences. Seeking his materials for the most part in the common paths of life—often in the humblest—he gives an importance to everything, and sheds a grace over all.' In 1825 Lamb was emancipated from the drudgery of his situation as clerk in the India house, retiring with a handsome pension of £450, which enabled him to enjoy the comforts and many of the luxuries of life. In a letter to Wordsworth he thus describes his sensations after his release: 'I came home for *ever* on Tuesday week. The incomprehensibleness of my condition overwhelmed me. It was like passing from life into eternity. Every year to be as long as three; that is to have three times as much real time—time that is my own—in it! I wandered about thinking I was happy, but feeling I was not. But that tumultuousness is passing off, and I begin to understand the nature of the gift. Holidays, even the annual month, were always uneasy joys, with their conscious fugitiveness, the craving after making the most of them. Now, when all is holiday, there are no holidays. I can sit at home, in rain or shine, without a restless impulse for walking. I am daily steadying, and shall soon find it as natural to me to be my own master, as it has been irksome to have had a master.' He removed to a cottage near Islington, and in the following summer went with his faithful sister and companion on a long visit to Enfield, which ultimately led to his giving up his cottage and becoming a constant resident at that place. There he lived for about five years, delighting his friends with his correspondence and occasional visits to London, displaying his social, racy humor and active benevolence."

In 1823 his essays appeared in book form. After five years of existence, the "London Magazine" came to an end, and he wrote but very little after that period. In 1830 he published a small volume of poems entitled "Album Verses." This, with an occasional article contributed to some literary journal, closed his life work. He died, as described, in 1834. "The sudden death of one so widely known, admired and beloved as Charles Lamb fell on the public, as well as on his own attached circle, with all the poignancy of a personal calamity and a private grief. His memory wanted no tribute that affection could bestow, and Wordsworth has commemorated in simple and solemn verse the genius, virtues, and fraternal devotion of his early friend."

It is chiefly as an essayist that Lamb holds his prominent place in literature. While there are great beauty and fine poetic feeling in some of his poems, yet his essays unite "wit, exquisite humor, a genuine and cordial vein of pleasantry, and heart-touching pathos" in a most happy manner. As an essayist he must ever stand by the side of Steele and Addison. His profound thought, simple language, and easy and entertaining style, are a constant source of interest and pleasure to the reader. We are always amply repaid for the time given to the volumes of Charles Lamb.

LAMARTINE.

ALPHONSE MARIE LOUIS DE PRAT DE LAMARTINE was born at Macon, October 21, 1790, and died at Passy, March 1, 1869.

The family of Lamartine was one of the best in France, the title of Prat having come from an estate in Franche Comte. His father was imprisoned during the Terror, but was subsequently released, when he removed to the country. The family participated in some of the most active and exciting scenes of French history, and at one time was the most popular in France.

Lamartine's education came chiefly from his mother. In 1805 he was sent to school at Lyons, but not being suited he was transferred to the care of the Peres de la Foi at Belley, where he remained till 1809. The next year he spent at home reading romantic and poetic literature. At the age of twenty he started on a journey to Italy, where he remained for two years. His family being strict royalists, he entered the Guards du Corps, and while the opposition held the government, took refuge in Switzerland at Aix en Savoil. While in refuge he fell in love, and, of course, gave to the world plenty of poetry in keeping with the feelings of a love-sick poet. After Waterloo he returned to Paris, where he mingled much in society. In 1818-19 he revisited Italy, Savoy and Switzerland. Learning of the death of his beloved he made it the subject of some quite creditable verses.

Applying himself more closely he soon had a volume of poetry written which he published in 1820, under the title of "The Meditations." The book became popular at once, thus not only encouraging him to greater study and effort, but helping him to secure position as well. Having left the army he entered the diplomatic service, and was appointed secretary to

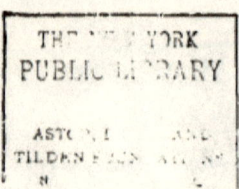

the embassy at Naples. This may be considered the beginning of his political life. On his way to Naples he married a young English lady, Marianne Birch, at Geneva, in 1823, and in the same year published his "Nouvelles Meditations." The lady was noted for her beauty and she possessed an ample fortune, which made their home pleasant and gave leisure for study. In 1824 he was transferred to Florence, where he remained for five years. In the succeeding year his "Last Canto to Childe Harold" appeared, a phrase in which led to a duel between him and an Italian officer by the name of Colonel Pepe.

"'The Harmonies Politiques et Religieuses' appeared in 1829 when he had left Florence. Having refused an appointment at Paris under the Polignac ministry (destined to be fatal to legitimism), he went on a special mission to Prince Leopold of Saxe-Coburg, who was not yet king of the Belgians, but was talked of as king of Greece. The next year he was elected to the Academy. Lamartine was in Switzerland, not in Paris, at the time of the revolution of July, and though he put forth a pamphlet on 'Rational Policy,' he did not take any active part in politics. In 1832 he set out with his wife and daughter for Palestine, having been unsuccessful in his candidature for a seat in the chamber. His daughter Julia died at Beyrout, and before long he received the news of his election by a constituency (Bergues) in the department of the Nord. He returned through Turkey and Germany, and made his first speech shortly after the beginning of 1834. Thereafter he spoke constantly, and acquired considerable reputation as an orator, bringing out, moreover, many books in prose and verse. His Eastern travels ('Souvenirs d'Orient') appeared in 1835, his 'Jocelyn' in 1836, his 'Chute d'un Ange' in 1838, and his 'Recueillments,' the last remarkable volume of his poetry, in 1839."

Lamartine began to modify his political views till he became quite democratic in his opinions. Commencing his greatest prose work, the "Historic des Girondins," he gave it to the world in periodical form first, but in book form in 1847. He made this work the model in politics, and he became at once one of the most important persons in France. "He was one of the first to declare for a provisional government, and became a member of it himself, with the post of minister for foreign affairs. He was elected for the new constituent assembly in ten different departments, and was chosen one of the five members of the Executive Committee. For a few months indeed, Lamartine, who for nearly sixty years had been a distinguished man of letters, an official of inferior rank in diplomacy, and an eloquent but unpractical speaker in parliament, became one of the foremost men in Europe. His own inexperience in the routine work of government, the utterly unpractical nature of his colleagues and of the constitution which they endeavored to carry out, and the turbulence of the Parisian mob proved fatal to his chances. During his brief tenure of office Lamartine gave some proofs of statesmanlike ability, notably in his reply to the deputation of United Irishmen who visited him in the hope that the new French democracy would take up the old hatred of the republic against England, and his eloquence was repeatedly called into requisition to pacify the Parisians. But no one can permanently carry on the government of a great country by speeches from the balcony of a house in the capital, and Lamartine found himself in a dilemma. So long as he held aloof from Ledru-Rollin and the more radical of his colleagues, the disunion resulting weakened the government; as soon as he effected an approximation to them, the middle classes, who more in France than any where else were and are the arbiters of governments, fell off from him. The quelling of the insurrection on the 15th of May was his last successful act. A month later the renewal of active disturbances brought on the fighting of June, and Lamartine's influence was extinguished in favor of Cavaignac. There is hardly another instance on record of so sudden an elevation and so rapid a fall. Before February in 1848 Lamartine was, as has been said, a private person of talent and reputation; after June in the same year he was once more the same, except that his chance of political pre-eminence was gone. He had been tried and found wanting, having neither the virtues nor the vices of his situation. In January, 1849, though he was nominated for the presidency, only a few thousand votes were given to him, and three months later he was not even elected to the legislative assembly."

Lamartine's misfortunes in political matters rendered the remainder of his life very melancholy. He had reached the age of fifty-nine. His money was gone, and his only hope left was found in his pen. He set to work most earnestly to repair his fortune, and the literature of his country was greatly enriched thereby. A series of "Confidences" soon appeared, also an autobiography, entitled "Raphael," treated his own experiences in a romantic form. He published "The History of the Revolution of 1848," "The History of the Restoration," "The History of Turkey," "The History of Russia," also a large number of biographical and miscellaneous works. A subscription was opened for him in 1858. In 1860 he revised all of his works and published them in forty-one volumes. The work took him five years, and in the meantime, in 1863, his wife died, thus leaving him, an old man, to fight the battle of life alone. He was about seventy-three; his powers were failing; public sentiment had changed so as to render his prose and poetry unpopular, hence his last hope had departed. He had anticipated that his literary labor would secure the means of comfort and independence, but the constantly changing sentiments of France ordered otherwise. Be it remembered, however, to the credit of France, that, in 1867, the government of the empire rewarded his literary labors with a donation of £20,000. The fact that Lamartine, with Quinet and Victor Hugo, was standing aloof from Napoleon's government, although Lamartine did not assume the active protesting attitude of the others, makes the donation all the more creditable to France. Party strife, however, arose to such a degree in the closing years of the reign of Napoleon III, as to give the donation a party color, and thus secure for him the censure of the extreme opposition. He lived only two years to enjoy his pension, and the empire died two years later.

"As a statesman, Lamartine was placed during his brief tenure of office in a position from which it would have been almost impossible for any man to emerge with credit who was not prepared and able to play the dictator. At no time in history, not even in the great revolution of sixty years earlier, were unpractical crotchets so rife in the heads of men as in 1848, and at no time was there such an absence of what may be called backbone in a nation as then in France. But Lamartine could hardly have guided the ship of state safely even in much calmer weather. For it does not appear that he had any settled political ideas. He was first an ardent legitimist, then a liberal royalist, then a constitutionalist of an indefinite type, then a republican; and it does not appear that any of the phases was the result of reasoned conviction, but rather of a vague kind of sentiment and of the contagion of popular and prevalent ideas." Thus we observe that Lamartine was a fitting representative of French instability. His opinions were no firmer than those of his neighbors. The government was as uncertain as the views of the people, and they shifted with every changing wind. But with all this he was a remarkable man for his time.

As a literary man he occupies an important place in French history. He is not the greatest writer, either in matter or manner, for Victor Hugo far excels him. He began writing at a time when the literary fields which he proposed to occupy were almost empty. For this reason he rose rapidly into popular favor, and, for a time, stood at the head of French letters. But he was soon entirely eclipsed by the brilliant and vigorous school who succeeded him, with Victor Hugo at their head. The study of French history, however, would be incomplete without a knowledge of Lamartine, the poet, historian and statesman.

LONGFELLOW.

Henry Wadsworth Longfellow, whom Griswold describes as the greatest American poet, was born at Portland, Maine, February 27, 1807, and he died at Cambridge, Massachusetts, March 24, 1882.

His father was of Puritan stock, and a lawyer by profession. He possessed the necessary wealth to give his children school opportunities.

At the age of fourteen young Longfellow was sent to Bowdoin College, where he graduated at eighteen. He was a close student, as shown by the testimony of his classmate, the talented Nathaniel Hawthorne, also by the

HENRY WADSWORTH LONGFELLOW.

recollections of Mr. Packard, one of his teachers. These glimpses that we catch of the boy reveal a modest, refined, manly youth, devoted to study, of great personal charm, and gentle manners. It is the boy that the older man suggested. To look back upon him is to trace the broad and clear and beautiful river far up the green meadows to the limpid rill. His poetic taste and faculty were already apparent, and it is related that a version of an ode of Horace which he wrote in his Sophomore year so impressed one of the members of the examining board that when afterward a chair of modern languages was established in the college, he proposed as its incumbent the young Sophomore whose fluent verse he remembered. Before his name was suggested for the position of professor of modern languages at Bowdoin, he had studied law for a short time in his father's office. The position was gladly accepted, for the young poet seemed more at home in letters than in law. That he might be better prepared for his work he studied and traveled in Europe for three and one-half years. For the purpose of becoming acquainted more thoroughly with the manners and literature of other countries, he visited France, Spain, Italy, Germany, Holland, and England. Returning home in 1829 he entered upon his duties at Bowdoin, where he remained for six years. Upon the death of Mr. George Ticknor, in 1835, Longfellow was appointed to the chair of modern languages in that eminent seat of learning. Again sailing for Europe he visited the Scandinavian countries, Germany and Switzerland. On this visit he became acquainted with the literature of northern Europe. Again returning to the United States, he entered upon his duties at Harvard. This position he held for nineteen years when he resigned, and was succeeded by James Russell Lowell. Thus, for twenty-five years, from 1829 to 1854, he was a college professor in addition to his ceaseless literary work.

At a very early age Longfellow gave evidences of poetic genius. Numerous stories are told of his childish effusions. From the commencement of his collegiate course it became evident to his teachers and fellow-students that literature would be his profession. While a youth his poems and criticisms, contributed to periodicals, attracted general attention. Hawthorne speaks of him as having scattered some delicate verses to the wind while yet in college. Among those youthful poems we may mention, "An April Day," a finished work that shows all of the author's flowing melody in later years.

In 1833 he published a translation of the Spanish verses called "Coplas de Manrique," which he accompanied with an essay upon Spanish poetry. This seems to have been his first studied effort and it showed wonderful grace and skill.

The genius of the poet steadily and beautifully developed, flowering according to its nature. The most urbane and sympathetic of men, never aggressive, nor vehement, nor self-asserting, he was yet thoroughly independent, and the individuality of his genius held its tranquil way as surely as the river Charles, whose placid beauty he so often sang, wound through the meadows calm and free. When Longfellow came to Cambridge, the impulse of transcendentalism in New England was deeply affecting scholarship and literature. It was represented by the most original of American thinkers and the typical American scholar, Emerson, and its elevating, purifying, and emancipating influences are memorable in our moral and intellectual history. Longfellow lived in the very heart of the movement. Its leaders were his cherished friends. He too was a scholar and a devoted student of German literature, who had drank deeply also of the romance of German life. Indeed, his first important works stimulated the taste for German studies and the enjoyment of its literature more than any other impulse in this country. But he remained without the charmed transcendental circle, serene and friendly and attractive. There are those whose career was wholly moulded by the intellectual revival of that time. But Longfellow was untouched by it, except as his sympathies were attracted by the vigor and purity of its influence. His tastes, his interests, his activities, his career, would have been the same had that great light never shone. If he had been the ductile, echoing, imitative nature that the more ardent disciples of the faith supposed him to be, he would have been absorbed and swept away by the flood. But he was as untouched by it as Charles Lamb by the wars of Napoleon.

From this period poems and essays and romances flowed from his inspired pen in almost endless profusion. In 1835 appeared "Outre Mer," being sketches of travel beyond the Atlantic; in 1839, "Hyperion, a Romance," which instantly became popular. In the same year with "Hyperion," came the "Voices of the Night," a volume of poems which contained the "Coplas de Manrique" and the translations, with a selection from the verses of the "Literary Gazette," which the author playfully reclaims, in a note, from their vagabond and precarious existence in the corners of newspapers—gathering his children from wandering in lanes and alleys, and introducing them decorously to the world. A few later poems were added and these, with the "Hyperion," showed a new and distinctive literary talent. In both of these volumes there is the purity of spirit, the elegance of form, the romantic tone, the airy grace, which were already associated with Longfellow's name. But there are other qualities. The boy of nineteen, the poet of Bowdoin, has become the scholar and traveler. The teeming hours, the ample opportunities of youth have not been neglected or squandered, but, like a golden-banded bee, humming as he sails, the young poet has drained all the flowers of literature of their nectar, and has built for himself a hive of sweetness. More than this he had proved in his own experience the truth of Irving's tender remark, that an early sorrow is often the truest benediction for the poet. At least two of the poems in "Voices," "Psalm of Life," and "Footsteps of Angels," penetrated the common heart at once, and have held it ever since. A young Scotchman saw them reprinted in some paper or magazine, and meeting a literary lady in London, he repeated them to her, and then to a literary assembly at her house; and the presence of a new poet was at once acknowledged. "The Psalm of Life" was the very heartbeat of the American conscience, and the "Footsteps of Angels" was a hymn of the fond yearning of every loving heart. Nothing finer could be written. They illustrate the fact that our inner consciousness breathes the air of immortality just as naturally as our lungs draw in the air of heaven.

In 1841 appeared "Ballads, and Other Poems;" in 1842, "Poems on Slavery;" in 1843, "The Spanish Student," a tragedy; in 1845, "Poets and Poetry of Europe;" 1846, "The Belfry of Bruges;" 1847, "Evangeline;" 1849, "Kavanaugh," a prose tale; in the same year, "The Seaside and the Fireside," a series of short poems; 1851, "The Golden Legend," a mediæval story in irregular rhyme; 1855, "The Song of Hiawatha," an Indian tale; 1858, the "Courtship of Miles Standish;" 1863, "Flower de Luce;" 1867, a translation of Dante; 1872, "The Divine Tragedy," a sacred but not successful drama; in the same year, "Three Books of Songs;" 1874, "Hanging of the Crane;" 1875, "The Masque of Pandora;" and 1878, "Keramos." The above gives an outline of his literary work, though he wrote numerous poems not mentioned, and made some excellent translations.

Among his short poems that have gone into every day literature, and are known in every home, may be mentioned "The Building of the Ship," "The Old Clock on the Stairs," "The Bridge," "The Builders," "The Day is Done," "The Ride of Paul Revere," "The Evening Star," "The Snow Flakes," "Excelsior," "Psalm of Life," and "Footsteps of Angels." Where can we find a more popular collection than that given above? Eminently, Longfellow is the poet of the domestic affections. He is the poet of the household, of the fireside, of the universal home feeling. The infinite tenderness and patience, the pathos and the beauty of daily life, of familiar emotion, and the common scene,—these are the significance of that verse whose beautiful and simple melody, softly murmuring for more than forty years, made the singer the most widely beloved of living men.

In 1868 he visited Europe for the third time. What a contrast between this and former visits! Cambridge University conferred upon him the degree of LL. D., and Oxford that of D. C. L. The Russian Academy of Science elected him a member, and he was also made a member of the Spanish Academy. He was received everywhere with marks of distinction. His fame had reached even the poor classes and the servants of nobility. It was known that he would visit the queen on a certain day, and as he passed along the streets and corridors leading to her reception room, he was surprised to see the number of persons looking from doors and peeping from windows to see him. The queen received him most cordially. She told him the persons he had noticed were her servants, that they had learned to love him, and that the poet who could thus command the affections of the poor and humble, as well as of the rich and great, surely wears a greater than an earthly crown. And why not love him? He is the poet, above all others, who has swept every chord of tenderness, beauty, and pathos; and he has lightened the sorrows and heightened the joys of every home. His poems are apples of gold in pictures of silver. The gentle influence of his poetry is sweetly and unconsciously expressed in one of his own poems:

> Come read to me some poem,
> Some simple and heart-felt lay,
> That shall soothe this restless feeling,
> And banish the thoughts of day.
>
> Not from the grand old masters,
> Not from the bard sublime,
> Whose distant footsteps echo
> Through the corridors of Time.
>
> *   *   *   *   *   *
>
> Such songs have power to quiet
> The restless pulse of care,
> And come like the benediction
> That follows after prayer.

Other fields were open for his muse, but with a steady and unerring purpose he held his pen close to the domestic heart. Scotland sings and glows in the verse of Burns, but the affections of the whole world shine in the verse of Longfellow.

A genial writer has paid our favorite a deserved compliment. He says that "in no other conspicuous figure in literary history are the man and the poet more indissolubly blended than in Longfellow. The poet was the man and the man was the poet. What he was to the stranger reading in distant lands, by

> 'The long wash of Australasian seas,'

that he was to his most intimate friends. His life and his character were perfectly reflected in his books. There is no purity, or grace, or feeling, or spotless charm in his verse which did not belong to the man. There was never an explanation to be offered for him, no allowance was necessary for the eccentricity, or grotesqueness, or willfulness, or humor of genius. Simple, modest, frank, manly, he was the good citizen, the self-respecting gentleman, the symmetrical man."

For a long time he lived at Cambridge, Massachusetts, in a house once occupied by General Washington as his headquarters; the highway running by his gate and dividing the smooth grass and modest green terrace about the house from the fields and meadows that sloped gently to the placid Charles, and the low range of distant hills that made the horizon. Through the little gate passed an endless procession of pilgrims of every degree and from every country to pay homage to their American friend. Every morning came the letters of those who could not come in person, and with infinite urbanity and sympathy and patience the master of the house received them all, and his gracious hospitality but deepened the admiration and affection of the guests. His nearer friends sometimes remonstrated at his sweet courtesy to such annoying "devastators of the day." But to an urgent complaint of his endless favor to a flagrant offender, Longfellow only answered, good-humoredly, "If I did not speak kindly to him, there is not a man in the world who would." On the day that he was taken ill, six days only before his death, three school-boys came out from Boston on their Saturday holiday to ask his autograph. The benign lover of children welcomed them heartily, showed them a hundred interesting things in his house, then wrote his name for them and for the last time.

Few men had known deeper sorrow—his first wife having died in Holland, in 1835; his second wife having been burned to death in 1861, by her clothes taking fire, accidentally, while she was playing with the children. But no man ever mounted upon his sorrow more surely to higher things. Blessed and beloved, the singer is gone, but his song remains, and its pure and imperishable melody is the song of the lark in the morning of our literature:

> "Type of the wise who soar but never roam,
> True to the kindred points of heaven and home."

JAMES RUSSELL LOWELL.

From an excellent article on Lowell, by F. H. Underwood, we make up the greater part of this sketch.

The Lowells are descended from Percival Lowell, of Bristol, England, who settled in Newbury, Massachusetts, in 1639. The father of the poet was Dr. Charles Lowell, an eminent clergyman (1782-1861); his grandfather, John Lowell (1743-1802), was an eminent judge, and the author of that section of the Bill of Rights by which slavery was abolished in Massachusetts.

Dr. Charles Lowell married Harriet Spence, a native of Portsmouth, New Hampshire, belonging to a Scotch family. Mrs. Harriet Spence Lowell had a great memory, an extraordinary aptitude for languages, and a passionate fondness for ancient songs and ballads. She had five children: Charles, Robert (the Rev. Robert Traill Spence Lowell, an author and poet), Mary Lowell Putnam (a lady of singular ability and learning), Rebecca, and James Russell, the subject of this sketch, who was the youngest, born February 22, 1819. The children were nurtured with romances and minstrelsy. The old songs were sung over their cradles, and repeated in early school-days, until poetic lore and taste—foreign grafts in many minds—were as natural to them as the bodily senses.

It seldom happens in this country that a lifetime is passed without change of residence; but, except during his visits abroad, Lowell has always lived in the house in which he was born.

Elmwood, though not very ancient, has an interesting history. The house was built by Peter Oliver, who was stamp-distributor just before the outbreak of the Revolution. The house was next occupied by Elbridge

Gerry, an eminent man in his day. After his death it became the property of Dr. Lowell, about a year before the birth of the poet. It is of wood, three stories high, and stands on the base-line of a triangle of which the apex reaches nearly to the gate of Mount Auburn cemetery. The ample grounds have an abundant growth of trees, most of them planted as a screen from the winds. There are a few native elms, but those which give the name to the estate are English, sturdy as oaks, standing in front of the house. In front, also, are large and beautiful ash trees.

The nearest neighbor to Elmwood in 1825 was William Wells, who kept a boys' school, and from him the poet got most of his early education; he was for a time, however, a pupil of a Mr. Ingraham, who had a classical school in Boston.

Lowell entered Harvard College in his sixteenth year, and graduated in 1838. His rank in scholarship was not a matter of pride. He has been used to say that he read almost everything—except the text-books prescribed by the faculty. To certain branches of study, especially mathematics, he had an invincible repugnance; and his degree was perhaps a tribute to his known ability, bestowed as an incentive to future diligence.

After leaving college Lowell entered the law school, and having finished the prescribed course, took his degree of LL. B. in 1840. He opened an office in Boston, but it does not appear that he ever seriously engaged in the practice of law.

A little before his twenty-second birthday he published a small volume of poems entitled "A Year's Life." The poems are naturally upon the subject that inspires youths of one-and-twenty; and though they do not appear in the author's "complete" collection, they are worthy of consideration. The unnamed lady who is celebrated in the poet's verse, and who afterward became his wife, was Miss Maria White, a person of beauty, refined in taste, sympathetic in nature, and the author of several exquisite poems. Notwithstanding the recollections of "A Year's Life" have been set aside by the severe judgment of the poet, the student will discover in them many intimations of the genius that shone out more clearly in later days.

In the domain of letters, dead magazines are the ruins, if wrecked air

JAMES RUSSELL LOWELL.

castles ever leave any ruins behind. Nearly every author has at some time felt a shock at the downfall of his castle, and happy is he who is not crushed thereby. In Lowell's case the name of the periodical was the "Pioneer." He was associated in the editorship with Robert Carter. The "Pioneer" survived but three months. Previous to this he had written some very striking literary essays for the Boston "Miscellany." About three years after "A Year's Life" another volume of poems appeared, well known to readers of to-day. The "Legend of Brittany" and "Prometheus" are the longest, but the most popular are "Rhoecus," "The Shepherd of King Admetus," "To Perdita Singing," "The Forlorn," "The Hermitage," "A Parable," etc.

There are several of the poems in this collection which now seem prophetic. They were bold utterances at the time, and were doubtless considered as the wild rhapsodies of a harmless enthusiast. The ode beginning:

> In the old days of awe and keen-eyed wonder,
> The Poet's song with blood-warm truth was rife,

may be regarded as a confession of faith. In force of thought and depth of feeling, and in the energy of its rhythmic movement, it is a remarkable production, whether for a poet of twenty-five or older. He decries the bards who seek merely to amuse, and deplores their indifference to human welfare:

> Proprieties our silken bards environ;
> He who would be the tongue of this wide land
> Must string his harp with chords of sturdy iron,
> And strike it with a toil-embrowned hand.

This stirring ode was a fit prelude to the part our poet was to perform.

The Mexican war was in progress, and the abolitionists declared that it was waged to obtain new territory for the extension of slavery, and thereby to counterbalance the growing power of the Northern States. President Polk had been elected to carry out the scheme. The appeal was to Congress, through the conscience of the nation, to stop the supplies.

Mr. Lowell wrote a letter to the Boston "Courier," purporting to come from Ezekiel Biglow, enclosing a poem in the Yankee dialect, written by his son Hosea, in which the efforts to raise volunteers in Boston were held up to scorn:

> Thrash away! You'll hev to rattle
> On them kittle-drums o' yourn;
> 'Tain't a knowin' kind o' cattle
> That is ketched with mouldy corn.

Society was puzzled. Critics turned the homely quatrains over with their claws as kittens do bottles, and doubted. Politicians thought them vulgar. For the first time in history the laugh was on the side of the reformers. The more cultivated of the abolitionists were in ecstacies. Some, however, did not quite understand the levity of tone. When Charles Sumner saw the first Biglow poem in the "Courier" he exclaimed to a friend: "This Yankee poet has the true spirit. He put the case admirably. I wish, however, he could have used good English."

The poems were finally gathered into a volume, which in comic completeness is without a parallel. The "work" begins with "Notices of the Press," which are delightful travesties of the perfunctory style both of "soft-soaping" and of "cutting up." There happening to be a vacant page, the space was filled off-hand by the first sketch of "Zekel's Courtship."

> Zekel crep' up quite unbeknown,
> An' peeked in thru the winder,
> An' there sot Huldy all alone,
> With no one nigh to hender.

This is the most genuine of our native idyls. Its appearance in the "Biglow Papers" was purely an accident; but it had the air of being an extract, and it was so greatly admired, that the poet afterward added new stanzas to fill out the picture. In the original sketch there were six stanzas; there are now twenty-four.

As the Yankee peculiarities of the "Biglow Papers" are evidently fresh studies, it might appear strange that they could be wrought out by a resident of Cambridge. For that city though rural is not in the least rustic. The primeval Yankee has become scarce everywhere; he is hardly obtainable as a rare specimen: he is a tradition; he and his bucolic manners and speech are utterly gone. As soon expect the return of Jacob and Rachel as to see again the originals of the poet's Zekel and Huldy. The old town as it was in Lowell's boyhood is sketched with rare humor and fine touches in an article by him published in "Putnam's Monthly" in 1853, entitled "Cambridge Thirty Years Ago." In this masterly picture we see a country village, silent and rural. There are old houses around the bare common, "and old women, capped and spectacled, still peered through the same windows from which they had watched Lord Percy's artillery rumble by to Lexington." One coach sufficed for the travel to Boston. It was "sweet Auburn" then, a beautiful woodland, and not a great cemetery. The "Old Road" from the square led to it, bending past Elmwood. Cambridgeport was then a "huckleberry pastur'," having a large settlement of old-fashioned taverns, with vast barns and yards, on the eastern verge. "Great white-topped wagons, each drawn by double files of six or eight horses, with its dusty bucket swinging from the hinder axle, and its grim bull-dog trotting silent underneath, brought all the wares and products of the country to Boston. These filled the inn yards, or were ranged side by side under broad-roofed sheds, and far into the night the mirth of the lusty drivers clamored from the red curtained bar-room, while the single lantern swaying to and fro in the black cavern of stables made a Rembrandt of the group of hostlers and horses below."

The provincial tone was evident. You have only to talk with an old Bostonian even now to see how it was. But the main thing was that up to 1830 the manners and speech of ordinary folk were those of the seventeenth century. The rustic Yankee was then a fact. In fifty years, by the aid of steam and electricity, Boston became a modern city, on equal terms with the Old World, a center of itself, and Cambridge was developed into a highly cultivated suburb. The rusticity was gone. The changes of two hundred years went by in a lifetime.

Recalling old Cambridge by the aid of Lowell's reminiscences, we see how the vernacular idioms and the humorous peculiarities of the people are so naturally reproduced in his comic verse.

Mr. Lowell was married December 26, 1844. His domestic life at Elmwood, like the "peace that passeth understanding," could be described only in simile. It was ideally beautiful. And nothing was wanting to perfect happiness but the sense of permanence. Mrs. Lowell was never very strong, and her ethereal beauty seemed too delicate for the climate of New England. Children were born to them, but all died in infancy excepting a daughter (now Mrs. Edward Burnett). Friends of the poet who were admitted to the study in the upper chamber remember the pairs of baby shoes that hung over a picture frame. From the shoes out through the west window to the resting-place of the dear little feet in Mount Auburn there was but a glance—a tender, mournful association, full of unavailing grief, but never expressed in words. Poems written in this period show the depth of parental feeling. Readers remember "The Changeling" and "She Came and Went:"

> "As a twig trembles which a bird
> Lights on to sing, then leaves unbent,
> So is my memory thrilled and stirred:
> I only know she came and went."

Mr. and Mrs. Lowell went to Europe in the summer of 1851, and spent a year, visiting Switzerland, France, and England, but living for the most part in Italy. They returned in the autumn of 1852. Mrs. Lowell was slowly, almost imperceptibly, declining. The end came in October, 1853, when like a breath her soul was exhaled.

On the day of Mrs. Lowell's death a child was born to Mr. Longfellow, and his poem "The Two Angels"—perhaps as perfect a specimen of his genius as can be cited—will remain forever as a most touching expression of sympathy:

> 'Twas at thy door, O friend, and not at mine,
> The angel with the amaranthine wreath,
> Pausing, descended, and with voice divine
> Whispered a word that had a sound like Death.
>
> Then fell upon the house a sudden gloom,
> A shadow on those features fair and thin,
> And softly, from that hushed and darkened room,
> Two angels issued, where but one went in.

Mrs. Lowell's poems were collected and privately printed in a memorial volume with a photograph from Page's portrait; many of them have been widely copied and have become a part of our literature.

Lowell's next important effort was "The Vision of Sir Launfal." This was composed in the space of about forty-eight hours. Its effect upon the reader is like that of the outburst of an inspired singer. The effect upon the public was immediate and powerful; the poem needed no herald nor interpreter.

About the same period came "The Present Crisis"—an ardent poem in a high prophetic strain, and in strongly sonorous measure. This has been often quoted by public speakers, and many of its lines are as familiar as the most trenchant of proverbs.

We will here merely mention "Ambrose," a beautiful legend with a lesson of toleration; "The Dandelion" and "The Birch Tree," both charming pictures already hung in the gallery of fame; "An Interview with Miles Standish," and "Beaver Brook," a fine specimen of an ideal landscape; "A Fable for Criticism," an excellent poem ranging the field of satire.

The "Fable" is as full of puns as a pudding of plums. The good ones are the best of their kind, strung together like beads, and the bad ones are so "atrocious" as to be quite as amusing. No poem of the kind in the language equals it in the two aspects of vivid genius and riotous fun. The "Fable" careers like an ice boat. Breezes fill the light sails as if toying with them, but the course is like lightning, and every movement answers to the touch of the helm.

In 1849 Mr. Lowell's poems were collected in two volumes. The "Biglow Papers," "A Fable for Critics," and "A Year's Life" were not included. In 1853, and for some years afterward, he was a frequent contributor to "Putnam's Monthly," conducted by George William Curtis and Charles F. Briggs. Some of his finest productions, both in prose and verse, appeared in that brilliant periodical. In the winter of 1854-'55 he delivered a course of twelve lectures on English poetry in the Lowell Institute.

It is probable that by this time our poet had begun to think of some connection with the university. The illustrious professor of belles-lettres, it was known, desired to retire from the chair, and public opinion pointed to

Lowell as a proper person for his successor. In the summer of 1855 Mr. Longfellow resigned, and Mr. Lowell was appointed in his place, with leave of absence for two years. He went to Europe to pursue his studies, and remained abroad, chiefly in Dresden, until the spring of 1857, when he returned and began his courses of lectures.

The germs of his literary criticism are to be found in his "Conversations on the Poets," published in his twenty-fifth year. The book is a valuable part of his literary biography. The sentences give an impression of prolixity at first, not so much of words as of teeming, struggling thought.

The volume "Fireside Travels" was published in 1864. The articles were written when Lowell was thirty-four. "Fireside Travels," among prose works, is the product of Lowell's best days. Pages appear like the soil of hot-house beds, with thoughts serious, jocose, learned, allusive, sprouting everywhere. It does not matter where the reader opens for every sentence has some salient or recondite charm.

In 1857 Lowell married Miss Frances Dunlap, of Portland, Maine. In the same year the "Atlantic Monthly" was started by some of the leading authors of New England, and Lowell became editor-in-chief, a position held by him until 1862. The "Monthly" was organized partly in the interest of the anti-slavery cause. Abraham Lincoln's election to the presidency settled the controversy so far as ballots were concerned, and transferred the struggle to the battle-field. The success of his "Biglow Papers," sent forth at the time of the Mexican war, led him to commence a second series shortly after the outbreak of the late war. The poems were all written in the Yankee dialect, and were unusually popular at the North. As different phases of the struggle were presented, they were caught up promptly by the poet and given in his inimitable style.

The prose works of Lowell consist of the "Fireside Travels," already referred to, and three volumes of essays, published in 1870, 1871, and 1876. Of these the one entitled "My Study Windows" will be found most interesting to general readers. The other two are entitled "Among My Books," and are of a purely literary character. A large number of his essays have appeared in magazines and reviews, and have not as yet been reprinted.

These essays of Lowell ("Among My Books," two volumes, "My Study Windows," one volume) cover a wide range of thought and observation, but all have the inevitable family likeness. Mention has been made of "Fireside Travels." Of a similar tone are "My Garden Acquaintance," "A Good Word for Winter," and "On a Certain Condescension in Foreigners." The last is a specimen of pure irony. "New England Two Centuries Ago," is a powerful historical article, in which the Puritans and Pilgrims are sketched.

Mr. and Mrs. Lowell visited Europe in 1873. He had never held office, though he has always had a warm interest in public affairs. It was therefore with gratification that his friends heard of his appointment as minister to Spain. After the retirement of Mr. Welsh Mr. Lowell was transferred to London. His reception in the metropolis of letters has been in the highest degree flattering to him, and a matter of just pride to his countrymen.

Lowell is great in prose, poetry and criticism, but his poems are the chief source of his fame. His serious poems are excellent, but as a humorist he appears at his best. He occupied a new field when he commenced the "Biglow Papers," and he cultivated the soil so as to bring it to its highest state of perfection.

Ordinarily it is difficult, while an author is yet living, to determine just what rank he must occupy in literature. But Lowell's rank is securely placed among the master writers of the age.

LORD MACAULAY.

THOMAS BABINGTON MACAULAY was born at Rothley Temple, Leicestershire, England, October 25, 1800. He died December 28, 1859, and was buried in Westminster Abbey, in Poets' Corner, near the statue of Addison, on January 9, 1860. His early death was caused by derangement of the action of the heart.

The ancestors of Lord Macaulay were long settled in the island of Lewis, Ross-shire. Zachary Macaulay (1768-1838), son of the Scottish minister, was sent when a boy to the West Indies. He was disgusted with the state of slavery in Jamaica, and afterward on his return to Great Britain, resided at Clapham, and became an active associate of Clarkson and Wilberforce. He married Selina, daughter of Mr. Thomas Mills, a bookseller in Bristol, and had, with other children, a son destined to take a high place among the statesmen, orators, essayists, and historians of England.

Before he was eight years of age the boy had written a "Compendium of Universal History," which gave a tolerably connected view of the leading events from the creation to 1800, and a romance in the style of Scott, in three cantos, called the "Battle of Cheviot." At a little later time the child composed a long poem on the history of Olaus Magnus, and a vast pile of blank verse entitled "Fingal, a Poem in Twelve Books." At the age of twelve he was placed under the care of the Rev. Mr. Preston, first at Shelford, afterward near Buntingford, in the neighborhood of Cambridge. In his nineteenth year he was entered at Trinity College, Cambridge; he gained two prizes for English verse, one in 1819, on "Pompeii," and one two years after on "Evening." He gained the Craven scholarship in 1821, took his degree of B. A. in 1822, became Fellow of his college in 1824, and took his degree of M. A. in 1825. He had distinguished himself by contributions to "Knight's Quarterly Magazine" in 1823 and 1824; and in August, 1825, appeared his celebrated article on Milton in the "Edinburgh Review." Having studied at Lincoln's Inn, Mr. Macaulay was called to the bar in 1826, and joined the Northern Circuit.

Three years afterward a distinguished Whig nobleman, the Marquis of Lansdowne, procured his return to parliament for the borough of Calne, and he rendered effective service in the Reform debates of 1831 and 1832. In 1832 he was appointed Secretary to the Board of Control, and the same year the citizens of Leeds returned him as their representative to the House of Commons. In 1834 he proceeded to India as legal advisor to the Supreme

Council of Calcutta. He returned to England in 1838, and in the following year was returned to parliament for the city of Edinburgh, which he continued to represent until 1847. In the Melbourne administration he held the office of Secretary of War, and in that of Lord John Russell, Paymaster of the Forces, with a seat in the cabinet. During this time he had written most of his essays, and published his "Lays of Ancient Rome." His law practice did not amount to a scanty support; but on the previous year he had associated himself with the "Edinburgh Review" in a series of brilliant essays that attracted the attention of prominent members of the government. His speech at the anti-slavery meeting in 1824 was described by the "Review" as a "display of eloquence of rare and matured excellence," which greatly spread his fame. He had also gained great reputation as a conversationalist.

Thus launched on the best that London had to give in the way of society, a commercial disaster overtook his father, in which the house of Babington & Macaulay lost its fortune of about £100,000. Our author was thus thrown wholly upon his own resources. His Trinity fellowship brought him £300 a year, but that expired in 1831. In 1828, however, he received temporary employment through an appointment as commissioner of bankruptcy, a position worth £400 per annum. A change in the ministry took this support from him in 1830. Macaulay now found himself a poor man, and was reduced to such straits that he had to sell his Cambridge gold medal.

In February, 1830, the doors of the House of Commons were opened to him in the only way in which a man without a fortune could enter them, through what was then called a "pocket borough." Lord Lansdowne, who had been struck by two articles on Mill (James) and the "Utilitarians" which appeared in the "Edinburgh Review" in 1829, offered the author the seat at Calne. The offer was accompanied by the express assurance that the noble patron had no wish to interfere with his freedom of voting. He thus entered parliament at one of the most exciting moments of English domestic history, when the compact phalanx of reactionary administration, which for nearly fifty years had commanded a crushing majority in the Commons, was on the point of being broken by the growing strength of the party of reform. Macaulay made his maiden speech on the 5th of April, 1830, on the second reading of the bill for the removal of Jewish disabilities. In July the king died and parliament was dissolved; the revolution took place in Paris. Macaulay, who was again returned for Calne, visited Paris, eagerly enjoying a first taste of continental travel. On March 1, 1831, the Reform Bill was introduced, and on the second night of the debate Macaulay made the first of his reform speeches. It was a signal success.

Encouraged by this first success, Macaulay now threw himself with ardor into the life of the House of Commons, while at the same time he continued to enjoy to the full the social opportunities which his literary and political celebrity had placed within his reach. For these reasons he dined out almost nightly, and spent many of his Sundays at the suburban villas of the Whig leaders, while he continued to supply the "Edinburgh Review" with a steady series of his most elaborate articles. On the triumph of Earl Grey's cabinet and the passing of the Reform Act in June, 1832, Macaulay, whose eloquence had signalized every stage of the conflict, became one of the commissioners of the Board of Control, and applied himself to the study of Indian affairs. His industry was untiring, and the amount of intellectual product which he threw off very great. Giving his days to India and his nights to the House of Commons, he could only devote a few hours to literary composition by rising at five when the business of the House had allowed of his getting to bed in time on the previous evening. Between September, 1831, and December, 1833, he furnished the "Review" with the following articles: "Boswell's Life of Johnson," "Lord Nugent's Hampden," "Burleigh and his Times," "Mirabeau," "Horace Walpole," "Lord Chatham," besides writing his ballad on the Armada for one of the Albums, annual publications of miscellanies then in fashion.

In the first reform parliament, January, 1833, Macaulay took his seat as one of the first two members for Leeds, which up to that date had been unrepresented in the House of Commons. He replied to O'Connell in the debate on the address, meeting the great agitator face to face with high, but not intemperate defiance. In July he defended the Government India Bill in a speech of great power, and to his aid was greatly due the getting the bill through the committee without unnecessary friction. When the abolition of slavery came before the house as a practical question, Macaulay had the prospect of being placed in the dilemma of having to surrender office or to vote for a modified abolition, viz., twelve years' apprenticeship, which was proposed by the ministry, but condemned by the abolitionists. He was prepared to make the sacrifice of place rather than be unfaithful to the cause to which his father had devoted his life. He placed his resignation in Lord Althorp's hands, and spoke against the ministerial proposal. But the sense of the House was so strongly expressed as unfavorable that, finding they would be beaten if they persisted, the ministry gave way and reduced apprenticeship to seven years, a compromise which the abolition party accepted, and Macaulay remained at the Board of Control.

Macaulay's reputation had reached a point where he could gain a support either in politics or literature; and at the same time his family's fortunes had sunk so that it became necessary for him to provide a support for his sisters. The pay in literature did not seem to be as great as in politics, hence he decided to accept the offer made him of a seat in the supreme council of India, a body which had been created by the India Act he had himself been instrumental in passing. The salary of the office was fixed at £10,000, an income out of which he calculated to be able to save in five years a capital of £30,000. His sister Hannah accepted his proposal to accompany him, and in February, 1834, the brother and sister sailed for Calcutta. Macaulay's appointment to India occurred at the critical moment when the government of the company was being superseded by government by the crown. His knowledge of India was, when he landed, but superficial. But at this juncture there was more need of statesmanship directed by general liberal principles than of a practical knowledge of the details of Indian administration. Macaulay's presence in the council was of great value; his minutes are models of good judgment and practical sagacity. The part he took in India has been described as "the application of sound liberal principles to a government which had till then been jealous, close and repressive." He vindicated the liberty of the press; he maintained the equality of Europeans and natives before the law; and as president of the committee of public instruction he inaugurated that system of national education which has since spread over the whole of the Indian peninsula.

Macaulay was also appointed president of a commission to inquire into the jurisprudence of England's eastern empire. His work was performed with eminent ability. The penal code which he sketched, and which was afterward completed by the aid of others, has been a practical success. His manners called out the ill-will of local English societies, but he met all efforts at political detraction by turning his thoughts to literature. He writes to his friend Ellis, "I have gone back to Greek literature with a passion astonishing to myself. I have never felt anything like it. I was enraptured with Italian during the six months which I gave up to it; and I was little less pleased with Spanish. But when I went back to Greek I felt as if I had never known before what intellectual enjoyment was." In thirteen months he read through, some of them twice, a large part of the Greek and Latin classics. The attention with which he read is proved by the pencil marks and corrections of press errors which he left on the margin of the volumes he used.

The fascination of these studies produced their inevitable effect upon his view of political life. He began to wonder what strange infatuation leads men who can do something better to squander their intellect, their health, and energy on such subjects as those which most statesmen are engaged in pursuing. He was already, he says, "more than half determined to abandon politics, and give myself wholly to letters, to undertake some great historical work, which may be at once the business and amusement of my life, and to leave the pleasures of pestiferous rooms, sleepless nights, and diseased stomachs to Roebuck and to Praed."

He and his sister, now Lady Trevelyan, returned to England in 1838, and Macaulay entered parliament as a member from Edinburgh. In 1839 he took a seat in the cabinet in Lord Melbourne's ministry, as secretary of war. This position compelled him to delay his great historical work for two years, when he was freed from office by the fall of Melbourne's ministry. In 1846 he accepted the position of paymaster of the forces under the administration of Lord John Russell. Within this time he had written his "Lays of Ancient Rome," one of his most popular volumes. To the neglect of politics he was working most earnestly upon his "History." In the sessions of 1846-'47 he spoke only five times, and at the general election of July, 1847, he lost his seat for Edinburgh upon issues which did not reflect credit upon that constituency. Over and above any political disagreement with the constituency, there was the fact that the balance of Macaulay's faculties had now passed to the side of literature. Lord Cockburn wrote in 1846: "The truth is, Macaulay, with all his knowledge, talent, eloquence and worth, is not popular. He cares more for his 'History' than for the jobs of constituents, and answers letters irregularly and with a brevity deemed contemptuous." At an earlier date he had relished crowds and the excitement of ever new faces; as years went forward and absorption in the work of composition took off the edge of his spirits, he recoiled from publicity. He began to regard the prospect of business as worry, and had no longer the nerve to brace himself to the social efforts required of one who represents a large constituency.

Macaulay retired into private life, not only without regret, but with a sense of relief. He gradually withdrew from general society, feeling the bore of big dinners, and country-house visits, but he still enjoyed close and constant intercourse with a circle of the most eminent men that London then contained. At that time social breakfasts were in vogue. Macaulay himself preferred this to any other form of entertainment. Of these brilliant reunions nothing has been preserved beyond the names of the men who formed them, —Rogers, Hallam, Sydney Smith, Lord Carlisle, Lord Stanhope, Nassau Senior, Charles Greville, Milman, Panizzi, Lewis, Van de Weyer. His biographer thus describes Macaulay's appearance and bearing in conversation: "Sitting bolt upright, his hands resting on the arms of his chair, or folded over the handle of his walking stick, knitting his eyebrows if the subject was one to be thought out as he went along, or brightening from the forehead downward when a burst of humor was coming, his massive features and honest glance suited well with the manly, sagacious sentiments which he set forth in his sonorous voice and in his racy and intelligible language. To get at his meaning people had never the need to think twice, and they certainly had seldom the time."

But, great as was his enjoyment of literary society and books, they only formed his recreation. In these years he was working with unflagging industry at the composition of his "History." His composition was slow, his corrections, both of matter and style, endless; he spared no research to ascertain the facts. He sacrificed to the prosecution of his task a political career, House of Commons fame, the allurements of society. The first two volumes of the "History of England" appeared in December, 1848. The success was in every way complete beyond expectation. The sale of edition after edition, both in England and the United States, was enormous. In 1852 when his party returned to power, he refused a seat in the cabinet, but he accepted a seat in parliament from Edinburgh. This was a complimentary amende paid by Edinburgh for his former defeat. But as his strength was diminishing, he only spoke once in parliament, preferring to save his small stock of force for the completion of his great work. In 1857 his eminent ability was recognized by his elevation to the peerage of Great Britain under the title of Baron Macaulay of Rothley.

In 1855 volumes three and four of the "History" appeared. No work, not being one of amusement, has in our day reached a circulation so vast. During the year ending June 25, 1857, the publisher sent out more than 30,000 copies of volume one; in the next nine years more than 50,000 copies of the same volume, and in the nine years ending with June, 1875, more than 52,000 copies. Within a generation of its first appearance upward of 140,000 copies of the "History" will have been printed and sold in the United Kingdom alone. In the United States no book except the Bible ever had such a sale. On the continent of Europe the sale of Tauchnitz editions was very large, a sale which did not prevent six rival translations in German. The "History" has been published in the Polish, Danish, Swedish, Hungarian, Russian, Bohemian, Italian, French, Dutch, and Spanish languages. Flattering marks of respect were heaped upon the author by the foreign academies. His pecuniary profits were on a scale commensurate with the reputation of the book; the cheque for £20,000 has become a landmark in literary history.

His health failed rapidly, hence he shortened the plan of his work to the reign of Queen Anne. Although "he brought down the narrative to the death of William III, the last half volume wants the finish and completeness of the earlier portions." In 1859 "he fell asleep and woke not again."

Macaulay never married, but his strong domestic affections found satisfaction in the attachment and sympathy of his sister, whose children were to him as his own. His life was eminently happy. He was profoundly versed in literature. Each item of information, as he acquired it, was properly labeled and stored away in the chambers of the mind, where he could reach it readily whenever needed for use. "His literary outfit was as complete as has ever been possessed by any English writer. Nor was the knowledge merely stored in his memory; it was always at his command. Whatever his subject, he pours over it his stream of illustration, drawn from the records of all ages and countries. Figures from history, ancient and modern, sacred and secular; characters from plays and novels, from Plautus down to Walter Scott and Jane Austen; images and similes from poets of every age and nation; shrewd thrusts from satirists, wise saws from sages, pleasantries, caustic or prophetic, from humorists,—all these fill Macaulay's pages with the bustle and variety of some glittering masque and cosmoramic revel of great books and heroical men. His style is before all else the style of great literary knowledge." His "Essays" are not merely instructive as history; they are, like Milton's blank verse, freighted with the spoils of all ages. They are literature as well as history. In their diversified contents the "Essays" are a library by themselves; for those who, having little time for study, want one book which may be a substitute for many, we should recommend the "Essays" in preference to anything else.

His composition is a model of rhetorical excellence. Were it not for the great knowledge displayed, we should weary with the excessive beauty of his diction. But the array of thoughts keeps up the charm, while the splendor and perfection of style lure us on to the close of his page.

Macaulay's works have been collected by his sister, and published in eight volumes. The first four are occupied by the "History;" the next three contain the "Essays" and the "Lives" which he contributed to the "Encyclopædia Britannica;" and the last contains his "Speeches," "The Lays of Ancient Rome," and some miscellaneous pieces. His diary still remains in manuscript in the hands of his family.

HORACE MANN.

HORACE MANN was born in Franklin, Massachusetts, May 4, 1796, and died at Yellow Springs, Ohio, August 2, 1859.

His father was a farmer of limited means, but possessing a just appreciation of the advantages of an education. Like Burns' parents, his father gave the encouragement of words and advice, which, in the majority of cases, is worth more than the encouragement of money.

His education was continued in district schools till he was twenty years of age, when he fitted himself to enter Brown University, at Providence, Rhode Island. Mann's college life was one of steady, solid work, and in 1819 he graduated with honor and with a thorough mastery of the subjects studied. The theme of his graduating oration, "The Progressive Character of the Human Race," foreshadowed his future career. Having graduated he became tutor of Latin and Greek in Brown University, a position he finally left to study law. He took a legal course of study in Litchfield, Connecticut, law school, where he was admitted to the bar in 1823. Mann then opened an office in Dedham, Massachusetts, where he gained considerable reputation as an advocate. His ability gained a ready recognition, but his heart seemed set upon educational matters.

In 1827 he was elected to the legislature of his State, and continued to be returned by large majorities as a representative from Dedham till 1833, when he removed to Boston, and entered into partnership with Edward G. Loring. At the first election after he became a citizen of Boston, he was chosen a member of the State senate, and by re-elections was continued a senator for four years. In 1836 and again in 1837 he was president of the senate. While in the legislature he was a member and for part of the time chairman of the committee for the revision of the statutes; and a large number of most salutary provisions were incorporated in the code at his suggestion. After the revised statutes were enacted, he was appointed, in conjunction with Judge Metcalf, to edit the work, for which he prepared the marginal notes and the references to judicial decisions.

At the organization of the Massachusetts board of education, June 30, 1837, he was elected its secretary, and for the next eleven years was annually re-elected. He introduced a thorough reform in the school system of the state; extensive changes in the law relating to schools were adopted; normal schools were established; school committees were paid; a system of county educational conventions was instituted; by means of "school registers" the actual condition of the schools was ascertained; and from the detailed reports of the school committees the secretary made valuable abstracts, which he embodied in his annual reports, forming several large volumes. In 1843 he visited Europe under the auspices of the board, but at his own expense, to examine schools and obtain such information as could be made available at home. His seventh annual report, made on his return, embodied the results of his tour. Many editions were printed, not only in Massachusetts, but in other states, sometimes by order of legislatures, sometimes by private individuals, and several editions were printed in England.

The "Common School Journal," which he edited, and much of which he wrote, consists of ten volumes, 8vo. He published a volume of lectures on education at the request of the board. He traveled over the state every year to hold conventions or teachers' institutes, at which he often taught during the day and lectured in the evening. From the above outline it must appear that Horace Mann was one of the most earnest and effective school workers the world has ever produced. He gave to Massachusetts her favorable standing in educational matters, and much of the school systems of other states is the outgrowth of his work.

In the spring of 1848 the circle of his labor was enlarged by his election to Congress to fill the vacancy caused by the death of John Quincy Adams. He took hold of the duties of the new office with a strong hand. On June 30th he made his first speech in maintenance of the right of Congress to legislate for the territories of the United States, and its duties to exclude slavery therefrom.

In 1852 he was the candidate of the Free Soil party for governor of Massachusetts, but failed in the election. On the day that he was nominated for governor he was also chosen president of Antioch College, a new institution just established at Yellow Springs, Green County, Ohio. He at once entered upon the work of building up the new college. The same zeal and intelligence that had characterized his labors in other fields were manifested at Antioch; and the institution became a powerful auxiliary to the educational interests of Ohio and the West. The college was carried through the pecuniary and other difficulties incident to a new school of the kind, and he satisfied himself and the public that a college for the common education of both sexes is entirely practicable. His annual reports became model school documents, and his lectures and controversial writings became the standard educational literature of the land. His lectures on education were translated into French by Eugene de Guer, in 1873, with a biographical sketch by Laboulaye.

His published works, besides those mentioned, are, "A Few Thoughts for a Young Man," which appeared in 1850; "Slavery: Letters and Speeches," 1851; "Lectures on Intemperance," 1852; "Powers and Duties of Women," 1853. His wife, Mary Peabody Mann, published the "Life of Horace Mann" in 1865. "Mann's Life and Works" appeared in two volumes at Cambridge in 1867, and "Thoughts selected from the Writings of Horace Mann," in 1869.

His style is very impressive and his diction is pure and elevated. His numerous illustrative paragraphs are aptly drawn,—are powerful and grand in their descriptions. His sentences have become proverbs in popular quotations, as may be illustrated in a few short examples.

"Lost, yesterday, somewhere between sunrise and sunset, two golden hours, each set with sixty diamond minutes. No reward is offered, for they are gone forever."

"Habit is a cable; we weave a thread of it each day, and it becomes so strong we cannot break it."

"Affectation hides three times as many virtues as charity does sins."

"It is well to think well. It is divine to act well."

His works should form a part of every library, as well for the purity of their style as for their noble and practical thoughts.

JOHN MILTON.

JOHN MILTON, the greatest English poet since Shakespeare, was born in London December 9, 1608, and he died on Sunday, November 8, 1674.

His father, Mr. John Milton, removed to London about 1586, where he lived for some time as a teacher of music. Later he opened an office on Bread Street, where, as scrivener, he drew up wills, marriage settlements and like legal documents, and received money from his clients for investment. He was known as a man of ingenious tastes, and he gained considerable reputation in London for his contributions to important musical publications. The father prospered so well in his work that he was enabled to give his children the advantages of the best school training.

Music was made a part of the education of the poet from his infancy. But three of six children survived—our poet, an elder sister, Anne, and Christopher, the youngest of the family. John Milton's domestic tutor was Thomas Young, afterward noted among the English Puritan clergy. At the age of ten, in addition to his private instruction, Milton attended at St. Paul's public schools, near his home. Here his teacher was Alexander Gill, an Oxford divine of high reputation. In 1624-'25, at the age of sixteen, Milton entered Christ's College, Cambridge. Milton had ample opportunity for the study of Latin and Greek, and to be thoroughly drilled in logic and philosophy. In 1630 his brother Christopher joined him in college. Milton's academic course lasted about seven and one-half years, when, at the age of twenty-four, he completed his course and took his M. A. degree. At the age of twenty he had taken the degree of B. A. The independence and spirit of Milton led him into a quarrel with his tutor, in the second year of his academic course. The master, Dr. Bainbridge, interfered, whereupon Milton left school for a time. Later a compromise was effected by which the youth returned and was placed under the tutorship of Nathaniel Tovey. His independent demeanor made him unpopular with the younger men of the college. He was nicknamed "The Lady," and was known among the students of the other branches of the university as "The Lady of Christ's College." Before leaving college, however, John Milton held the fullest respect of all, and his intellectual pre-eminence was acknowledged by all. With a certain degree of self-esteem, he was not ignorant "of his own parts," and he anticipated his possibilities. He had gone through the prescribed work with exceptional applause, and to the regular Latin and Greek he had added a knowledge of French, Italian and Hebrew. He returned to his father's home, where he spent five years in studying classical literature. Thus with rare mental powers well trained, health, beauty and grace of person, Milton stepped into the literary arena there to contend with Shakespeare for the mastery of the English tongue. At the age of thirty he started for a tour on the continent. While abroad he formed many valuable acquaintances, and his society was courted by the choicest Italian wits. He visited the great Galileo, then a prisoner of the Inquisition.

Upon the breaking out of the Civil War, Milton returned home and espoused the cause of the Puritans. He was made Latin secretary on a salary of £300 per annum, and his pen did excellent service for Cromwell. Upon the Restoration Milton was forced into retirement, where he pursued

his studies and won an immortal literary fame, both in his poetic and prose writings.

His "Mask of Comus" is a play partially in imitation of Shakespeare's style. It contains, also, traces of Beaumont and Fletcher's style. "Samson Agonistes" is a dramatic poem of merit. "L'Allegro" and "Il Penseroso" are excellent poems, the former a cheerful, merry man, and the latter a thoughtful, melancholy man. His numerous shorter "Poems," "Sonnets" and "Psalms" are full of merit, but we turn to "Paradise Lost," published in 1669, as his greatest poem. Next to the poems of Homer and Virgil this is the greatest poem of its kind produced in any age. "Paradise Regained" followed in due time. For his great master piece he received only about fifteen pounds. In addition to his poetical works he produced powerful tracts, essays and books in prose. The best of these is his "Areopagitica, a Plea for Unlicensed Printing." His other prose writings were mainly upon political and church matters, and a strong discussion of the question of divorces.

Milton's diction is peculiarly rich and pictorial in effect. In force and dignity he towers over all his contemporaries. He is of no class of poets; "his soul was like a star and dwelt apart." The style of Milton's verse was moulded on classic models, chiefly the Greek tragedians, but his musical tastes, his love of Italian literature, and the lofty and solemn cast of his own mind, gave strength and harmony to the whole. His minor poems alone would have rendered his name immortal, but there still wanted his great epic to complete the measure of his fame and the glory of his country."

Milton's prose style is lofty, clear, vigorous, expressive, and frequently adorned with profuse and glowing imagery. "It is to be regretted," says Lord Macaulay, "that the prose writings of Milton should in our time be so little read. As compositions, they deserve the attention of every man who wishes to become acquainted with the full power of the English language. They abound with passages compared with which the finest declamations of Burke sink into insignificance. They are a perfect field of cloth of gold. The style is stiff with gorgeous embroidery. Not even in the earlier books of 'Paradise Lost' has he ever risen higher than in those parts of his controversial works in which his feelings, excited by conflict, find a vent in bursts of devotional and lyric rapture. It is, to borrow his own majestic language, 'a seven-fold chorus of hallelujahs and harping symphonies.'"

In 1643 Milton married Mary Powell, but within a month she left him. Her parents were strong Royalists and Milton was a Republican, hence the separation. Later she returned, and although his tracts on divorce had been published with the intention of repudiating her, yet, like his own Adam, "he was fondly overcome with female charm," and received her as his wife. In 1652 his wife died. He was married twice after this. Milton was blind—"dark, dark, irrecoverably dark"—in 1652, and his "Paradise Lost" was not begun till 1658, hence his most important literary work was done while he was blind. His daughters, wife and visiting friends rendered him valuable aid in writing while he composed. A neat monument, lately erected to perpetuate his memory, now marks his resting place near St. Giles' church. Dryden passes his opinion of Milton by associating him with Homer and Virgil in the following lines:

> "Three poets in three distant ages born,
> Greece, Italy and England did adorn;
> The first in loftiness of thought surpassed,
> The next in majesty, in both the last.
> The force of Nature could no further go;
> To make a third she joined the former two."

D. G. MITCHELL.

DONALD GRANT MITCHELL was born in Norwich, Connecticut, in April, 1822.

He entered Yale College from which he graduated in 1841. He then

DONALD G. MITCHELL.

enriched his mind by traveling in Europe. Returning to this country, he studied law in New York.

Mitchell commenced his career as an author in 1847 by the publication of "Fresh Gleanings, or a New Sheaf from the Old Fields of Continental Europe." This work appeared under the assumed name of "Ik Marvel," a name well known to the literary public. Again in Europe, in 1848, he wrote "The Battle Summer," which was published in New York in 1849. In 1850 he published a satirical work in two volumes, entitled "The Lorgnette." The work appeared anonymously. In the same year appeared "The Reveries of a Bachelor, by Ik Marvel," which was regarded as one of his best volumes. Indeed, it is one of the most entertaining books in the English language. "Dream-Life" followed in 1851. By this time Mitchell's reputation was thoroughly established, and he was regarded as one of the most popular of American writers.

In 1853 he became United States consul at Venice, a position he filled with ability till in 1855, when he returned to his own country. He immediately removed to his farm near New Haven, which he named "Edgewood." This delightful retreat has been his home ever since, and from this place have gone forth several of his best works. In 1869 "The Hearth and Home," a New York weekly, was established, and Mitchell assisted as one of its editors for several years. He has been before the public for many years as a public lecturer, in which field he has won an enviable reputation.

In 1854 appeared "Fudge Doings" in two volumes; 1863, "My Farm of Edgewood;" 1864, "Wet Days at Edgewood;" also, in 1864, "Seven Stories, with Basement and Attic;" 1866, "Doctor Johns," in two volumes; 1867, "Rural Studies;" 1869, "Pictures of Edgewood."

Donald G. Mitchell's style is noted for its grace and beauty. His word-pictures, especially in "The Reveries," are charming. Having commenced one of his sketches, the reader cannot lay the book aside till he has finished reading it. His knowledge of human nature is such that his writings seem personal to each reader. You feel as if Mitchell were acquainted with you and knew your history, else he could not have said so many things that seem to apply to your life, or that you have realized in your own experiences. Then what he says is presented in a manner so natural and so graceful that the reader is captivated by the manner as much as by the matter of his writings. Another attractive feature in Mitchell's books is the purity of sentiment—the absence of everything low, mean, or morally unhealthy. His humor is not boisterous, but is mellowed into a rich and delicate hue that makes all his works lively and interesting and instructive. If the reader cannot obtain all of Mitchell's works, he should at least get "The Reveries of a Bachelor" and "Dream-Life" and read them. If he loves beauty and grace and naturalness of style he must be charmed even to a second and a third reading of these works. Mitchell deserves to rank as one of the most delightful writers of the national period of our literature.

JOAQUIN MILLER.

Joaquin Miller, whose real name is Cincinnatus Hiner Miller, was born in Indiana, November 10, 1841.

Mr. Miller is an excellent example of a self-made man. His writings fell into poetic measure even before he became acquainted with the laws of versification or the rules of grammar. Without the refinement of classic culture he has yet gained an enviable reputation both in the New and Old World.

When he was about eleven years old his father emigrated to Oregon. Three years later the boy went to California to seek his fortune. His verses at this time attracted some attention although they betrayed an utter lack of school training. He wandered about for some time, then returned home in 1860 and commenced the study of law at Eugene, Oregon. In the succeeding year he became express messenger in the gold-mining district of Idaho. This position he soon relinquished to take charge of the "Democratic Register." For its political sentiments this paper was suppressed during the late war, whereupon Miller opened a law office in Canon City, Oregon, in 1863. From his experiences and study his mind had become thoroughly disciplined, and his style had become polished and refined.

In 1866 he was elected judge of Grant County, a position he held till in 1870. In this period he commenced to write poetry which at once became popular in his locality. He first published a volume of his verses in paper cover, under the title of "Specimens." His next volume appeared with the title "Joaquin et al.," from which he derived the name by which he is most popularly known. In 1870 he was divorced from his wife whom he had married in 1863. He immediately started for London, where, in 1871, he published his "Songs of the Sierras." The subject of the book and the attractive manner in which the songs were given made the work deservedly popular, and gained a favorable poetic standing for the author. In 1872 appeared "Songs of the Sun Lands;" and in 1873 a prose volume entitled "Life among the Modocs: Unwritten History." These volumes showed excellent literary ability and were very favorably received. He has also published "The Ship in the Desert." Perhaps his most popular individual poems are "The Isles of the Amazons," the "The Arizonian," and "Burns and Byron."

"Mr. Miller's poems are often unnatural and extravagant, but there is in them a certain wild freedom and passion in perfect keeping with the life and scenery from which he drew his inspiration with a tropical richness of imagery and an almost cloying sweetness of rhythm and rhyme."

THOMAS MOORE.

THOMAS MOORE was born at Dublin, Ireland, May 28, 1779, and his brilliant career was brought to a close by his death, February 26, 1852.

His father was a Dublin grocer of respectability. We have no account of Moore's early life except that given by himself. He was born in the prescribed sect of Catholics, whose exclusion from the society of the castle produced a closer union among their varied ranks, and thus, from the first, Moore was no stranger to the more refined gayeties of social intercourse. It was, upon the whole, a gay life in Catholic society, though the conspiracy of the United Irishmen was being quietly formed beneath the surface. Amateur theatricals was one of their favorite diversions, and gifts of reciting and singing were not likely to die for want of applause. Moore's school-master was a leader in these entertainments, a writer of prologues and epilogues and incidental songs, and at a very early age Master Thomas Moore was one of his show boys, ardently encouraged in all his exercises by a very affectionate mother at home. Before he left school he had acquired fame in his own circle as a song writer, and had published in the "Anthologia Hibernica," verses "To Zelia, on her charging the author with writing too much on love." This was in 1793. In that year the prohibition against Catholics entering Trinity College was removed, and the next year Moore took advantage of the new freedom. As one of the first Catholic entrants, he had an exceptional stimulus to work, and there industriously acquired a classical scholarship.

He crossed St. George's Channel in 1799, to study law in the Middle Temple, carrying with him a translation of the "Odes of Anacreon," which he wished to publish by subscription. In a very short time he had enrolled half the fashionable world among his subscribers, and had obtained the permis-

sion of the Prince of Wales to dedicate the work to him. The mere power of writing graceful and fluent amatory verses would not alone have enabled the poet to work this miracle. Moore's social gifts were of the most engaging kind. He charmed all whom he met, and charmed them, though he was not a trained musician, with nothing more than with his singing of his own songs. The piano and not the harp, was his instrument, but he came nearer than anybody else in modern times to Bishop Percy's romantic conception of the minstrel.

In 1800 we find Moore a leading element in London society. The ruling aspiration of his life seemed to be the hope of applause. He could not bear the shortest banishment from fashionable drawing-rooms without uneasy longings. If prudence whispered that he was frittering away his time and dissipating his energies, he persuaded himself that his conduct was thoroughly worthy of a solid man of business; that to get a lucrative appointment from his political friends he must keep himself in evidence, and that to make his songs sell he must give them a start with his own voice. But his mind was seemingly not much troubled either with sordid care or with sober prudence; he lived in the happy present, and he liked fashionable society for its own sake,—and no wonder, seeing how he was petted, caressed, and admired. Through Lord Moira's influence he was appointed registrar of the admiralty court in Bermuda in 1803. He went there to take possession, but four or five months of West India society, jingling piano-fortes, and dusky beauties bored him excessively, and he appointed a deputy and returned to London, after little more than a year's absence. The office continued to bring him about £400 a year for fourteen or fifteen years, but at the end of that time embezzlement by the deputy, for whom he was responsible, involved him in serious embarrassment. This was the only political patronage Moore ever received. He sought position, but failing to get anything desirable, he was forced to settle down to literature as a profession.

In 1801 he ventured on a volume of original verse, many of the poems having been written before he was eighteen. The work appeared under the assumed name of "Thomas Little,"—referring to his diminutive stature. In after years he was ashamed of this work of his youth, but much of these early writings proved to be excellent.

He seems to have spent a good deal of time in the libraries of the great houses that he frequented; Moira, Lansdowne, and Holland were all scholarly men and book-collectors. It might be asked,—What had "passion's warmest child," whose "only books were woman's looks," to do with obscure mediæval epigrammatists, theologians and commentators? But it would seem that Moore took the hints for many of his lyrics from books, and, knowing the great wealth of fancy among mediæval Latinists, turned often to them as likely quarters in which to find some happy word-play or image that might serve as a motive for his muse. The public, of course, was concerned with the product and not with the process of manufacture, and "Little's" songs at once became the rage in every drawing-room.

In 1806 he published two volumes of "Odes and Epistles," written mostly in Bermuda. The "Edinburgh" contained a savage review of this publication, by Jeffrey. The criticism so aroused Moore that he challenged Jeffrey to fight a duel. But as an illustration of our author's impressive personality, we call attention to the fact that a few minutes' conversation with Jeffrey changed a bitter critic to a life-long friend. However, Jeffrey had praised his satirical epistles, and Moore continued the vein of the epistles in "Corruption" and "Intolerance" in 1808, and the "Skeptic," a philosophical satire, 1809. About this time he undertook a work that was perfectly suited to his powers. The publisher, Power, engaged him to write words for a collection of "Irish Melodies." The first number appeared in 1807, and it proved so successful that for the next twenty-seven years writing words for music was Moore's steadfast source of income, Power paying him £500 per annum. Six numbers of "Irish Melodies" were published before 1815; then they turned to sacred songs and national airs, issuing also four more numbers of "Irish Melodies" before 1834. The most characteristic moods of Irish feeling, grave and gay, plaintive and stirring, were embodied in these airs, and their variety touched the whole range of Moore's sensitive spirit. Divorced from the music, many of them are insipid enough, but they were never meant to be divorced from the music; the music was meant, as Coleridge felt when he heard them sung by the poet himself, to twine round them and overtop them like the honeysuckle.

Since all hope of office had deserted him, he commenced to write political squibs. Feeling that the prince regent, to whom he had dedicated his first volume, was the cause of his failure to secure political advancement, Moore opened fire upon his highness. The prince's defects and foibles, his fatness, his huge whiskers, his love for cutlets and curacoa, and practical jokes, were ridiculed with the lightest of clever hands. Moore opened fire in the "Morning Chronicle," and crowned his success next year (1813) with a thin volume of "Intercepted Letters, The Two-penny Post Bag." A very little knowledge of the gossip of the time enables us to understand the delight with which Moore's sallies were received in the year which witnessed the imprisonment of Leigh Hunt for more outspoken attacks on the regent. Moore received every encouragement to work the new vein. He was at one time in receipt of a regular salary from the "Times;" and his little volumes of squibs published at intervals—"The Fudge Family in Paris," 1818; "The Journal of a Member of the Procurate Society," 1820; "Fables for the Holy Alliance," 1823; "Odes on Cash, Corn, Catholics and Other Matters," 1828; "The Fudges in England," 1835—went through many editions. The prose "Memoirs of Captain Rock," 1824, may be added to the list.

"Lalla Rookh" appeared in 1817. Moore, as was his habit, made most laborious preparation, reading himself slowly into familiarity with Eastern scenery and manners. He retired to a cottage in Derbyshire, near Lord Moira's library at Donington Park, that he might work uninterruptedly, safe from the distractions of London society; and there, "amid the snows of a Derbyshire winter," as he put it, he patiently elaborated his voluptuous pictures of flower-scented valleys, gorgeous gardens, tents and palaces, and houris of ravishing beauty. Moore's contemporaries were dazzled and enchanted with "Lalla Rookh." There was not a single image or allusion in it that an ordinary Englishman could understand without a foot-note. High testimonies were borne to the correctness of the local coloring, and the usual stories circulated of Oriental natives who would not believe that Moore had never traveled in the East. And for more than twenty years his promise to write would secure almost any amount of money in advance. The "Loves of the Angels," another Orientalism none the less popular than "Lalla Rookh," appeared in 1822. For a short time Moore lived in Paris, whither he was forced to go to avoid arrest for the sum embezzled by his deputy at Bermuda. His friends came forward with the necessary money to settle the matter and give Moore time to pay it from the sales of his books. In June, 1822, the sales from "Loves of the Angels" netted him £1,000, and "Fables for the Holy Alliance" £500, thus paying in full for the deputy's rascality. While abroad he visited Lord Byron at Venice, and the last named work was written while he was with Byron.

Upon returning to England he engaged to write political squibs for the "Times" at a salary of £400. He published "Captain Rock" and his latest imaginative work, "The Epicurean," an Eastern tale in prose. Moore completed his "Memoirs of Sheridan" in 1825, "Life of Lord Byron," in two volumes, in 1830, and "Memoirs of Lord Edward Fitzgerald," 1831. In 1833 his political friends secured him a pension of £300, that he might spend his remaining days in comparative comfort.

It was a misfortune for the comfort of the last twenty years of Moore's life that he allowed himself to be drawn into the project of writing the "History of Ireland" in "Lardner's Cyclopedia." Scott and Mackintosh scribbled off the companion volumes on Scotland and England with very little trouble, but Moore had neither their historical training nor their dispatch in writing. Laborious conscientiousness and indecision are a fatal combination for a man who undertakes a new kind of task late in life. The history sat like a nightmare on Moore for fifteen years, and after all was left unfinished on the melancholy collapse of his powers in 1845. From the time that he burdened himself with it Moore did very little else, beyond a few occasional squibs and songs, the last flashes of his genius, and the "Travels of an Irish Gentleman in Search of a Religion," although he had tempting offers of more lucrative, and, it might have been thought, more congenial work. Moore's character had a deeper manliness and sincerity than he often gets credit for; and his tenacious persistence in this, his last task, was probably due to an honorable ambition to connect himself as a benefactor with the history of his country by opening the eyes of the English people to the misgovernment of Ireland.

Upon the death of his last child in 1845 Moore became a total wreck, but he lingered along till 1852, when the once prime favorite of London and deeply beloved benefactor of Ireland passed to his rest.

He kept an extensive diary to be published upon his death, for the benefit of his wife. The work, extending to eight volumes, was published in 1852-'56, from which Mrs. Moore received £3,000.

One effect of the genius of Moore has been to elevate the feelings and occurrences of ordinary life into poetry, rather than dealing with the lofty, abstract elements of the art. The combinations of his wit are wonderful. Quick, subtle, and varied, ever suggesting new thoughts or images, or unexpected turns of expression—now drawing resources from classical literature or the ancient fathers—now diving into the human heart, and now skimming the fields of fancy—the wit or imagination of Moore (for they are compounded together) is a true Ariel, "a creature of the elements," that is ever buoyant and full of life and spirit. His very satires "give delight and hurt not." They are never coarse, and always witty. When stung by an act of oppression and intolerance he could be bitter or sarcastic enough, but some lively thought or sportive image soon crossed his path, and he instantly followed it into the open and genial region where he loved most to indulge. He never dipped his pen into malignity.

J. L. MOTLEY.

JOHN LOTHROP MOTLEY, one of the three great American historians, was born at Dorchester, Massachusetts, April 15, 1814, and after having been singularly honored in both the New and the Old World, he died in Dorsetshire, England, May 29, 1877.

He entered Harvard in 1827, at the age of thirteen, and graduated four years later, making him only seventeen when he finished his first collegiate course. He immediately repaired to Gottingen, thence to Berlin, in each of which places he studied for about a year. Motley next spent some time in traveling in Italy and other parts of southern Europe, after which he returned to the United States in 1834. Immediately taking up the study of law he was called to the bar, but subsequently made literature his profession. In 1837 he married, and two years later published a two-volume novel entitled "Morton's Hope, or the Memoirs of a Young Provincial." The work appeared anonymously, and attracted little or no attention. It proved to be a failure. In 1840 he was appointed secretary of the legation to the American Embassy to Russia. Not being suited with the atmosphere of St. Petersburg, he soon resigned and turned his attention to literature.

His next work consisted of historical and critical essays contributed to the "North American Review." These essays gave him considerable reputation. In 1849 he again came forward with a novel entitled "Merry Mount, a Romance of the Massachusetts Colony." This work appeared anonymously, and, like his first effort, fell heavily on the market. From the two failures in the field of romance he probably came to the conclusion that he was not adapted to that vein of literature. He also took the hint from the success of his historical essays, and in 1846 the project of writing a history of Holland had begun to take shape in his mind, and he had already prepared a considerable quantity of MSS., when, finding the materials at his disposal in the United States quite inadequate for the completion of his work, he resolved to migrate, along with his family, to Europe in 1851. The next five years were spent at Berlin, Dresden, Brussels, and the Hague in laborious investigation of the archives preserved in those capitals, and resulted in 1856 in the publication of "The Rise of the Dutch Republic, a History" (London and New York, 3 vols. 8vo). This work, which, after a large historical introduction, minutely follows the history of the Low Countries from the abdication of Charles in 1555 down to the assassination of William the Silent in 1584, immediately became highly popular by its graphic manner and the warm and sympathetic spirit in which it was written, while at the same time it was frankly recognized by scholars as a painstaking and conscientious piece of original work. It speedily passed through many English editions, was translated into French (with an introduction by Guizot) in 1859, and also into Dutch (with introduction and notes by Bakhinzen van den Brink, himself a distinguished historian), as well as into German and Russian. Pursuing his researches in England, France, Belgium and Holland, Motley was able to publish in 1860 the first two volumes of the "History of the United Netherlands," covering the period from the death of William the Silent, in 1584, to shortly after the destruction of the Armada, by which the Spanish project for subjugating England and reconquering the Netherlands was finally defeated. This work, which was on a somewhat larger scale than the preceding, embodied the results of a still greater amount of original research, not only in the Dutch archives, in the copies of the Simancas archives, and in the portions of those archives still retained in Paris, but also in the London State Paper Office, and in the MS. department of the British Museum. By two new volumes, published in 1868, the work was brought down to the twelve years' truce in 1609, and it was announced that the author was engaged in writing a continuation which should embrace the history of the Thirty Years' War. Meanwhile Motley, from the close of 1861 to 1867, had held the post of United States minister to Vienna; in 1869 he was appointed to a similar position at the court of St. James, but was recalled in 1870. After a short visit to Holland he again took up his residence in England, where "The Life and Death of John Barneveld, Advocate of Holland, with a view of the Primary Causes of the Thirty Years' War" (2 vols.) appeared in 1874. Ill health now began to interfere with sustained literary work, and, after a protracted period of failing vigor, he died in 1877.

There is no doubt about Motley's place as a historian. He occupies a front rank. The story is told in an easy, attractive and clear manner. The narrative once commenced, you can hardly lay down the book till the conclusion is reached. Macaulay gained renown by the sparkle of a highly polished and rhetorical literary style, but Motley gained friends by the clear, unvarnished manner in which the story fell from his pen. America is justly proud of her trio of great historians, Prescott, Bancroft and Motley.

JAMES MONTGOMERY.

This distinguished poet and journalist was born at Irvine, Ayrshire, Scotland, November 4, 1771. His eventful life closed at Sheffield, April 30, 1854, at the age of eighty-three.

His father was a Moravian missionary, who died whilst propagating Christianity in the Island of Tobago. From him James received the strong religious sentiments that formed the groundwork for much of his excellent poetry.

He was educated at the Moravian school of Fulneck, named after the original home of the Moravians. Having refused to become a priest, James was apprenticed to a grocer at Mirfield. At the age of sixteen, with less than a dollar in money, he ran off from Mirfield, and after some suffering, secured employment as shop-boy in the village of Wath, in Yorkshire. In a short time he left this place and started for London. He carried with him a collection of his poems, but failing to find a publisher, took a situation as clerk in a newspaper office in Sheffield, in 1791. This position proved to be both pleasant and profitable, and was the beginning of his journalistic career. Upon his master's failure, Montgomery, with the aid of friends, started "The Sheffield Iris," a weekly journal, which he edited until 1825, a period of more than thirty years. His course did not always run smooth. In January, 1794, amidst the excitement of that agitated period, he was tried on the charge of having printed a ballad, written by a clergyman of Belfast, on the demolition of the Bastile in 1789, which was interpreted into a seditious libel. The poor poet, notwithstanding the innocence of his intentions, was found guilty and sentenced to three months imprisonment in the castle of York, and to pay a fine of £20. In January, 1795, he was tried for a second imputed political offense—a paragraph in his paper which reflected on the conduct of a magistrate in quelling a riot at Sheffield. He was again convicted, and sentenced to six months imprisonment in York Castle, to pay a fine of £30, and to give security to keep the peace for two years. From our stand-point the charges against him were absurdly forced and unfair.

Montgomery's first volume of poetry, entitled "The Wanderer of Switzerland and Other Poems," appeared in 1806. The volume was mercilessly ridiculed by the "Edinburgh Review," and though the popularity of the book had already carried it into the third edition, the "Review" predicted that "The Wanderer of Switzerland," and the other poems of the collection would never be heard of again. As a singular illustration of the unfairness of critics, we call attention to the fact that, within eighteen months of the prophecy, another edition was passing through the same press that printed the "Review," and it has now reached twenty editions.

His next poem, "The West Indies," published in 1810, was written in honor of the abolition of African slave trade by the English legislature in 1807. The poem is considered superior to any of his former productions. "Prison Amusements" next appeared. As the title indicates, the poems of this collection were written while he was confined in York Castle. In 1812-'13 he came forward with an elaborate poem entitled "The World Before the Flood." In this poem he draws pictures of the happiness of the antediluvian patriarchs, and treats in a sweet and touching manner traditional or historical incidents belonging to that period. "Thoughts on Wheels" appeared in 1817, an excellent work issued to overcome many of the evils of the day, and directed against the state lotteries. "The Climbing Boy's Soliloquies" written by different authors, was published at this time. This book sought to overcome the cruel practice of employing boys as chimney sweeps, and it finally accomplished its object. He published "Greenland" in 1819, an excellent sketch of the ancient Moravian Church, and the origin of its missions to Greenland. Its beautiful descriptions rendered it at once popular. "Songs of Zion" appeared in 1822; "The Pelican Island," 1827, suggested by a passage in "Captain Flinders' Voyage to Terra Australis," describing the existence of the ancient haunts of the pelican in the small island on the coast of New Holland.

In 1825 he retired from his newspaper, and thereafter lived a quiet and happy life in literature. In 1830 and 1831 Mr. Montgomery was selected to deliver a course of lectures at the Royal Institution on Poetry and General Literature, which he prepared for the press and published in 1833. A pension of £200 per annum was, at the instance of Sir Robert Peel, conferred upon Montgomery, which he enjoyed till his death in 1854, at the ripe age of eighty-three.

The inspiring force of Montgomery's poetry was the humanitarian sentiment which has been such a power in the political changes of this century, and the pulse of this sentiment is nowhere felt beating more strongly than in his verse. His poetry has thus a historical interest altogether apart from its intrinsic value as poetry. Strictly speaking, Montgomery was more of a rhetorician than a poet, but his imagination was bold, ardent, and fertile. At the close of his career as a journalist, when all parties agreed in paying him respect, he claimed for his poetry that it was at least not imitative, and the claim was just as regarded conception and the choice of subjects, but as regards diction and imagery the influence of Campbell is very apparent in his earlier poems, and the influence of Shelley is supreme in the "Pelican Island," his last and best work as a poet. His "Lectures on Poetry and General Literature," published in 1833, show considerable breadth of sympathy and power of expression. "Memoirs" of him were published in seven volumes in 1856-'58. They furnish valuable materials for the history of English provincial politics in the nineteenth century.

John Howard Payne

J. H. PAYNE.

John Howard Payne was born in New York, June 9, 1792, and died in Tunis, April 10, 1852.

His mind matured early as seen in the fact that at the age of thirteen, while a clerk in a counting house, he edited a weekly journal known as the "Thespian Mirror;" and while attending Union College he published another periodical called "The Pastime."

At the age of seventeen he became an actor in the Park Theatre, of New York. He appeared as "Young Marvel," and at other times acted in Boston, Philadelphia, Baltimore and other large places. At the age of twenty-one he appeared at Drury Lane Theatre, London, as "Young Marvel," and for twenty years he pursued a career of varied success in England as actor, manager and playwriter. He translated French dramas and produced original plays and adaptations, including "Brutus," "Therese, or the Orphan of Geneva," and "Clari." The first, produced in 1818, with Edmund Kean in the principal part, still holds possession of the stage. "Clari," which was produced as an opera, contains the celebrated song, "Home, Sweet Home," which alone preserves Payne's name from oblivion. He also produced "Charles the Second."

Returning to the United States in 1832, he was appointed American consul at Tunis in 1841. This office he held at the time of his death in 1852.

"Home, Sweet Home" touched the popular affections of the people, hence the world will never let it die; and with that beautiful home poem must forever be associated the name of John Howard Payne. Without that song he must have been forgotten, as he was only a precocious youth and a man of ordinary ability. But the one inspiration sang his name into immortal life.

EDGAR ALLEN POE.

EDGAR ALLEN POE was born in Boston, January 19, 1809, and after a tempestuous life of forty years, he died in the city of Baltimore, October 7, 1849.

His father, the son of a distinguished officer in the Revolutionary army, was educated for the law, but having married the beautiful English actress, Elizabeth Arnold, he abandoned law, and in company with his wife, led a wandering life on the stage. The two died within a short time of each other, leaving three children entirely destitute. Edgar, the second son, a bright, beautiful boy, was adopted by John Allen, a wealthy citizen of Richmond. Allen, having no children of his own, became very much attached to Edgar, and used his wealth freely in educating the boy. At the age of seven he was sent to school at Stoke Newington, near London, where he remained for six years. During the next three years he studied under private tutors, at the residence of the Allens in Richmond. In 1826 he entered the University of Virginia, where he remained less than a year.

After a year or two of fruitless life at home, a cadetship was obtained for him at West Point. He was soon tried by court-martial and expelled from school because he drank to excess and neglected his studies. Thus ended his school days.

In 1829 he published "Al Aaraaf, and Minor Poems." "This work," says his biographer, Mr. Stoddard, "was not a remarkable production for a young gentleman of twenty." Poe himself was ashamed of the volume.

After his stormy school life, he returned to Richmond, where he was kindly received by Mr. Allen. Poe's conduct was such that Mr. Allen was

obliged to turn him out of doors, and, dying soon after, he made no mention of Poe in his will.

Now wholly thrown upon his own resources, he took up literature as a profession, but in this he failed to gain a living. He enlisted as a private soldier, but was soon recognized as the West Point cadet and a discharge procured.

In 1833 Poe won two prizes of $100 each for a tale in prose, and for a poem. John P. Kennedy, one of the committee who made the award, now gave him means of support, and secured employment for him as editor of the "Southern Literary Messenger" at Richmond. After a short but successful editorial work on "The Messenger," his old habits returned, he quarreled with his publishers and was dismissed. While in Richmond he married his cousin, Virginia Clem, and in January, 1837, removed to New York. Here he gained a poor support by writing for periodicals.

His literary work may be summed up as follows: In 1838 appeared a fiction entitled "The Narrative of Arthur Gorden Pym;" 1839, editor of Burton's "Gentleman's Magazine," Philadelphia; next, editor of "Graham's Magazine;" 1840, "Tales of the Grotesque and Arabesque," in two volumes; 1845, "The Raven," published by the "American Review;" then sub-editor of the "Mirror" under employment of N. P. Willis and Geo. P. Norris; next associate editor of the "Broadway Journal."

His wife died in 1848. His poverty was now such that the press made appeals to the public for his support.

In 1848 he published "Eureka, a Prose Poem."

He went to Richmond in 1849, where he was engaged to a lady of considerable fortune. In October he started for New York to arrange for the wedding, but at Baltimore he met some of his former boon companions, and spent the night in drinking. In the morning he was found in a state of delirium, and died in a few hours.

The most remarkable of his tales are "The Gold Bug," "The Fall of the House of Usher," "The Murders of the Rue Morgue," "The Purloined Letter," "A Descent into Maelstrom," and "The Facts in the Case of M. Valdemar." "The Raven" and "The Bells" alone would make the name of

Poe immortal. The teachers of Baltimore placed a monument over his grave in 1875.

Poe has been severely censured by many writers for his wild and stormy life, but we notice that Ingram and some other prominent authors claim that he has been willfully slandered, and that many of the charges brought against him are not true. His ungovernable temper and high spirit led him into disputes with his friends, hence he was not enabled to hold any one position for a great length of time. Like Byron and Burns, he had faults in personal life, but his ungovernable passions are sleeping, while the sad strains of "The Raven," the clear and harmonious tones of "The Bells," and the powerful images of his fancy live in the immortal literature of his time.

ALEXANDER POPE.

ALEXANDER POPE was born in London, May 21, 1688, and he died at Twickenham, May 30, 1744.

Pope claimed to be of gentle blood, and that his father was of a gentleman's family in Oxford, "the head of which was the Earl of Downe." The poet's mother was the daughter of William Turner, Esq., of York. In 1677 Pope's father carried on business in London, as a linen merchant. Having acquired a competency in addition to the property gained by his marriage with Edith Turner, he retired from business about 1688 to a small estate at Binfield, near Windsor.

Alexander's education was commenced by the family priest. After the boy had made some proficiency under his private tutor, he was sent to a Catholic seminary at Twyford, near Winchester. In this school young Pope lampooned his teacher, was severely whipped, and finally removed to a small school near London. He returned home in about his thirteenth year. Here

he devoted himself to an enthusiastic study of literature and private instruction. Pope, even from his youth, was an admirer of Dryden. He wrote verses before he was twelve years of age.

> As yet a child, and all unknown to fame,
> I lisped in numbers, for the numbers came.

He had commenced his "Pastorals" at the age of sixteen, and had translated parts of "Statius." In 1709 his "Pastorals" were published, and in 1711 appeared his "Essay on Criticism." Addison reviewed the "Essay" in the "Spectator" and praised it very cordially. The ripeness of judgment displayed by one so young was considered very remarkable, and not only the "Essay" rose into great popularity, but from that time Pope's life was that of a popular poet. Even at that early age his style was formed and complete. He selected Dryden as the master of his versification; but in point of brevity, accuracy and melody, he improved greatly upon his original. In 1712 the "Essay" was followed by the "Rape of the Lock." This poem, with the addition made a year later, is probably the most perfect specimen we have of Pope's genius and art. The poem is referred to so frequently, that we venture to give its origin. Lord Petre ventured to steal a lock of hair from Miss Arabella Fermor, his lady-love, and a beauty of the day. The act was taken seriously, and it caused an estrangement between the families. Pope, as he suggests, intended to make a jest of the affair, and laugh them together. While he failed to "laugh them together again," he added greatly to his fame by the production. "Windsor Forest" appeared in 1713, and "Temple of Fame" in 1715. These are full of fine pictures of forest scenes and external nature. Pope now commenced the work of translating the "Iliad," which was published at intervals between 1715 and 1720. By this translation, he made about £5,320. Part of this sum was given by the upper classes to reward his literary merit. Pope's exclamation,

> "And thanks to Homer, since I live and thrive,
> Indebted to no prince or peer alive,"

was hardly just. The "Odyssey" was not finished, even by the help of his friends Broome and Fenton, till in 1725. For the two translations Pope received between eight and nine thousand pounds. In 1716 Pope's father having sold his estate at Binfield, removed to Chiswick, where he died in 1716, leaving his aged wife to the care of her son. While residing here Pope collected his poems into a book. In this volume first appeared "Elegy to the Memory of an Unfortunate Lady," also the "Epistle of Eloisa to Abelard." "The delicacy of the poet in veiling over the story of Abelard and Eloisa and at the same time preserving the ardor of Eloisa's passion, the beauty of his imagery and descriptions, the exquisite melody of his versification, rising and falling like the tones of the Æolian harp, as he successively portrays the tumults of guilty love and the deepest penitence and the highest devotional rapture, have never been surpassed." About 1718 the poet removed with his aged mother to Twickenham, where he resided during the remainder of his life. Here he had taken a lease of a house and grounds which he improved very tastily, and here he was visited by the ministers of state, wits, poets and beauties. This classic spot was the center of attraction, and remained so while Pope lived. In 1725 he brought out an edition of Shakespeare in six quarto volumes. This work was not considered a success. Next, in conjunction with his friend Swift, he published three volumes of "Miscellanies" in 1727-'28. The treatment which the author received on account of these volumes led to "The Dunciad," which, as enlarged and published in 1729, is an elaborate and splendid satire. In this satire he is often merciless and unjust toward the poets and critics against whom he waged war. In 1731-'35 Pope published his "Essay on Man." This is in four Epistles, and worthy of the author's fame. It is full of splendid passages and lines of mingled sweetness and dignity, as seen in the following:

> "Hope springs eternal in the human breast;
> Man never is, but always to be blessed.
> The soul, uneasy and confined from home,
> Rests and expatiates in a life to come."

From this time Pope confined himself chiefly to satire. In 1735-'39 he brought out his "Imitations of Horace." In 1742, he added a fourth book to "The Dunciad," which, in its complete form, he published in 1743.

Political events now combined to agitate the last days of Pope. The government issued a proclamation prohibiting Catholics from coming within ten miles of London. This was done in anticipation of the approach of the Pretender. He soon answered another proclamation; this time "from the Highest of all Powers." Uttering the death sentiment, "I am so certain of souls being immortal that I seem to feel it within me as it were by intuition," he obeyed the proclamation from on high, and passed to his final rest.

Pope was a remarkable man, considering the circumstances of his life. He was of delicate frame and health, and was quite badly deformed from birth. On account of his physical condition, he was kept from any active pursuit. Being deformed, his vanity was over-indulged, which probably led to his hasty and irritable temper. With all his outward faults we admire him, and here append his own words: "To err is human, to forgive, divine." His "wit, fancy and good sense are as remarkable as his satires," and his elegance has scarcely been equaled.

PRESCOTT

WILLIAM HICKLING PRESCOTT, one of the three great American historians, was born at Salem, Massachusetts, May 4, 1796. When sitting alone in his study he experienced a shock of paralysis, from the effects of which he died in less than two hours. At his death, on January 28, 1859, a cloud of deep mourning settled over the entire country, and a vast concourse of people followed the remains to the grave.

Prescott's father was an eminent judge and lawyer. Appreciating the advantages of a good education, he gave William every opportunity for study that the best schools could afford. He entered Harvard College where he distinguished himself in his studies. His collegiate life was greatly interrupted by an accident which threatened to render him totally blind. A fellow-student threw a crust of bread, which accidentally struck Prescott in the eye. For a long time he was almost wholly blind. Partly for medical advice and partly for pleasure, he visited England, France and Italy. After an absence of two years, he returned to the United States, when he married and settled in Boston. An essay on "Italian Narrative Poetry," contributed to the "North American Review" in 1824, was his first literary effort. The essay was followed by numerous valuable papers from his pen, published in the "Review." The favor with which his papers were received led him to turn his attention wholly to letters. The peculiar charm which the public pointed out in his historical narratives, indicated to him that he could best succeed in the realm of history. He lost no time in experimental novel writing, but at once commenced to prepare for his life-work by studying the literature and history of Spain. He had decided to write the history of Ferdinand and Isabella's reign, and had begun the work, when his eye gave out entirely, and for several years he had no use of it in reading.

His literary enthusiasm, however, was too strong to be subdued even by this calamity; he engaged a reader, dictated copious notes, and from these notes constructed his composition, making in his mind those corrections which are usually made in the manuscript. Instead of dictating the work thus composed, he used a writing-case made for the blind, which he thus describes: "It consists of a frame of the size of a piece of paper, traversed by brass wires as many as lines are wanted on the page, and with a sheet of carbonated paper, such as is used for getting duplicates, pasted on the reverse side. With an ivory or agate stylus, the writer traces his characters between the wires on the carbonated sheet, making indelible marks which he cannot see on the white sheet below." In this way the historian proceeded with his task, finding, he says, his writing-case his best friend in his lonely hours. The sight of his eye partially returned, but never sufficiently to enable him to use it by candle-light.

In 1837 appeared his history of "Ferdinand and Isabella," in three volumes, and the work was eminently successful on both sides of the Atlantic. In 1843 "The Conquest of Mexico," three volumes, and in 1847 "The

Conquest of Peru," two volumes, still further extended Mr. Prescott's reputation, and it is calculated that latterly he received from £4,000 to £5,000 a year from the sale of his writings.

He next commenced work upon his "History of Philip II," and about the same time made a visit to England. The mother country received him with great favor and distinction, and Oxford conferred upon him the honorary degree of LL. D. Prescott proposed to carry his "History of Philip" through six volumes, and the British government had contracted to pay him £1,000 per volume for the copyright. When a part of the "History" was ready for the press in 1854, a decision of the House of Lords annulled the bargain. There being no protective international copyright law, it was decided that Prescott could claim no protection for his work unless he resided in England at the time of its publication. But he would not take this course. At a great pecuniary sacrifice he preferred to present to the world one signal example more of the injustice to which the writers of England and America are exposed by the want of a reasonable system of international copyright. English writers claim that the American government is responsible for the want of such a system of protection to authors. In 1855 appeared two volumes of "Philip II," and the third in 1858. In the interval Prescott received a shock from paralysis, which was followed by another in 1859, resulting in his death.

Prescott is one of the few literary men who determined, without error, on a proper sphere of action. From the first he gave forth no uncertain sound. His first articles gave evidence of genius, and success crowned every step of his life. While Americans are proud of him, and are willing to accept no rank for him except that of the first, English writers are equally just in their estimates of him. The following is English authority: "As a historian Prescott may rank with Robertson as a master of the art of narrative, while he excels him in the variety and extent of his illustrative researches. He was happy in the choice of his subjects. The very names of Castile and Arragon, Mexico and Peru, possess a romantic charm, and the characters and scenes he depicts have the interest and splendor of the most gorgeous fiction. To some extent the American historian fell into the error of Robertson in palliating the enormous cruelties that marked the career of the Spanish conquerors, but he is more careful in citing his authorities, in order, as he says, to put the reader in a position for judging for himself, and thus for revising, and, if need be, for reversing the judgments of the historian."

T. B. READ.

THOMAS BUCHANAN READ was born in Chester County, Pennsylvania, March 12, 1822, and died in New York, May 11, 1872.

Mr. Read commenced his life work as an artist, intending to make painting a business. When he was but seventeen years of age he entered the studio of a sculptor in Cincinnati, Ohio, where he remained about two years. In 1841 he went to New York, and, after a few months, removed to Boston, where he began his career as a painter. While he gained distinction as an artist, yet he is known to the general public as a poet, and to his pen must we look for the chief source of his fame.

While in Boston he contributed numerous poems to the "Courier," which were received with so much favor as to induce him to cultivate his poetic faculties. He abandoned entirely the study of sculpture, and gave his whole time to poetry and painting. In 1846 he settled in Philadelphia, where he remained until 1850, when he went to Florence, Italy. In that sunny clime he remained, with an occasional visit to the United States, till in the spring of 1872. On the latter date he returned to America, but died shortly after his arrival.

He won fame as a painter, his most important works being portraits. His literary record is brief, but it is one of unusual merit. He published his "Lays and Ballads" at Philadelphia in 1848; "The New Pastoral," 1856; "The Waggoner of the Alleghenies," 1862; "A Summer Story, and Other

Poems," 1865; and "Poetical Works," in three volumes, in 1866. Read has written a few poems that have become a part of the current literature of the land, and have been reproduced in school readers and popular selections till they can be repeated from memory by most lovers of poetry. Among these we may mention "Drifting," perhaps his most beautiful poem, and "Sheridan's Ride," the most popular.

Read's poetry is true to nature. The thoughts seem to suggest the appropriate words in which to clothe them, so that his sentences are a perfect mirror in which the thoughts are reflected. He usually selects subjects that are real, hence you can appreciate pen sketches of actual persons, places, and events. Ordinarily his poems close in a few sweet and tender thoughts. Simplicity, also, is a feature of his writings, as may be illustrated by a short selection entitled

THE OLD HOME.

Between broad fields of wheat and corn
Is the lowly home where I was born;
The peach-tree leans against the wall,
And the woodbine wanders over all.
There is the barn,—and as of yore,
I can smell the hay from the open door,
And see the busy swallows throng,
And hear the peewee's mournful song.
Oh, ye who daily cross the sill,
Step lightly, for I love it still!
And when you crowd the old barn eaves,
Then think what countless harvest sheaves
Have passed within that scented door,
To gladden eyes that are no more.

JOHN RUSKIN.

John Ruskin, author of several works on art, was born in London in 1819, the only son of a wealthy wine merchant. He was entered at Christ Church College, Oxford, where he graduated, and in 1839 took the Newdegate prize for English poetry. Impressed with the idea that art was his vocation in life, he studied painting under Copley Fielding and J. D. Harding; but the pencil has long since become merely the auxiliary of the pen. In 1843 appeared the first portion of his "Modern Painters, by an Oxford Graduate," which, though published when the author was only twenty-four years of age, bears the impress of deep thought. The second part was published in 1846, and the third and fourth volumes ten years later, in 1856. Many other works appeared in the interval. Indeed, Mr. Ruskin is now one of the most voluminous writers of the day; but it may be a question if he has ever risen to the level of the first two volumes of "Modern Painters." Latterly his works have been little more than hurriedly written pamphlets, reviews, and revisals of popular lectures, which, though often rising into passages of vivid description and eloquence, and possessing the merit of great clearness, are generally loose and colloquial in style. "The Seven Lamps of Architecture," 1849, and the "Stones of Venice," three volumes, 1851-'53, are the principal of Mr. Ruskin's works, besides the "Modern Painters," but we may also mention the following: "Letters in Defense of the Pre-Raphaelites," published at various times since 1851; "The Construction of Sheep-folds" (the discipline of the church), 1851; "The Opening of the Crystal Palace," 1854; "Notes on the Academy Exhibitions," published in the month of May for the last few years; "The Elements of Drawing," 1857; "The Political Economy of Art," 1858; "The Two Paths," 1859; besides contributions to the

JOHN RUSKIN.

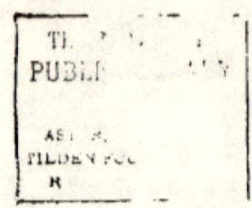

"Quarterly Review," the "Art Journal," the "Scotsman," etc. In 1861 a selection from the works of Mr. Ruskin was published in one volume—a treasure to all young literary students and lovers of art. His subsequent works have been numerous: "Lectures on Civilization," 1866; "The Queen of the Air, Being a Study of the Greek Myths of Cloud and Storm," 1869; "Lectures on Art," delivered before the University of Oxford in 1870, etc. Mr. Ruskin made a munificent offer of £5,000 for the endowment of a master of drawing in Oxford, which was accepted by the university authorities in November, 1871.

Mr. Ruskin's influence upon art and art literature has been remarkable. The subject has received a degree of consideration among general readers that it had not previously enjoyed in our day, or perhaps in any period of our history; and to Mr. Ruskin's veneration for every work of creation, inculcated in all his writings, may be ascribed the origin of the society of young artists known as the Pre-Raphaelites. Protesting against what they conceived to be lax conventionalism in the style of most modern painters, the innovators went back, as they said, to Nature, preferring her, in all her moods and phases, to ideal visions of what she occasionally might, or ought to appear. Mr. Ruskin seems often to contradict himself, but upon this point his own mind is easy. "I never met a question yet," he says in the inaugural address to the Cambridge School of Art, "which did not need, for the right solution of it, at least one positive and one negative answer, like an equation of the second degree. Mostly matters of any consequence are three sided or four sided, or polygonal; and the trotting round a polygon is severe work for people any way stiff in their opinions. For myself, I am never satisfied that I have handled a subject properly till I have contradicted myself at least three times."

Parents can do their children no greater service than to put into their hands the writings of Ruskin. His style is pure and his works are free from dangerous sentiments. Having read Ruskin, the young man or young woman has noble thoughts of God and his works in nature, and elevated ideas of life.

JOHN GODFREY SAXE.

J. G. SAXE was born in Highgate, Franklin County, Vermont, June 2, 1816. We have not learned that his youth was marked by any points of interest. With habits of industry and a desire for learning, he advanced steadily from the beginning to the end of his school work, "each day gaining and always retaining" valuable information.

In 1839 he completed a course of study in Middlebury College. In 1843 he was admitted to the bar at St. Albans. He practiced law in his native county till in March, 1850. During the next six years Saxe was editor and proprietor of the "Burlington Sentinel." In the year 1856 he was State's Attorney. Three years later, in 1859-'60, he was the candidate of his party for governor of Vermont. From the time of his admission to the bar he was actively engaged in literary work, although his first published book did not appear till in 1846.

Saxe's books include "Progress, a Satire," published in 1846; "New Rape of the Lock," 1847; "The Proud Miss McBride," 1848; "The Times," 1849; "The Money King, and other Poems," 1859; "Clever Stories of Many Nations," 1864; "The Masquerade and other Poems," 1866; "Fables and Legends in Rhyme," 1872; and "Leisure Day Rhymes," 1875. The collection of poems, "The Times," published in Boston in 1849, has passed through forty editions.

Saxe is one of our best humorous poets. In some respects he resembles Hood, "being remarkably quick in seeing the ludicrous side of things, and very felicitous in the use of puns and other oddities of speech."

At present he resides in Brooklyn, N. Y.

SIR WALTER SCOTT.

Sir Walter Scott was born in Edinburgh, Scotland, August 15, 1771, and he breathed his last on September 21, 1832.

His father, a writer to the "Signet," encouraged literature. His mother, Anna Rutherford, daughter of the professor of medicine in the Edinburgh University, was a lady of fine culture, also well related. The excellent ancient Scottish kinsmen of both his parents centered in our poet. To those who understand the impulses of a Scotchman, it is easy to understand the pleasure that Scott felt at his ability to trace his ancestral line back to the best ancient families of his beloved Scotia.

Apparently the most important part of his education came incidentally from his physical condition, by the following circumstances: Delicate health, arising chiefly from lameness, led to his being placed under the charge of some relations in the country; and when a mere child, yet old enough to receive impressions from country life and border stories, he resided with his grandfather at Sandy-Knowe, a romantic situation a few miles from Kelso, and there at the age of thirteen he first read Percy's Reliques. This work had great effect in making him a poet. He passed through the high school of his native town, and the Edinburgh University. In these schools he acquired a good knowledge of Latin, and became proficient in ethics, moral philosophy, and history, but his aversion to Greek prevented him from acquiring the rich treasures of that classic mine. For the purposes of general literature, he acquired a sufficient knowledge of the German, French, Italian and Spanish languages. His great appetite for books led him to store his mind with a vast variety of general knowledge. The greater part of this information he acquired during the sickness of his youth. He was particularly fond of romances, and he became familiar with the ballads of his country, and the stories of border life. He also formed the habit of inventing stories and telling them to the great pleasure of his audience. His gentle and pleasing manners made him a welcome guest wherever he went. Even in early life he had acquired some skill in writing verse. Some of his productions in this line were secured by Dr. Adams of the high school which our youthful poet was attending, and wrapped in a cover inscribed " Walter Scott, July, 1783."

Having completed his literary training in school, he was apprenticed to his father as a writer, but he afterward studied law and was admitted to the bar in his twenty-first year. By this time his health was completely restored and he was vigorous and robust. Numerous "raids," as Scott called them, were made into the country, in which valuable knowledge of rural life, character, traditions and anecdotes was acquired. Scott joined the Tory party, and when the dread of an invasion agitated the country he became one of a band of volunteers, "brothers true," in which he held the rank of quartermaster. His exercises as a cavalry officer and the jovialities of the mess-room occupied much of his time; but he still pursued, though irregularly, his literary studies, and an attachment to a Perthshire lady—though ultimately unfortunate—tended still more strongly to prevent his sinking into idle frivolity or dissipation. In 1796 he published translations of Burger's "Lenore" and "The Wild Huntsman," ballads of singular wildness and power. Next year, while fresh from his first-love disappointment, he was prepared, like Romeo, to "take some new infection to his eye," and meeting at Gilsland, a watering-place in Cumberland, with a young lady of French parentage, Charlotte Margaret Carpenter, he paid his addresses to her, was accepted, and married on the 24th of December.

The lady possessed a small fortune and with this the young couple settled in a neat little cottage at Lassawade, where their happiness was complete. By this time Scott had passed the lighter period of life; his hopes for the future were all ablaze. In 1799 he published his translation of Goethe's tragedy, "Goetz von Berlichingen," and was appointed sheriff of Selkirkshire, at a salary of £300 per annum. With this income added to

WALTER SCOTT.

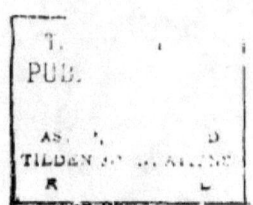

the receipts of his pen he was enabled to begin gathering the material for his books. He visited Liddesdale and collected the ballad poetry of the Border, and in 1802 gave to the world "Minstrelsy of the Scottish Border." The work at once pointed out the great power which afterward appeared so strongly in his novels. His next task was editing the metrical romance of "Sir Tristrem," supposed to have been written by Thomas the Rhymer, or Thomas of Ercildoune, who flourished about the year 1289. At length, in January, 1805, appeared "The Lay of the Last Minstrel." His conception of the Minstrel was inimitable, and won all hearts—even those who were indifferent to the supernatural part of the tale, and opposed to the irregularity of the ballad style.

Scott's regular income had now reached about £5,000 per annum. But the now famous Scotchman was not satisfied with a mere competence. He had an ambition to found a family that should be as honorable as the ancient Border names he so much venerated. To do this he must become a land-owner with an estate large enough to yield a steady and princely income. He must also maintain a liberal hospitality. They proved a snare to him, as we shall see before closing this sketch.

He now took up his residence in a beautiful locality on the banks of the Tweed, that he might be in the county for which he was acting as sheriff. He also formed a partnership with his schoolfellow, an extensive printer in Edinburgh. A publishing house was soon connected with the establishment. The firm drew heavily upon Scott to meet the immense outlay of the new concern, and thus he became mixed up with the pecuniary transactions of the concern to quite an extent. However, one of his strong friends secured him the appointment, in 1806, of one of the principal clerkships of the Court of Sessions at a salary of about $6,500 per annum. His share of the printing business and the income from the new appointment enabled him to lay up a magnificent fortune for his family. In 1808 he published his great poem, "Marmion," the best of his chivalrous tales, for the copyright of which he received one thousand guineas; also an edition of Dryden. "The Lady of the Lake," the most popular of his works then published, appeared in 1810; "The Vision of Don Roderick," 1811; "Rokeby," 1813; "The Bridal of Triermain," 1813; "The Lord of the Isles," 1814; "The Field of Waterloo," 1815; and "Harold the Dauntless," 1817. It will be seen by the above that books were falling annually from the pen of the Great Minstrel, but the style had become familiar to the world and had lost some of its popularity. So he turned from poetry to prose, and the long and magnificent series of "Waverly" followed. Before considering his novels we will call attention to his efforts to found a family that should be permanent and honorable in the history of Scotland. Scott had now removed from his pleasant cottage at Ashestiel; the territorial dream was about to be realized. In 1811 he purchased a hundred acres of moorland on the banks of the Tweed, near Melrose. The neighborhood was full of historical associations, but the spot itself was bleak and bare. Four thousand pounds were expended on this purchase, and the interesting and now immortal name of Abbotsford was substituted for the very ordinary one of "Cartley Hole." Other purchases of land followed, generally at prices considerably above their value. From these farms was formed the estate of Abbotsford. In his baronial residence the poet received innumerable visitors—princes, peers, and poets—men of all ranks and grades. His mornings were devoted to composition—for he had long practiced the invaluable habit of early rising—and the rest of the day to riding among his plantations, thinning or lopping his trees, and in the evening entertaining his guests and family. The honor of the baronetcy was conferred upon him in 1820 by George IV, who had taste enough to appreciate his genius. Never, certainly, had literature done more for any of its countless votaries, ancient or modern.

As early as 1805 Scott had begun the composition of "Waverly," but being dissatisfied with his work he threw it aside. In 1813 he accidentally came across the unfinished manuscript in a drawer with his fishing tackle, and resolved to complete it. The work was finished in 1814. The book appeared anonymously, as did most of his subsequent works, but the world was reasonably certain of their authorship. In 1815 "Guy Mannering" appeared. Bearing some marks of haste, yet the interest of the tale is sustained throughout with dramatic skill and effect. "The Antiquary," bringing out Scott's knowledge of the middle and lower ranks of Scottish life, was published in 1816. This year also witnessed the appearance of "The Black Dwarf" and "Old Mortality." Although Scott made an extra effort to keep the authorship of these novels a secret, by changing to a new publisher, yet the universal voice assigned them to the author of "Waverly." "Old Mortality" came laden with the rich spoils of history, and was pronounced the greatest of Scott's performances. In 1818 "Rob Roy" and "The Heart of Mid-Lothian" were published. "Rob Roy" presented beautiful pictures of Highland scenery and manners, and aroused the old enthusiasm that greeted "The Lady of the Lake." "The Bride of Lammermoor," a story of sustained and overwhelming pathos, appeared in 1819, conjointly with "The Legend of Montrose." "Ivanhoe," the historical romance, was published in 1820. The scene of this novel belongs to the time of Richard I of England. In 1820 "The Monastery" and "The Abbot" appeared, and in the succeeding year "Kenilworth," which ranked next to "Ivanhoe." "The Fortunes of Nigel," an English historical romance of the time of James I, belongs to 1822, and to the succeeding year, the following three works of fiction: "Peveril of the Peak," "Quentin Durward," and "St. Ronan's Well." "Quentin Durward" was a raid into French history. "The French nation exulted in this new proof of the genius of Scott, and led the way in an enthusiastic admiration of the work." In 1824 he published "Redgauntlet;" "The Tales of the Crusaders" in 1825, being two tales entitled "The Betrothed" and "The Talisman," the latter a splendid eastern romance.

At this time came the break in Scott's fortunes, to which we referred in speaking of his connection with the publishing house. The commercial distresses of 1825-'26 fell upon publishers as on other classes, and the bankruptcy of Constable & Company involved the poet in losses and engagements to a very large amount. His wealth, indeed, had been almost wholly illusory, for he had been paid for his work chiefly by bills, and these ultimately proved valueless. In the management of his publishing house, Scott's sagacity seems to have forsaken him; unsalable works were printed in thousands; and while these losses were yearly accumulating, the princely hospitalities at Abbotsford knew no check or pause. Heavy was the day of reckoning—terrible the reverse; for when the spell broke in January, 1826, it was found that, including the Constable engagements, Scott's commercial liabilities exceeded £120,000, and there was a private debt of £10,000. He would listen to no overtures of composition with his creditors—his only demand was for time. He ceased "doing the honors for all Scotland," sold off his Edinburgh house, and taking lodgings there labored incessantly at his literary tasks. "The fountain was awakened from its inmost recesses, as if the spirit of affliction had troubled it in its passage." Before his death the commercial debt was reduced to £54,000. Our strongest admiration is aroused by the terrible energy with which he continued his work. "The Life of Napoleon," in nine volumes, appeared in 1827; "The Two Drovers," "The Highland Widow," and "The Surgeon's Daughter," in the beginning of 1828. This constituted the first series of "The Chronicles of Canongate," and in the latter part of the same year he published the second series, entitled "The Fair Maid of Perth." At the same time Scott was preparing his "Tales of a Grandfather," "History of Scotland," for Lardner's "Cyclopedia," "Letters on Demonology," and collected numerous notes for his novels. In 1829 he was ready with the romance entitled "Anne of Geierstein."

Disease was fast taking his strength, but his pen never faltered. It produced less rapidly, perhaps, but retained most of its power. After repeated shocks of paralysis and apoplexy he wrote "Count Robert of Paris," "Castle Dangerous," and published them in 1831. These tales were imperfect, but they closed the work of the noble mind that had so long swayed the sceptre of romance. "In April, 1831, he suffered a still more severe attack, and he was prevailed upon, as a means of withdrawing him from mental labor, to undertake a foreign tour. The Admiralty furnished a ship of war and the poet sailed for Malta and Naples. At the latter place he resided from the 17th of December, 1831, to the 16th of April following. He still labored at unfinished romances, but his mind was in ruins. From Naples the poet went to Rome. On the 11th of May, he began his return homeward, and reached London on the 13th of June. Another attack of apoplexy, combined with paralysis, had laid prostrate his powers, and he was conveyed to Abbotsford a helpless and almost unconscious wreck. He lingered on for some time, listening occasionally to passages read to him from the Bible, and from his favorite author, Crabbe. Once he attempted to write, but his fingers would not close upon the pen. He never spoke of his literary labors or success. At times his imagination was busy preparing for the reception of the Duke of Wellington at Abbotsford, at other times he was exercising the functions of Scottish judge, as if presiding at the trial of members of his own family. His mind never appeared to wander in its delirium toward those works which had filled all Europe with his fame. This fact is of interest in literary history. But the contest was soon to be over; 'the plough was nearing the end of the furrow.' 'About half-past one, P. M.,' says Mr. Lockhart, 'on the 21st of September, 1832, Sir Walter breathed his last, in the presence of all his children. It was a beautiful day—so warm that every window was open—and so perfectly still that the sound of all others most delicious to his ear, the gentle ripple of the Tweed over its pebbles, was distinctly audible as we knelt around the bed, and his eldest son kissed and closed his eyes.' "

Upon his death his life insurance reduced his debt to £30,000. The publisher of his works, Mr. Robert Cadell, assumed the debt in return for the copyright of Scott's works. The estate of Abbotsford was freed from all incumbrances, through the sale of the great author's works. Not only this, but the publisher was enabled to buy himself an estate, and leave his family a fortune of about half a million dollars. The unexpired copyrights Mr. Cadell sold just before his death, to Adam Black & Co., for £17,000. It is a marvelous comment on the popularity of Scott's works. A debt of over half a million paid within twenty years, and a fortune of nearly an equal amount piled up from the pen of the "Great Wizard of the North."

SCHILLER.

JOHANN CHRISTOPH FRIEDRICH VON SCHILLER, one of the greatest of German national poets, was born at Marbach, Germany, on the banks of the Nectar, on the 10th of November, 1759. He died on the 9th of May, 1805, at the age of forty-five.

His father, Johann Caspar Schiller, for a time was a surgeon in the Bavarian army, and served in the Netherlands during the Succession War. The Peace of Paris put an end to his military employment, but he was retained in the service of the Duke of Wurtemberg, and moved from one establishment to another from time to time.

Friedrich followed the movements of his parents for some time, and had to glean his learning from the various masters. His first teacher was Moser, in the village of Lorch, for three years. In the public school at Ludwigsburg he spent four years, where his studies were regulated with a view to preparing him for the ministry. Through the influence of the Duke of Wurtemberg he abandoned this idea and entered a seminary at Stutgard. At this same college he turned his attention for a time to the study of medicine. His first production was an epic poem entitled "Moses," and written at the age of thirteen. It was not till in 1783, however, that he adopted literature as a profession. For two years he was writer at the theatre at Mannheim. Here it was that he wrote his tragedy of "Fiesco." With the appearance of "Fiesco" and its companion, "Kabale und Liebe," the first period of Schiller's literary history may be said to conclude. In 1789 Goethe recommended him for the professorship of history at Jena University and he was successful in securing it. Two years later he produced his "History of the Thirty-Years' War." This by many is con-

sidered his chief performance in this line of literature, although competent critics affirm that had "The Revolt of the Netherlands" been completed, it would have been its equal if not its superior; but either would have placed him in the first rank among historians. In 1789 he brought forth his masterpiece, the tragedy of "Wallenstein." One year later he took up his abode in Weimar. It was near this time that he consummated a scheme that had been in his mind for ten years—the editing of the "Thalia." This was, in 1793, merged into the "Horen." While living at Weimar he gave to the world "Mary Stuart," which appeared in 1800, "Maid of Orleans," 1801, and "The Bride of Messina." "William Tell," one of the very finest and probably the most well known of all Schiller's dramas, was sent out in 1804. Although it lacks unity of interest and of action, is less comprehensive than "Wallenstein," and not so ethereal as the "Jungfrau," still it ably sustains the high place among his writings which is claimed for it. It is given on good authority that the ballads of Schiller are the finest of their kind in the German language. As has been stated, he died on Friday, May 9, 1805, and was buried between midnight and one o'clock Sunday morning.

WILLIAM SHAKESPEARE.

WILLIAM SHAKESPEARE was born at Stratford-on-Avon, in the county of Warwick, in April, 1564, and having gained a competency of fortune and fullness of fame in London, he retired to his native town, where he died on the 23d of April, 1616.

But very little is known of Shakespeare's early life or of the history of his ancestors. His father, John Shakespeare, is traced to a family occupying lands near Warwick. John Shakespeare was settled near Stratford, where he became a wool-comber. His social position was improved by his marriage to Mary Arden, a rustic heiress to an estate valued at about six hundred dollars per annum. He arose to be high bailiff and chief alderman of Stratford, but becoming involved, he mortgaged his wife's estate and was thus reduced to poverty. Of the six surviving children William was the oldest.

The only school education he received was what he could gather in a short grammar school course. From this school he was soon called home to assist in his father's business. A blank of several years here occurs in his history. While we can gain no incidents of his life in this period, yet we may take it for granted that he was busy with his studies and reflections, for he came out of this period with a breadth and depth of thought and knowledge scarcely surpassed in his time.

While Shakespeare's fame rests mainly upon his work as a dramatist, yet, with the exception of "The Faerie Queene," his poems are unequaled in the "Elizabethan Age." His "Venus and Adonis" appeared in his twenty-ninth year, and the "Rape of Lucrece" the year following. Shakespeare dedicated these poems to Henry Wriothesley, Earl of Southampton, in the

following modest words: "I know not how I shall offend in dedicating my unpolished lines to your lordship, nor how the world will censure me for choosing so strong a prop to support so weak a burden; only, if your honor seems but pleased I account myself highly praised and vow to take advantage *of all idle hours* till I have honored you with some graver labor. But if the *first heir of my invention* prove deformed, I shall be sorry it had so noble a godfather, and never after ear [till] so barren a land." Later, it is claimed, the Earl of Southampton presented Shakespeare with 1,000 pounds to complete a purchase which he wished to make. Objections are urged against the above poems on the ground of their excessive coloring and licentiousness. His sonnets, 154 in number, were first printed in 1609. While many of them are beautiful, yet they reflect no great credit on their author. Partially pleased and not wholly displeased, we turn from Shakespeare the poet to Shakespeare the dramatist. We but repeat the universal opinion when we say that Shakespeare reigns supreme in the dramatic world. Here he is at home. The circumstances of his youth were such as to cultivate his dramatic genius. While he resided at home, London players were in the habit of making frequent visits to Stratford. Burbage, the greatest performer of his day,—the future Richard, Hamlet, and Othello—was from Warwickshire. The circumstance of his father's being high bailiff would probably give William an opportunity to meet these noted performers and from them and their plays to receive the "first stirrings of his immortal dramatic genius." At the age of eighteen Shakespeare married Ann Hathaway. This lady was seven years older than her husband, but the union seems to have been a harmonious one. About 1586 our poet removed to London where his ambition had full scope. As an actor he was always spoken of favorably, but "the source of his unexampled success was his immortal dramas, the delight and wonder of his age." Up to 1611 the whole of Shakespeare's plays, thirty-seven in number, according to the first folio edition, are supposed to have been produced. One year after the completion of the last of these plays he retired to his country house. Here he lived for four years, a perfect "picture of calm felicity and satisfied ambition," when he died at the age of fifty-two. His widow survived him seven years. Three children had been born to them, but no lineal representatives of the great poet remain.

The autograph signature of the poet to a mortgage deed was sold in 1858 for the British Museum, in London, for the sum of three hundred guineas. The enormous sum paid for this single signature of the great Shakespeare shows the estimation placed upon mementoes of him, and illustrates, to a certain extent, the esteem in which his memory is held in England. The signature is so obscured that the spelling cannot be determined.

P. B. SHELLEY.

Percy Bysshe Shelley was born at Field Place, near Horsham, in Sussex, August 4, 1792; and his eventful life came suddenly to a sad termination. He had gone out in a boat to Leghorn to welcome Leigh Hunt to Italy, and while returning on the eighth of July, 1822, the boat sank in the Bay of Spezia, and all on board perished. When his body floated to shore a volume of Keats' poetry was found open in Shelley's coat pocket. The remains were reduced to ashes and deposited in the Protestant burial ground at Rome, near those of a child he had lost in that city.

His father was a member of the House of Commons. The family line could be traced back to one of the followers of William of Normandy. Thus in noble blood Shelley was more fortunate than most of his brother poets, considering the estimate that England placed upon the distinction of caste. He had all the advantages of wealth and rank, and hence much was expected of him.

At the age of ten Shelley was placed in the public school of Sion House, but the harsh treatment of instructors and school-fellows rendered his life most unpleasant. Such treatment might have been called out by his

Percy B Shelley

fondness for wild romances and his devotion to reading instead of more solid school work. While very young he wrote two novels, "Zastrozzi" and "St. Irvyne, or the Rosicrucian," works of some merit. Shelley was next sent to Eton, where his sensitive nature was again deeply wounded by ill usage. He finally revolted against all authority, and this disposition manifested itself strongly in Eton.

Shelley next went to Oxford, but he studied irregularly, except in his peculiar views, where he seemed to be constant in his thought and speculations. At the age of fifteen, he wrote two short romances, threw off various political effusions, and published a volume of political rhymes entitled "Posthumous Poems of My Aunt Margaret Nicholson," the said Margaret being the unhappy maniac who attempted to stab George III. He also issued a syllabus of Hume's "Essays," and at the same time challenged the authorities of Oxford to a public discussion of the subject. He was only seventeen at the time. In company with Mr. Hogg, a fellow-student, he composed a treatise entitled "The Necessity of Atheism." For this publication, both of the heterodox students were expelled from the college in 1811. Mr. Hogg removed to York, while Shelley went to London, where he still received support from his family.

His expulsion from Oxford led also to an inexcusable confusion in his social life. He had become strongly attached to Miss Grove, an accomplished young lady, but after he was driven from college her father prohibited communication between them. He next became strongly attached to Miss Harriet Westbrook, a beautiful lady of sixteen, but of social position inferior to his. An elopement soon followed, and a marriage in August, 1811. Shelley's father was so enraged at this act that he cut off his son's allowance. "An uncle, Captain Pilfold—one of Nelson's captains at the Nile and Trafalgar—generously supplied the youthful pair with money, and they lived for some time in Cumberland, where Shelley made the acquaintance of Southey, Wordsworth, De Quincey and Wilson. His literary ambition must have been excited by this intercourse; but he suddenly departed for Dublin, whence he again removed to the Isle of Man, and afterward to Wales. After they had been married three years and two children were born to them they separated. In March, 1814, Shelley was married a second time to Harriet Westbrook, the ceremony taking place in St. George's Church, Hanover Square. Unfortunately, about this time the poet became enamoured of the daughter of Mr. Godwin, a young lady who could 'feel poetry and understand philosophy,' which he thought his wife was incapable of, and Harriet refusing to agree to a separation, Shelley, at the end of July in the same year, left England in the company of Mary Wollstonecraft Godwin."

Upon his return to London, it was found that by the deed, the fee-simple of the Shelley estate would pass to the poet upon his father's death. Accordingly he was enabled to raise money with which he purchased an annuity of £1,000 from his father. He again repaired to the continent in 1816, when he met Lord Byron at Lake Geneva. Later he returned to England and settled at Great Marlow, in Buckinghamshire. His unfortunate wife committed suicide by drowning herself in the Serpentine River in December, 1816, and Shelley married Miss Godwin a few weeks afterward (December 30).

Leaving his unfortunate social career, we come now to consider his poetical works. At the age of eighteen he wrote "Queen Mab," a poem containing passages of great power and melody. In 1818 he produced "Alastor, or the Spirit of Solitude," full of almost unexcelled descriptive passages; also the "Revolt of Islam." Shelley was most earnest in his attentions to the poor. A severe spell of sickness was brought on by visiting the poor cottages in winter. Poor health induced him to go to Italy, accordingly on the twelfth of March, 1818, he left England forever.

In 1819 appeared "Rosalind and Helen," and "The Council," a tragedy dedicated to Leigh Hunt. "As an effort of intellectual strength and an embodiment of human passion it may challenge a comparison with any dramatic work since Otway, and is incomparably the best of the poet's productions." In 1821 was published "Prometheus Unbound," which he had written while resident in Rome. "This poem," he says, "was chiefly written upon the mountainous ruins of the Baths of Caracalla, among the flowery glades and thickets of odoriferous blossoming trees, which are extended in ever-winding labyrinths upon its immense platforms and dizzy arches suspended in the air. The bright blue sky of Rome, and the effect of the vigorous awakening of spring in that divinest climate, and the new life with which it drenches the spirits even to inspiration, were the inspiration of this drama." Shelley also produced "Hellas," "The Witch of Atlas," "Adonais," "Epipsychidion," and several short works with scenes translated from Calderon and the "Faust of Goethe." These closed his literary labors, for he died as described in the beginning of this sketch, in 1822.

A complete edition of "Shelley's Poetical Works" with notes by his widow was published in four volumes in 1839, and the same lady gave to the world two volumes of his prose "Essays," "Letters from Abroad," "Translations and Fragments." Shelley's was a dream of romance—a tale of mystery and grief. That he was sincere in his opinions and benevolent in his intentions is now undoubted. He looked upon the world with the eyes of a visionary bent on unattainable schemes of intellectual excellence and supremacy. His delusion led to misery and made him, for a time, unjust to others. It alienated him from his family and friends, blasted his prospects in life, and distempered all his views and opinions. It is probable that, had he lived to a riper age, he might have modified some of those extreme speculative and pernicious tenets, and we have no doubt that he would have risen into a purer atmosphere of poetical imagination. The troubled and stormy dawn was fast yielding to the calm noonday brightness. He had worn out some of his fierce antipathies and morbid affections; a happy domestic circle was gathered around him, and the refined simplicity of his tastes and habits, joined to wider and juster views of human life, would imperceptibly have given a new tone to his thoughts and studies. The splendor of his lyrical verse—so full, rich and melodious—and the grandeur of some of his conceptions, stamp him a great poet. His influence on the succession of English poets since his time has been inferior only to that of Wordsworth. Macaulay doubted whether any modern poet possessed in an equal degree the "highest qualities of the great ancient masters." His diction is singularly classical and imposing in sound and structure. He was a close student of the Greek and Italian poets. The descriptive passages in "Alastor" and the river-voyage at the conclusion of the "Revolt of Islam," are among the most finished of his productions. His better genius leads him to the pure waters and the depth of forest shades, which none of his contemporaries knew so well how to describe. Some of the minor poems, "The Cloud," "The Skylark," etc., are imbued with a fine lyrical and poetic spirit.

THE CLOUD.

I bring fresh showers for the thirsting flowers,
    From the seas and the streams;
I bear light shade for the leaves when laid
    In their noonday dreams.
From my wings are shaken the dews that waken
    The sweet birds every one,
When rocked to rest on their mother's breast,
    As she dances about the sun.
I wield the flail of the lashing hail,
    And whiten the green plains under;
And then again I dissolve it in rain,
    And laugh as I pass in thunder.

MRS. SIGOURNEY.

LYDIA HUNTLEY SIGOURNEY was born in Norwich, Connecticut, September 1, 1791, and died in Hartford, June 10, 1865.

Having completed her studies, she opened a private school in Hartford, in 1814. In the succeeding year she published "Moral Pieces in Prose and Verse," a work of some merit. In 1819 she married Charles Sigourney, a merchant of Hartford. Her life passed pleasantly between her home duties and her books till in 1840, when she visited Europe. In 1842 the reminiscences of her visit were published in a volume entitled "Pleasant Memories of Pleasant Lands," and the work was well received.

Her principal works are "Letters to Young Ladies," "Pocahontas, and Other Poems," "Letters to my Pupils," "Letters to Mothers," "Letters of Life," "Post Meridian," "The Man of Uz, and other Poems," "Indian Names," "Death of an Infant." The list is too long to be given in full, as she published nearly sixty volumes of poems, prose, and selections. Her autobiography appeared in 1866, the year after her death, under the title of "Letters of Life."

Mrs. Sigourney is regarded by a large class of critics as the most gifted authoress America has yet produced. She possessed a pleasant and agreeable style, and her works are deservedly popular.

ROBERT SOUTHEY.

Robert Southey, LL.D., poet laureate of England, was born at Bristol, August 12, 1774, and he died at Greta, March 21, 1843.

His father was a respectable linen draper, but Robert was indebted to his uncle for an education. At the age of fourteen he was sent to the Westminster School, where he remained about four years. Southey and some of his school associates started a periodical called "The Flagellant," in which they published a sarcasm upon corporal punishment. Dr. Vincent, the headmaster, commenced a prosecution against the publishers, which forced Southey to withdraw from the school. Like Shelley, he was somewhat disgusted with the institutions of his country, but the effect upon their lives was far different. The effect finally wore off from Southey. In 1792 he entered Balliol College, Oxford. He became an excellent scholar, including a knowledge of Greek, Latin, Spanish, and Portuguese languages. While at Oxford he formed literary plans enough for the work of several long and busy lives. He was one of the most studious men that ever lived. His life was spent almost entirely in his magnificent library. Referring to his books, and he had one of the finest private libraries in the realm, he said:

> My days among the dead are passed;
> Around me I behold,
> Where'er these casual eyes are cast,
> The mighty minds of old;
> My never-failing friends are they,
> With whom I converse night and day.

Southey's literary career commenced in 1794, when he published a volume of poems in conjunction with Robert Lovell, under the names of Moschus and Bion. At the same time he composed his drama of "Wat Tyler," a revolutionary pamphlet, "which was long afterward published surreptitiously by a knavish book-seller to annoy its author." Afterward Southey expressed his excuse for "Wat Tyler" as follows: "In my youth, when my stock of knowledge consisted of such an acquaintance with Greek and Roman history as is acquired in the course of a scholastic education—when my heart was full of poetry and romance, and Lucan and Akenside were at my tongue's end—I fell into the political opinions which the French revolution was then scattering throughout Europe; and following these opinions with ardor wherever they led, I soon perceived that inequalities of rank were a light evil compared to the inequalities of property, and those more fearful distinctions which the want of moral and intellectual culture occasions between man and man. At that time, and with those opinions, or rather feelings (for their root was in the heart and not in the understanding), I wrote 'Wat Tyler,' as one who is impatient of all the oppressions that are done under the sun. The subject was injudiciously chosen, and it was treated as might be expected by a youth of twenty at such times, who regarded only one side of the question."

"Joan of Arc," published in 1793, is full of the same political sentiment. In 1795 he married Miss Edith Fricker, of Bristol, but they parted immediately after the ceremony was performed, the lady returning to her parents, while Southey finished his studies.

The death of his brother-in-law and brother-poet, Lovell, occurred dur-

ing his absence abroad, and Southey on his return set about raising something for his young friend's widow. She afterward found a home with Southey—one of the many generous and affectionate acts of his busy life. In 1797 he published his "Letters from Spain and Portugal," and took up his residence in London, in order to commence the study of law. A college friend, Mr. C. W. W. Wynn, gave him an annuity of £160, which he continued to receive until 1807, when he relinquished it on obtaining a pension from the crown of £200.

His health failing, he again visited Portugal, and after a year's absence, returned to England much improved. For a short time he resided at Bristol, then took a journey into Cumberland to visit Coleridge. He found his poetic friend at Greta Hall, Keswick, where Southey remained during the greater part of the rest of his life. About the same time he was appointed private secretary to Mr. Cory, chancellor of the exchequer of Ireland, at a salary of £350 per year. The work was not congenial, hence after about six months of bondage, he returned to his home and entered upon his career as a professional author. "Thalaba, the Destroyer," appeared in 1801, an Arabian fiction of great beauty and magnificence, for which he received 100 guineas. Abandoning entirely his revolutionary views, he became greatly devoted to the church and state, and settled on the banks of the river Greta, near Keswick. A volume of "Metrical Tales" appeared in 1804; "Madoc," an epic poem, founded on a Welsh story, in 1805; "The Curse of Kehama," his greatest poetical work, in 1810. Some of the scenes of this strangely magnificent theatre of horrors are described with the power of Milton.

In 1814 he published "Roderick, the Last of the Goths," a noble and pathetic poem. Accepting the office of poet laureate in 1813, he published some courtly strains that added nothing to his fame. His "Carmen Triumphale" appeared in 1814, and "The Vision of Judgment," 1821. These works were ridiculed at the time, and especially by Lord Byron, who published another "Vision of Judgment," in which he punishes the laureate most severely. His last poetical work was a volume of narrative verse, "All for Love," and "The Pilgrim of Compostella," published in 1829. He was offered a baronetcy and a seat in parliament, both of which he prudently declined. His fame and his fortune, he knew, could only be preserved by adhering to his solitary studies, but these were too constant and uninterrupted. The poet forgot one of his own maxims, that "frequent change of air is of all things that which most conduces to joyous health and long life."

In 1833-'37 Southey edited and published the works of Cowper in fifteen volumes. In the meantime his wife became a mental imbecile in 1834, in which sad condition she remained about three years. Southey bore up under the affliction, but his health was greatly shattered. After a brief time he married Miss Bowles, the poetess, but his mind became clouded in the course of a few years, and he died in 1843.

Wordsworth, writing to Lady Frederick Bentinck in July, 1840, says that on visiting his early friend he did not recognize him till he was told. "Then his eyes flashed for a moment with their former brightness, but he sank into the state in which I had found him, patting with both hands his books affectionately like a child." Three years were passed in this deplorable condition, and it was a matter of satisfaction rather than regret that death at length stepped in to shroud this painful spectacle from the eyes of affection as well as from the gaze of vulgar curiosity. He died at Greta on the 21st of March, 1843. He left at his death a sum of about £12,000, to be divided among his children, and one of the most valuable private libraries in the kingdom. The life and correspondence of Southey have been published by his son, the Rev. Charles Cuthbert Southey, in six volumes. His son-in-law, the Rev. J. Wood Warter, published his "Commonplace Book," four volumes, and "Selections from His Letters," four volumes. In these works the amiable private life of Southey, his indefatigable application, his habitual cheerfulness and lively fancy, and his steady friendships and true generosity, are strikingly displayed. The only drawback is the poet's egotism, which was inordinate, and the hasty, uncharitable judgments sometimes passed on his contemporaries, the result partly of temperament and partly of his seclusion from general society. Southey was interred in the churchyard of Crosthwaite, and in the church is a marble monument to his memory, a full-length recumbent figure, with the following inscription by Wordsworth on the base:

WORDSWORTH'S EPITAPH ON SOUTHEY.

Ye vales and hills, whose beauty hither drew
The poet's steps, and fixed him here, on you
His eyes have closed; and ye, loved books, no more
Shall Southey feed upon your precious lore,
To works that ne'er shall forfeit their renown,
Adding immortal labors of his own;
Whether he traced historic truth with zeal
For the state's guidance, or the church's weal;
Or Fancy, disciplined by studious Art,
Informed his pen, or Wisdom of the heart
Or Judgments sanctioned in the patriot's mind
By reverence for the rights of all mankind.
Large were his aims, yet in no human breast
Could private feelings find a holier nest.
His joys, his griefs, have vanished like a cloud
From Skiddaw's top, but he to heaven was vowed
Through a life long and pure, and steadfast faith
Calmed in his soul the fear of change and death.

EDMUND SPENSER.

EDMUND SPENSER was born at East Smithfield, England, about 1553; and, impoverished and broken-hearted, he died on Saturday, January 13, 1599.

The poet's father came from the family of Spenser, which settled at Hurstwood, in Lancashire, where it flourished until 1690. His exact relation to the ancient and noble house of Spenser cannot be ascertained.

In 1569 young Edmund was entered a sizar of Pembroke College, Cambridge. Although entered as one of the humblest class of students, he pursued his studies for seven years, taking the degree of M. A. in June, 1576. While Spenser was attending college Gabriel Harvey, the future astrologer, was at Christ's College. An intimacy was formed between them which lasted during the poet's life and was of great advantage to him. Harvey induced Spenser to go to London, and there introduced him to Sir Philip Sidney, one of the very diamonds of her majesty's court.

Sir Philip afterward patronized our poet and recommended him to the powerful Earl of Leicester. Spenser's literary life commenced in 1579, by the publication of his "Shepherd's Calendar," dedicated to Sidney. This is a pastoral poem and it shows some faults, such as obsolete uncouth phrases, but its numerous beautiful passages exhibit the "germs of that tuneful harmony and pensive reflection in which Spenser excelled."

In the next ten years Spenser was not before the public. Within this time he seems to have been corresponding with Harvey and Sir Philip Sidney, concerning the literary innovation of banishing rhymes and introducing the Latin prosody into English verse. The scheme, however, was soon abandoned, and he took up the "Faerie Queene" and carried it forward in the sweet music of his verse "and the endless flow and profusion of his fancy."

Like Chaucer, Spenser had to depend upon the patronage of certain nobles and upon court favors for support. In his struggles he met with numerous reverses, but he toiled on in poverty till Lord Grey was sent to Ireland as lord-deputy, when Spenser was selected as his secretary. After two years of service, the appointment was recalled, and our poet returned to England. Finally, in 1586, the crown showed an appreciation of Spenser's ability, and granted him 3,028 acres of land in the county of Cork, Ireland. This grant was made from a tract of land forfeited by the Earl of Desmond. Twelve thousand acres had been granted previously to Sir Walter Raleigh. In fulfillment of one of the conditions of the grant, our poet removed to his estate. Here, near Doneraile, in Kilcolman Castle, he took up his abode, and received the numerous visits of the illustrious Raleigh, whom he styled "the Shepherd of the Ocean." "The poet's castle stood in the midst of a large plain, by the side of a lake. The river Mull ran through his grounds, and a chain of mountains in the distance seemed to bulwark in the romantic

retreat." At this place he wrote most of the "Faerie Queene," and with his noted friend Raleigh, read the manuscript while sitting

> "Amongst the cooly shade
> Of the green alders, by the Mulla's shore."

This masterly poem appeared in January, 1589-'90, dedicated to Her Majesty, and was enthusiastically received. The queen now settled a pension of fifty pounds per annum upon Spenser. Next appeared his smaller poems, such as "The Tears of the Muses," "Mother Hubbard," etc., in 1591; "Daphnaida," 1592; "Amoretti" and "Epithalamium," 1595. The last named related to his courtship and marriage.

About the same time appeared "Elegy of Astrophel," on the death of the lamented Sidney. In the excitement incident to the rebellion in Ireland, Spenser met with reverses that reduced him to poverty. The English settlers who occupied the crown lands, were the objects of the hatred of the natives. Spenser, with the others, had been often harsh and oppressive, and he was an advocate of arbitrary power in the government of Ireland. At length the storm burst upon him. The insurgents attacked Kilcolman, and having robbed and plundered, set fire to the castle. In the excitement Spenser and his wife escaped, but an infant child of the poet perished in the flames.

Spenser then went to London, where he died as stated in the beginning of this sketch, and was buried in Westminster Abbey, near the tomb of Chaucer. The Earl of Essex defrayed the funeral expenses, and his hearse attendants were his brother poets, who threw "mournful elegies" into his grave. Thirty years later, Anne, Countess of Dorset, erected a monument over his grave. "Spenser is the most luxuriant and melodious of all our descriptive poets," and in his style he has never been surpassed.

HARRIET BEECHER STOWE.

HARRIET ELIZABETH BEECHER STOWE was born in Litchfield, Connecticut, June 15, 1812. Her father was Dr. Lyman Beecher, a distinguished clergyman. In 1833, with her father, she removed to Cincinnati, where, in 1836, she was married to the Rev. Calvin Stowe, who afterward became professor at Bowdoin College and at Andover Theological School.

Several stories which she had written for the Cincinnati "Gazette" and other periodicals, were collected and published in a volume entitled "The Mayflower." In 1851 she commenced "Uncle Tom's Cabin," in the Washington "National Era." The story was afterward published in Boston in two volumes. "Its success was without a parallel in the literature of any age. Nearly half a million copies were sold in this country, and a considerably larger number in England. It was translated into every language of Europe, and into Arabic and Armenian. It was dramatized and acted in nearly every theatre in the world." In 1853 she visited Europe and was received with gratifying attention. "Sunny Memories of Foreign Lands" was published upon her return from Europe. In 1856 appeared "Dred, a Tale of the Great Dismal Swamp." This work produced but slight impression. The success of "Uncle Tom's Cabin" probably removed the charm of novelty in the subject of her new story. "The Minister's Wooing" appeared in book form in 1859. "Agnes of Sorrento" and "The Pearl of Orr's Island" were published in 1862; "House and Home Papers," in 1864; "The Chimney Corner," in 1865; "Little Foxes," 1865; "Queer Little People," 1867; "Oldtown Folks," 1869; "Pink and White Tyranny," 1871; "My Wife and I," 1872. Probably the great mistake in her literary work was made in pub-

HARRIET BEECHER STOWE.

lishing "The True Story of Lady Byron's Life." If true it should not have been told, but the story is thought not to be true.

Mrs. Stowe has written very extensively, and her published works entitle her to a place among the greatest authors of fiction. While her fame rests upon her first great book, yet all of her works contain excellent qualities. Her genius is rare and original. For several years she has spent the greater part of her time in her Florida home, in company with her husband and daughters.

It is customary with most authors to classify female writers as the wife or sister or some other relative of some man. Mrs. Stowe, however, needs not the name of her husband, nor the world-wide fame of the Beechers, to give her a place in the front ranks of literature. The world knows her as well as it knows her relatives, and its admiration for her is richly merited.

E C. STEDMAN.

EDMUND CLARENCE STEDMAN, one of the popular living American poets and critics, was born in Hartford, Connecticut, October 8, 1833.

In 1849 he entered Yale College, but was suspended in 1852 and did not return. The success of his literary labor, however, induced the trustees of Yale to restore the poet to his class in 1871, and bestow upon him the degree of A. M.

He commenced his literary life first by editing the "Norwich Tribune," and later the "Winsted Herald." In 1855 he settled in New York, and four years later became a writer for the "Tribune." Upon the breaking out of the late war he became an army correspondent for the "World," a position he held until 1863, when he became private secretary to Attorney General

Bates at Washington. All of the trusts thus far imposed on him were discharged with credit to himself and employers.

In 1860 he published "Poems, Lyric and Idyllic;" in 1864, "Alice of Monmouth, an Idyl of the Great War, and Other Poems." In 1864 he also entered New York as a stock broker, and has continued the banking business in connection with his literary work. In 1869 he published "The Blameless Prince;" 1873, his "Complete Poems;" and "Victorian Poets," a volume of critical studies, in 1875.

He has written numerous poems that are not only very popular, but are the product of a high order of genius. Among them we may mention, "The Doorstep," "Pan in Wall Street," "At Twilight," "John Brown of Ossawatomie," "The Blameless Prince," and "Alice of Monmouth." He has also shown himself to be one of our best living critics. Occasionally we meet with an excellent article from his pen, and we are always delighted with his easy, graceful style. In the reviews he frequently makes of prominent literary characters he is just and impartial, never measuring them by the rules of personal fancy or prejudice, but always by the accepted standards of excellence.

JONATHAN SWIFT.

JONATHAN SWIFT was born in Dublin, Ireland, November 30, 1667, and he died October 19, 1745.

His parents were of English descent. His grandfather, vicar of Goodrich, in Herefordshire, lost his fortune through his activity in the cause of Charles I, in the Civil War. "Three of the vicar's sons settled in Ireland, and Jonathan Swift, father of the celebrated author, was bred to the law in Dublin, but died in great poverty before the birth of his distinguished son." Although born into poverty and orphanage, Swift afterward became one of the most remarkable men of his age. His entire dependence upon his uncle for support is a circumstance that seems to have made a deep impression upon his haughty soul. Sir Walter Scott tells us that Swift observed his birthday as an occasion "not of joy, but of sorrow," and he was accustomed to spending the day in sorrowful laments that he was thus born.

Swift was sent to Trinity College, Dublin, where, at the age of twenty-one, he was permitted to receive his degree by special favor. Sir William Temple, a distant relative of Swift's mother, received him into his own house. In 1692 he entered Oxford, where he took his M. A. degree. His first intention was to make the ministry a profession, and for this purpose he procured a position in the Diocese of Comar in Ireland, at an income of £100 per annum. Soon disgusted with the life and poor pay of an obscure country clergyman, he abandoned his former intention and returned to Moor Park, the house of Sir William Temple. Upon the death of Temple in 1699, Swift accompanied Lord Berkley to Ireland as chaplain. From this nobleman he obtained the rectory of Aghar and other appointments amounting in all to £200 per annum.

As a political writer Swift sided with the Whigs, and when in England associated with Addison, Steele and Halifax. In 1704 the "Tale of a Tub" was published. This is "the wildest and wittiest of all polemical or controversial works." Not receiving the attention of the ministry that he thought due him, he left the Whigs and went over to the Tory administration. Here he was received with open arms, and he at once passed into the inner chamber of the hearts of the new people. "He carried with him shining weapons for party warfare—irresistible and unscrupulous satire, steady hate, and a dauntless spirit." His new allies gave him the deanery of St. Patrick's in 1713. At first Swift was greatly disliked by the Irish people, but by the "Drapier's Letters" and other works he soon gained great popularity. He received all the heart of the Irish people, and became more than king of the rabble. In dealing with the people, "kisses and curses were alternately on his lips."

Finally his reason gave way after several attacks of giddiness and deafness. The fits of lunacy were followed by the *dementia* of old age. For three years before his death he was unable to utter more than a few words and broken exclamations. Soon this wreck of a mighty intellect sank into speechless silence, his spirit passed away, and he was buried in St. Patrick's Cathedral, amidst the tears and prayers of his countrymen. Swift seems to have had a presentiment of the sad close of his life. While in company with Young and some other friends he was observed standing and gazing upward at a noble elm which in its uppermost branches was much decayed. Pointing to it he said: "I shall be like that tree; I shall die at the top." Most of his fortune of £10,000 he left to found a lunatic asylum at Dublin.

Swift wrote much poetry which is excellent. He succeeded in his work because he never attempted to rise above this visible diurnal sphere. However, we must ever look to "Gulliver's Travels" and the "Tale of a Tub" as the chief corner-stones of Swift's fame. The purity of his prose style renders it a model of English composition. He could wither with his irony and invective; excite to mirth with his wit and invention; transport as with wonder at his marvelous powers of grotesque and ludicrous combination, his knowledge of human nature—piercing quite through the deeds of men—and his matchless power of feigning reality and assuming at pleasure different characters and situations in life. In 1814 his works were published by Sir Walter Scott, in nineteen volumes.

BAYARD TAYLOR.

BAYARD TAYLOR was born in Kennett Square, Chester County, Pennsylvania, January 11, 1825, and died in Berlin, December 19, 1878, while serving as United States minister to Germany.

At the age of seventeen he became an apprentice in a printing office, where he received important training. This business, however, was soon

JAMES BAYARD TAYLOR.

abandoned, for, at the age of nineteen, with only $140 in his pocket, he set out for a tour in Europe. From 1844 to 1845 he made a pedestrian tour on the continent. Being a close observer, he filled his mind with valuable and interesting information, the result of which appeared in 1846, in "Views Afoot, or Europe Seen with the Knapsack and Staff." This work showed Taylor to be unusually happy in the use of the pen. The favor with which it was received indicated that he might win success as a traveler and an author.

Upon returning to this country he edited a newspaper in Phoenixville, Pennsylvania, for one year; then removing to New York he wrote for the "Literary World" for a short time. Subsequently he joined the editorial staff of the "Tribune," in which paper many of his works of travel were first printed. In 1849 he went to California, and visited Mexico on his way home, the result of which appeared in 1850 in "A Voyage to California."

In 1851 he set out on an extended tour in the East, in the course of which he ascended the Nile to lat. 12° 30′ N., and afterward traversed large portions of Asia Minor, Syria, and Europe; and in the latter part of 1852 he made a new departure from England, crossing Asia to Calcutta, and thence proceeding to China, where he joined the expedition of Commodore Perry to Japan. After this he made several other journeys. In 1862-'63 he was secretary of legation at St. Petersburg, and part of the time charge d' affairs. In 1874 he revisited Egypt, and attended the millennial celebration in Iceland. In February, 1878, he was appointed minister to Germany, where he had previously resided for several years at intervals. Taylor had become a fine German scholar, and his appointment as minister gave great satisfaction to that people. The above gives a brief outline of his travels. He also gained a reputation as a public lecturer.

His literary labors were extensive and valuable, as will be seen by the following list of published works: besides "Views Afloat," he published "El Dorado, or Adventures in the Path of Empire," in two volumes, in 1850; "A Journey to Central Africa," 1854; "The Lands of the Saracen," 1854; "A Visit to India, China, and Japan," 1855; "Northern Travel: Summer and Winter Pictures of Sweden, Denmark, and Lapland," published in London in 1857, and in New York, 1858; "Travels in Greece and Russia," 1859; "At Home and Abroad, a Sketch of Life, Scenery and Men," 1859, and a second series in 1862; "Colorado, a Summer Trip," 1867; "By-ways of Europe," 1869; and "Egypt and Iceland," 1874. The above works, which record the results of his travels, are valuable and interesting, yet they only close one line of his authorship. Still more important is the record of his muse.

His volumes of poems are: "Ximena, or the Battle of the Sierra Morena, and Other Poems," published at Philadelphia in 1844; "Rhymes of Travel, Ballads, and Other Poems," 1848; "The American Legend," a poem delivered before the Phi Beta Kappa Society of Harvard University, in 1850; "Book of Romances, Lyrics and Songs," 1851; "Poems and Ballads," 1854; "Poems of the Orient," 1855; "Poems of Home and Travel," a selection from his early lyrics, published at Boston in 1855; "The Poet's Journal," 1862; "The Pictures of St. John," 1866; "The Ballad of Abraham Lincoln," 1869; "The Masque of the Gods," 1872; "Lars, a Pastoral of Norway," 1873; "The Prophet, a Tragedy," 1874; and "Home Pastorals, Ballads, and Lyrics," 1875. In addition to the above works, he also published the following novels: "Hannah Thurston, a Story of American Life," in 1863; "John Godfrey's Fortunes," 1864; "The Story of Kennett," 1866; and "Joseph and His Friend," 1870. He also translated in the original metres both parts of Goethe's "Faust," in 1870-'71; edited a "Cyclopedia of Modern Travel," 1856; and an "Illustrated Library of Travel, Exploration, and Adventure," 1872-'74. Other translations and works appeared which we need not mention here. At the time of his death he was engaged in writing the life of Goethe.

Taylor's works have been very popular throughout the literary world, and they continue to hold the public favor. They have been translated into the German, French and Russian languages. He is considered as one of the greatest of modern travelers. His observations always appeared in interesting and instructive volumes. He also won high rank as a novelist. While he gained renown in several lines of authorship, yet we must turn to his poetry as the chief source of his fame. Much of his poetical writings is of a high order. His "Centennial Ode," which he read on July 4, 1876, is a masterpiece, worthy of his country and his genius.

Bayard Taylor deserves rank among the most useful and popular authors of his time.

BENJAMIN F. TAYLOR.

BENJAMIN FRANKLIN TAYLOR, one of America's most gifted and entertaining authors and lecturers, was born in Lowville, New York, in 1822. He received his education at Madison University, New York, under the tutorship of his father, who was at that time president of the institution. Mr. Taylor has been an active and popular worker in the literary field. "The Attractions of Language" appeared in 1845, and "January and June," in 1853. No one who admires beautiful word-pictures, fine sentiment, and a clear and entertaining literary style, can afford to be without the volumes of B. F. Taylor.

For many years he was literary editor of the Chicago "Evening Journal." During the late war he was the "Journal's" principal war correspondent. Many of his letters have been gathered together and published under the title of "Pictures in Camp and Field."

His pictures are so perfect, and his words so admirably selected, that in reading them we live again our soldier life. We hear the rattle of musketry, and the roar of artillery, and see the advancing columns and terrible conflict as the armies contest in a hand-to-hand struggle; and when the winds have lifted the black smoke, we see the terrible work of battle, and we again earnestly pray a kind Father to spread the mantled mourning of night over the scene.

Mr. Taylor published "The World on Wheels" in 1873, and "Old Time Pictures and Sheaves of Rhyme" in 1874. All of his works have passed through several editions. He has been very popular on the lyceum platform.

It will pay us, kind friends, to read the volumes of Taylor. They contain the beautiful wish that " our lives and his may not be composed of random 'scores,' but be a beautiful anthem, harmony in all its parts, melody in all its tones; not a strain wanting, not a note out of tune; till 'the daughters of music are brought low,' and the life-anthem is ended."

"But isn't it a pleasant thought that perhaps somebody may take up the tune, when we are dead—not a note lost, nor a jar, nor a discord, but all swan-like harmony? Perhaps! perhaps! There is something hollow, like a knell, in that word. The veil that hides the future is woven of 'perhaps;' in it the greatest ills have their solace, the brightest joys their cloud."

ALFRED TENNYSON.

ALFRED TENNYSON was born at Somersby, near Spilsby, England, August 6, 1810 (given 1809 by some, and January 12, 1810, by others). His father was the Rev. George Clayton Tennyson, LL. D., a Lincolnshire clergyman, who is described as "a tall, striking and imposing man, full of accomplishments and parts, a strong nature, high souled, high tempered." Alfred's mother was the daughter of the Rev. Stephen Fyche. To the Rev. Tennyson were born eleven or twelve children, seven of whom were sons. The three eldest, Frederick, Charles and Alfred, formed a brotherhood of poets, though Alfred is the only one who gained great literary distinction.

Tennyson was fortunate in the influence of his home. The children were a noble little clan of poets and knights, coming from a

ALFRED TENNYSON.

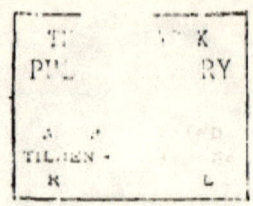

knightly race. Somersby was so far away from the world, so behindhand in its echoes, that though the early part of the century was stirring with the clang of legions, few of its rumors seem to have reached the children. They never heard, at the time, of the battle of Waterloo. They grew up together, playing their own games, living their own life; and where is such life to be found as that of a happy, eager family of boys and girls, before Doubt, the steps of Time, the shocks of Chance, the blows of Death, have come to shake their creed? Mrs. Tennyson, the mother of the family, was a sweet and gentle and most imaginative woman; so kind-hearted that it passed into a proverb, and the wicked inhabitants of a neighboring village used to bring their dogs to her windows and beat them, in order to be bribed by the gentle lady to leave off, or to make advantageous bargains by selling the worthless curs. She was intensely, fervently religious. After her husband's death (he had added to the rectory and made it suitable for his large family) she still lived at Somersby with her children. The daughters were growing up; the older sons were going to college. Frederick, the eldest, went first to Trinity, Cambridge, and his brothers followed him there in turn. Life was opening for them, they were seeing new aspects and places, and making new friends and bringing them home to their Lincolnshire rectory.

At an early age Tennyson showed signs of poetic powers. On one occasion, when the members of the family were going to church, Charles handed Alfred a slate and gave him a subject for a poem. Upon returning home, Alfred took the slate to his brother, with a poem covering both sides. Charles scanned the lines, then handed the slate back with the encouragement, "Yes, Alfred, you can write." The next instance was not so encouraging. Upon the death of his grandmother the young poet was asked to write an elegy that would be appropriate. The task was performed, whereupon Alfred's grandfather handed the boy ten shillings, saying, "There, that is the first money you have earned by your poetry, and, take my word for it, it will be the last." But the youth persevered, and, before he was nineteen, published a volume of poems conjointly with his brother Charles. In 1829 he gained the Chancellor's medal for an English prize poem, his subject being "Timbuctoo."

Referring to Tennyson's early days, William Howitt has written: "You may hear his voice, but where is the man? He is wandering in some dreamland, beneath the shade of old and charmed forests, by far-off shores, where

> 'all night
> The plunging seas draw backward from the land
> Their moon-led waters white;'

by the old mill-dam, thinking of the merry miller and his pretty daughter; or wandering over the woodlands where

> 'Norland whirlwinds blow.'

"From all these places—from the silent corridor of an ancient convent, from some shrine where a devoted knight recites his vows, from the dreary monotony of 'the moated grange,' or the forest beneath the 'talking oak'—comes the voice of Tennyson, rich, dreamy, passionate, yet not impatient, musical with the airs of chivalrous ages, yet mingling in his song the theme and spirit of those that are yet to come."

His fame was established in 1830, when he published "Poems, Chiefly Lyrical, by Alfred Tennyson." From that date to this—a period of fifty-five years—he has been a distinguished character in English letters. In 1833 he issued another volume, giving unusual signs of poetic power. This volume was handled severely by critics, which was the cause, perhaps, of the delay of nearly nine years before his next volume appeared. The young poet received the criticism in a true scholarly spirit, and set about correcting his faults. The two volumes which he brought out in 1842 raised him to the position of absolute superiority. These volumes, entitled "Poems," contained many of his first poems completely revised and many new ones. The following appeared in the list: "Morte d'Arthur," "Godiva," "The May Queen," "Dora," "Talking Oak" and "Locksley Hall." These poems are among the best in the language, and they alone would render the author's name immortal. "Locksley Hall" is Tennyson's most finished work.

From the date of the above works Tennyson has stood at the head of English poetry. In 1847 appeared "The Princess, a Medley;" 1850, "In

Memoriam," a volume of short poems written as a tribute of respect to his beloved friend, Arthur Hallam, who died in his twenty-third year.

"At the time Arthur Hallam died he was engaged to be married to a sister of the poet. She was scarcely seventeen. One of the sonnets addressed by Hallam to his betrothed was written when he began to teach her Italian:

> 'Lady, I bid thee to a sunny dome,
>   Ringing with echoes of Italian songs;
>   Henceforth to thee these magic halls belong,
> And all the pleasant place is like a home.
> Hark, on the right, with full piano tone,
>   Old Dante's voice encircles all the air;
>   Hark yet again, like flute-tones mingling rare
> Comes the keen sweetness of Petrarca's moan.
> Pass thou the lintel freely; without fear
>   Feast on the music. I do better know thee
>   Than to suspect this pleasure thou dost owe me
> Will wrong thy gentle spirit, or make less dear
> That element whence thou must draw thy life—
> An English maiden and an English wife.'

"As we read the pages of this little book we come upon more than one happy moment saved out of the past, hours of delight and peaceful friendship, saddened by no foreboding, and complete in themselves.

> 'Alfred, I would that you behold me now,
> Sitting beneath an ivied mossy wall.
>   *   *   *   *   Above my head
> Dialates immeasurable a wild of leaves,
> Seeming received into the blue expanse,
> That vaults the summer noon.'

"There is something touching in the tranquil ring of the voice calling out in the summer noontide with all a young man's expansion." The young friends had played and studied and traveled together, and they had anticipated a brilliant and happy life in the society of each other. But the spell was broken by Arthur's sudden death while traveling with his father in Austria. The memory of his friend is tenderly embalmed by Tennyson in "In Memoriam."

By this time the poet's fame was so thoroughly established that, upon the death of Wordsworth, in 1850, the queen appointed Alfred Tennyson Poet Laureate. In 1852 he wrote an "Ode on the Death of the Duke of Wellington;" 1855, "Maud, and other Poems;" 1859, The "Idyls of the King." The last named is a great connected poem, dealing with the very highest interests of man. The work at once took its place among the greatest poems in the English language. "Enoch Arden, and other Poems" appeared in 1864; "The Holy Grail," "Pelleas and Etarre," and "The Windows, or Songs of Wrens," set to music, 1870; "The Tournament," and "Gareth and Lynette," 1872.

At Somersby Tennyson met Miss Sellwood, and their acquaintance resulted in their marriage. Miss Sellwood came from an ancient and honorable family, her mother being a sister of Sir John Franklin. Shortly after their marriage they settled at Freshwater, in the Isle of Wight, where they still live. In addition to this home they own an estate in Surrey, to which they retreat when the tourists and visitors become too oppressive in the Isle of Wight.

It is not difficult to determine that Tennyson occupies the front rank in the literature of England. Further than this, an estimate cannot be made. For more than a quarter of a century the hearts of the English people have been beating time to the music of his verse. When the spell is broken by his death we shall realize more fully the hold he now has upon the public. He seems to have brought poetry up to its highest standard of perfection; at least he is the representative of his age. He shows wide culture, deep and analyzing thought, and great beauty of expression. The measure and flow of his verse are always adapted to the thought, and the sound to the sense. No library is complete without the volumes of Tennyson.

THACKERAY.

WILLIAM MAKEPEACE THACKERAY was born at Calcutta in 1811, and died suddenly on December 24, 1863.

His family was originally from Yorkshire. His father, at the time of his death being but thirty years of age, was secretary to the Board of Revenue at Calcutta.

The son, with his widowed mother, left India, and arrived in England in 1817. "When I first saw England," he said in one of his lectures, "she was in mourning for the young Princess Charlotte, the hope of the empire. I came from India as a child, and our ship touched at an island on the way home, where my black servant took me a walk over rocks and hills, till we passed a garden where we saw a man walking. 'That is he,' said the black man; 'that is Bonaparte. He eats three sheep every day, and all the children he can lay hands on.' There were people in the British dominions besides that poor black who had an equal terror and horror of the Corsican ogre." Young Thackeray was placed in the Charterhouse School of London, which had formerly received as grown boys or scholars the melodious poets Crashaw, Addison, Steele, and John Wesley. From the Charterhouse Thackeray went to Trinity College, Cambridge, and, whilst residing there in 1829, he made his first appearance as an author. In conjunction with a college friend he carried on for a short time a light humorous weekly miscellany entitled "The Snob."

In 1830-'31 he was one of "at least a score of young English lads who used to live at Weimar for study, or sport, or society," and who were received with the kindest hospitality by the Grand Duke and Duchess. He did not remain at college to take his degree. His great ambition was to be an artist, and for this purpose he studied at Rome and Paris. On attaining his majority he became possessed of considerable fortune, but some losses and speculations reduced his patrimony. Thackeray first became known through "Frazer's Magazine," to which he was for several years a regular contributor under the names of "Michael Angelo Titmarsh," "George Fitz-Boodle, Esquire,""Charles Yellowplush," etc.—names typical of his artistic and satirical predilections. Tales, criticisms, descriptive sketches and poetry were dashed off by his ready pen. They were of unequal merit, and for some time attracted but little attention; but John Sterling, among others, recognized the genius of Thackeray in his tale of "The Hoggarty Diamond," and ranked its author with Fielding and Goldsmith. His style was that of the scholar combined with the shrewdness and knowledge of a man of the world. "Titmarsh" had both seen and read much. His school and college life, his foreign travels and residence abroad, his artistic and literary experiences, even his losses, supplied a wide field for observation, reflection and satire. He was thirty years of age or more ere he made any bold push for fame.

In 1836 Thackeray joined with his step-father and others in starting "The Constitutional," a daily newspaper, which, not being a paying investment, was suspended in about a year. He entered the Middle Temple, and was admitted to the bar in 1848, but did not make law a profession. Under assumed names, he published "The Paris Sketch-Book," two volumes, in 1840; "The Second Funeral of Napoleon" and "The Chronicles of the Drum," 1841; and "The Irish Sketch-Book," 1843. These works were not popular, although they contained some fine passages. About the same time "Barry Lyndon," one of his best short satires, appeared in "Frazer's Magazine." "Punch," the wittiest of English journals, was started in 1841, and Thackeray contributed to its columns. His articles signed "The Fat Contributor" became famous. Next appeared "Jeames's Diary" and the "Snob Papers," noted for their irony and wit. He visited the East, and wrote "Notes of a Journey from Cornhill to Grand Cairo, by way of Lisbon, Athens, Constantinople and Jerusalem, by M. A. Titmarsh," which was published in 1846. In the following year appeared a small Christmas book

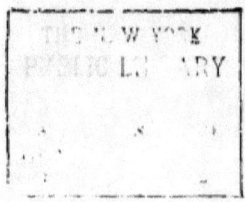

entitled "Mrs. Perkins' Ball." In February, 1847, he commenced "Vanity Fair, a Novel Without a Hero." This work was published in monthly parts, and illustrated by himself. As the story advanced it grew in interest, till its immense popularity had placed the author among the greatest of English novelists and social satirists. From that time he wrote over his proper name. In 1848 appeared "Our Street," another Christmas volume, to which "Dr. Birch and His Young Friend" was added in 1849, as a companion volume. In 1849-'50 he published his second great work, "The History of Pendennis," as a monthly serial, in which he describes the gentleman of the present age. In 1851 Thackeray published "The Kickleburys on the Rhine," a Christmas tale written by M. A. Titmarsh. This bitter satire was reviewed by the "Times" newspaper, and it was charged that the novelist represented only the dark side of life. Thackeray replied in "An Essay on Thunder and Small Beer," prefixed to a second edition of the Christmas volume.

In the summer of 1851 Thackeray appeared as a lecturer. His subject was "The English Humorists of the Eighteenth Century;" and all the rank and fashion, with no small portion of the men of letters of London, flocked to Willis' rooms to hear the popular novelist descant on the lives and works of his great predecessors in fiction from Swift to Goldsmith. The lectures were afterward repeated in Scotland and in America; and they are now published, forming one of the most delightful little books in the language. To Swift Thackeray was perhaps too severe, to Fielding too indulgent; Steele is painted *en beau* in cordial love, and with little shadow; yet we know not where the reader will find in the same limited compass so much just and discriminating criticism, or so many fine thoughts and amusing anecdotes as those which this loving brother of the craft has treasured up regarding his fellows of the last century. The Queen Anne period touched upon in these lectures formed the subject of Thackeray's next novel, "Esmond," published in three volumes in 1852. The work is in the form of an autobiography. The hero, Col. Henry Esmond, is a cavalier and Jacobite, who, after serving his country abroad, mingles with its wits and courtiers at home, plots for the restoration of the Chevalier St. George, and finally retires to Virginia, where, in his old age, he writes this memoir of himself and of the noble family of Castlewood, of which he is a member. It is a grand and melancholy story.

In 1852 he published in monthly parts, "The Newcomes: Memoirs of a Most Respectable Family. Edited by Arthur Pendennis, Esq." This work is considered his masterpiece. The leading theme or moral of the story is the misery occasioned by ill-assorted marriages.

In 1855-'56 he again entered the lecture field. Crossing the Atlantic he made a tour of the United States. He had prepared four new lectures upon "The Four Georges," which he delivered here to large audiences. Returning to his home, he repeated his lectures in England and Scotland. In 1857 appeared "The Virginians," a tale of the time of George II. In 1860-'62 Thackeray conducted the "Cornhill Magazine," and in the pages of this popular miscellany appeared his "Roundabout Papers"—a series of light, graceful essays and sketches; also two novels, "Lovel, the Widower," and "Philip on His Way Through the World," which were scarcely worthy of his reputation. He had commenced another story, "Denis Duval," of which four monthly portions were published; and he contemplated Memoirs of the reign of Queen Anne, as a continuation of Macaulay's History. All of his schemes, however, were frustrated by his sudden and lamentable death. His health had long been precarious, and on the day preceding his death he had been in great suffering. Still he moved about; "he was out several times," says Shirley Brooks, "and was seen in Palace Gardens, Kensington, reading a book. Before the dawn on Thursday, December 24, 1863, he was where there is no night." "Never more," said the "Times," "shall the fine head of Mr. Thackeray, with its mass of silvery hair, be seen towering among us." He had died in bed alone and unseen, struggling, as it appeared, with a violent spasmodic attack, which had caused the effusion on the brain, of which he died.

Thackeray and Dickens are two important characters in social history. The former possessing the greater culture, and dealing with the follies of the higher classes, did much for English society, while the latter, with greater genius, accomplished the same results by holding up to ridicule the vices of the poor.

ISAAC WATTS.

Dr. ISAAC WATTS was born at Southampton, July 17, 1674, of parents remarkable for their piety and sanctity, and died, after a long life of unusual activity and usefulness, seventy-five years later, on the 25th day of November, 1748.

But for his early inclination to adopt the views of the Dissenters, Watts would have been placed in the university, but on account of the interest taken in this peculiar body he was educated at one of their institutions, under the charge of the Rev. Thomas Rowe. At Stoke Newington, in 1698, he was chosen assistant minister of an Independent congregation, and four years later he assumed entire control. The onerous duties incumbent upon one placed in his position soon told upon his health, however, and he was compelled to require the services of an assistant. But the force and vigor of his vital powers seemed on the wane, and he was compelled to resign the pastorate entirely, and in 1712 a benevolent gentleman, Sir Thomas Abney, of Abney Park, offered him a place in his household. This Watts accepted, and here, surrounded by loving and watchful friends, and in a home of peace and contentment, he passed the remaining thirty-five years of his life.

When he had lived at Abney Park eight years, he suffered the loss of his much-loved friend and benefactor, Sir Thomas Abney. His widow, however, accorded to Watts the same privileges and benefits he had enjoyed before his death, and no change occurred. The most of his time, while living in this retirement, was spent in study, but he occasionally preached. Nearly all his writings are well known and highly prized, both in prose and poetry. His treatise on "Logic, or the Right Use of Reason," and "Improvement of the Mind,"—the latter a supplement of the former,—will always be valued for their force of argument and facility of comparison. The greater part of his poetry consists of devotional hymns, which find their way to the hearts of the people by their unaffected simplicity, their powerful imagery, and the zeal they are well calculated to excite.

J. G. WHITTIER.

JOHN GREENLEAF WHITTIER was born at Haverhill, Massachusetts, December 17, 1807. He is unmarried, and for the last forty-five years has made his principal home at Amesbury, Massachusetts. He belongs to the Society of Friends, or Quakers, and is the greatest representative of that denomination.

Nothing is known of his ancestors except that they were Friends and in full sympathy with the traditions and doctrines of that peace-loving organization. Of course they were bitterly opposed and persecuted by the Puritans. In the Massachusetts Bay Colony the persecutions were most bitter, and the "drab coats and broad-brimmed hats were as hateful to the colonists as the features and war paint of the Indians. They were not to be exterminated, however, for there was an invincible strength in the doctrines of peace which they professed and practiced, and in the simple goodness of their lives. Shunned at first, it was not long before they were tolerated, and before their influence was felt in the milder manners of their Puritan neighbors, who gradually forgot the senseless animosities of their ancestors. Such I conceive to be the early colonial history of the Quakers, who succeeded in establishing themselves in Massachusetts and elsewhere."

At first Whittier received but a brief common school education. He worked on his father's farm in the summer and helped to make shoes in the winter. His entire school opportunities were confined to a district school,

JOHN GREENLEAF WHITTIER

which was open only about twelve weeks in the year, and to one year of academic study. His chances for study at home were limited to about a score of volumes, mostly relating to the doctrines of his sect, and the lives of its founders.

Mr. Whittier's literary life commenced by his contributions to the "Haverhill Gazette." At the age of twenty-one he was selected editor of the "American Manufacturer," a protective tariff journal. The questions that were discussed in this journal necessarily required unusual ability; but Whittier showed so much mental strength in its columns that in 1830 he was chosen editor of the "New England Review." Although a young man, he yet sustained himself in the editorial chair formerly occupied by George D. Prentice and J. G. C. Brainard. In the "Review" he published a "Life of Brainard," "Legends of New England," and "Mollie Pitcher." In 1833 appeared an essay entitled "Justice and Expediency, or Slavery considered with a View to its Abolition."

For a short time he returned from his literary labor to his farm and took an active interest in politics. In 1835 he was elected to the Massachusetts legislature. In 1839 he became secretary of the Anti-slavery Society, and also editor of the "Pennsylvania Freeman," at Philadelphia. He returned to Amesbury in 1840, and from that date has been known as a man of letters. Before this, however, Whittier had written an Indian poem entitled "Mogg Megone," in 1835. This was followed in 1836 by "Voices of Freedom," a series of excellent poems, the last of which appeared in 1848. "Leaves from Margaret Smith's Journal" appeared in 1836; "Lays of Home," 1843; "The Stranger in Lowell," 1845; and "Supernaturalism in New England," 1847, the last two being prose; "Old Portraits and Modern Sketches," being biographical, and one of his best prose works, 1850. In 1850 or 1851 appeared a collection entitled "Songs of Labor and Other Poems."

"The Songs of Labor" are followed, in the complete edition of Mr. Whittier's poetical works, by upward of fifty poems which are ranged under the head of "Miscellaneous." They are divided into classes or groups, "The Angels of Buena Vista," "Barclay of Ury," "The Legend of St. Mark," and "Calef in Boston," ranking among legendary poems; "Worship," "Lines Accompanying Manuscript Presented to a Friend," "Channing," "To the Memory of Charles B. Storrs," and "Memoirs," among personal poems; and "The Reward," "To Pius IX," "The Men of Old," "The Peace Convention at Brussels," "Seed-time and Harvest," among didactic poems. There is a ripeness of thought about these productions which we do not find in Mr. Whittier's earlier verse, and a noticeable grace and beauty of expression which leave nothing to be desired. "The Chapel of the Hermit" appeared in 1853; "Literary Recreations," another of his excellent prose works, 1854; "The Panorama, and Other Poems," 1856; "Home Ballads," 1859; "In War Times," 1864; "Snow-Bound," 1865. "If I wished to give an intelligent foreigner an idea of Mr. Whittier's genius, and an idea of the characteristics of American poetry at the same time, I should ask him to read Mr. Whittier's 'Snow-Bound.' This exquisite poem has no prototype in English literature, unless Burns' 'Cottar's Saturday Night' be one, and it will be long, I fear, before it has a companion-piece. The materials upon which 'Snow Bound' is based are of the slightest order, and the wonder is that any poet, even the most skillful one, could have made a poem out of them. But Mr. Whittier has made a poem which will live, and can no more be rivaled by any winter poetry that may be written hereafter, than 'Thanatopsis' can be rivaled as a meditation on the universality of death. The characters in this little idyl are carefully drawn, and the quiet of the homestead during the storm is in striking contrast to the out-door bustle which succeeds it. There is no evidence anywhere that the poem cost a moment's labor; everything is naturally introduced, and the reflections, which are manly and pathetic, are among the finest that Mr. Whittier has ever written. 'Snow Bound' at once authenticated itself as an idyl of New England life and manners."

In 1867 appeared "The Tent on the Beach, and Other Poems;" 1868, "Among the Hills;" 1870, "Miriam, and Other Poems;" 1872, "The Pennsylvania Pilgrim, and Other Poems." Whittier's "Legends of New England" were afterward worked out in several beautiful poems and presented in "Mogg Megone," "Bride of Pennacook," "Cassandra," "Southwick," and "Mary Garvin." His fame is secured even by his shorter poems. Everybody knows "Randolph of Roanoke," "Maud Muller," "Skipper Ireson's Ride," "Telling the Bees," "Barbara Fritchie," "My Psalm," "The Barefoot Boy," and "My Playmate." "The Hermit of Thebaid" is nearly faultless.

"Mr. Whittier is one of the few American poets who have succeeded in obtaining the suffrages of the reading public and of the literary class. Men of letters respect his work for its sincerity, simplicity, and downright manliness, and average readers of poetry respect it because they can understand it. There is not a grown man or woman in the land who does not readily enter into the aspiration and discontent of "Maud Muller," and into the glowing patriotism of "Barbara Fritchie." Whether the incident which is the inspiration of the latter ever occurred, is more than doubtful; nevertheless, the poem is one that the world will not willingly let die. The reputation of such poems is immediate and permanent, and beyond criticism, favorable or otherwise; the touch of nature in them is beyond all art. I should never think of comparing 'Barbara Fritchie' with Bryant's 'O Mother of a Mighty Race,' but I am sure that it has a thousand readers where Bryant's poem has one. Bryant seldom reached the hearts of his countrymen, but his best poems appealed to what was loftiest in their intellects."

Before closing this sketch, we will make brief reference to the poet as he is at present considered aside from his literary work. At seventy-seven years and over one can be said to have the beauty only of age, striking as that is in Mr. Whittier's case, with the dark eye and full beard, where black lines still appear among the silver, while his form is as straight, and his step is as firm and elastic as ever. But the poet's youthful beauty is reported to have been extraordinary; very tall, erect, and well knit, with fine features, dark skin, and flashing, deep-set eye, he could not have looked the Quaker to any extent; and in fact we think he is more of a Quaker in affection than anything else. He has himself recognized that

"Over restless wings of song
His birthright garb hung loose,"

and even though he clings to the form of the sect in many respects, using the plain language generally, and tells somewhere why he prefers the silence of the meeting for worship rather than any solitude of wood or wild where Nature speaks to him with a thousand voices, and catches him with a thousand hands, yet he dresses so nearly like men of the world in cut and color, that only practiced eyes could detect the slight difference in the shape of the coat, and his feelings about such matters are entirely liberal. When his little niece wanted the scarlet cap that other children wore, and there was objection in the house on account of the Quaker custom, Mr. Whittier insisted that she should be gratified, although, sooth to say, poet as he is, he himself cannot tell red from green till sunlight falls upon it. Once, indeed, the liberal fire, of which he is so fond, having damaged the border of the wall paper, he matched the pattern and triumphantly replaced it before detection, only to learn that he had substituted for the green vine, one of a bright autumnal crimson. Yet so strong is the poet's imagination that this defect of vision is nowhere evident in his work, although one might gather there that while, as he says, "his eye was beauty's powerless slave," yet light and shade please him more than variety and depth of hue.

After the loss of his sister, his niece kept his house until her marriage to Mr. Pickard, of the Portland "Transcript," a gentleman who has written most appreciatingly of Mr. Whittier, and to whom we are indebted for many facts of his life. There was a pleasant coincidence attending this marriage of his niece, as her husband was the nephew of the old schoolmaster and dearest friend of the poet, Joshua Coffin, the historian of Newbury. But the marriage broke up his home, in a measure, and not long afterward he went to Danvers, a town about twenty miles from Boston, where he makes his home at Oak Knoll, with some charming and genial cousins. The Amesbury residence, however, occupied by old friends, remains nearly as it always has been.

Although a great man in the true sense of the term, Mr. Whittier's life has not been marked by any great events. He did not flash into the literary skies like a brilliant meteor, to glide out of sight and be remembered only as a startling visitor; but he took his place in the literary constellation of his country as a fixed star of the first magnitude. The champion of right, and the enemy of wrong, he took hold of his life work with a firm grasp, and has never faltered in the least. In his patriotic lyrics he has written with a terrible energy. "He seems," as Whipple says, "to have poured out his life blood with his lines." Since Longfellow's death Whittier is the most popular American poet. In true poetic genius he surpasses the lamented Longfellow. "No living poet can more safely rest his works and his memory to the keeping of that august power, Posterity, than John Greenleaf Whittier."

E. P. WHIPPLE.

Edwin P. Whipple was born in Gloucester, Massachusetts, March 8, 1819.

He was educated to business, first as a clerk in a bank at Salem, where he commenced work at the age of fifteen, then, three years later, at a bank in Boston, where he became chief clerk. He was also made superintendent of the reading room of the Merchants' Exchange at the time of its foundation, a position he held till in 1860.

Whipple's literary record commenced at the age of twenty-one, when he delivered a humorous poem before the Mercantile Library Association of Boston. In 1850 he delivered a fourth of July oration before the city authorities on "Washington and the Principles of the American Revolution." In 1848 he published two volumes of "Essays and Reviews," which at once established his reputation as a popular critic and essayist. The style was pleasing, and the judgment proved to be as good as that of any of the standard authorities. In the same year he published "Lectures on Subjects Connected with Literature and Life;" in 1860 he prefixed a life of Macaulay to an edition of his essays. In 1867 "Character and Characteristic Men" appeared; and

"Literature in the Age of Elizabeth," a course of lectures, delivered before the Lowell Institute in 1869.

Whipple is noted for his good taste, sound judgment, agreeable style; and he is one of the most popular of living writers. We are occasionally pleased to find a popular review of some author, from his ready pen, and we always accept it as reliable. The beauty of his style may be illustrated in a paragraph of his upon "The Influence of Books:"

"From the hour of the invention of printing, books, and not kings, were to rule the world. Weapons forged in the mind, keen-edged, and brighter than a sunbeam, were to supplant the sword and battle-axe. Books! lighthouses built on the sea of time! Books! by whose sorcery the whole pageantry of the world's history moves in solemn procession before our eyes. From their pages great souls look down in all their grandeur, undimmed by the faults and follies of earthly existence, consecrated by time."

WALT WHITMAN.

Walt Whitman was born in Westhills, Long Island, May 31, 1819, in a farm-house overlooking the sea. While yet a child his parents moved to Brooklyn, where he acquired his education. He learned type-setting at thirteen years of age; two years later he taught a country school. He contributed to the "Democratic Review" before he was twenty-one years old. At thirty he traveled through the Western States, and spent one year in New Orleans editing a newspaper. Returning home he took up his father's occupation of carpenter and builder, which he followed for a while. During the War of the Rebellion he spent most of his time in the hospitals and camps, in the relief of the sick and disabled soldiers. For a time he was a department clerk in Washington.

WALT WHITMAN.

In 1856 he published a volume entitled "Leaves of Grass." This volume shows unquestionable power, and great originality, and contains passages of a very objectionable character, so much so, that no defense that is valid can be set up. His labors among the sick and wounded necessarily made great impressions; these took form in his mind and were published under the title of "Drum Taps."

His poems lack much of coming up to the standard of recognized poetic measure. He has a style peculiar to himself, and his writings are full of meaning, beauty and interest. Of his productions, Underwood says: "Pupils who are accustomed to associate the idea of poetry with regular classic measure in rhyme, or in ten-syllabled blank verse or elastic hexameters, will commence these short and simple prose sentences with surprise, and will wonder how any number of them can form a poem. But let them read aloud with a mind in sympathy with the picture as it is displayed, and they will find by nature's unmistakable responses, that the author is a poet, and possesses the poet's uncommunicable power to touch the heart."

N. P. WILLIS.

NATHANIEL PARKER WILLIS was born in Portland, Maine, January 20, 1806, and died at Idlewild, near Newburgh, New York, January 21, 1867.

His father was Nathaniel Willis, a noted journalist, who was born in Boston, in 1780, and who died there in 1870, at the advanced age of ninety. The father established and edited several different journals, and always with ability. In 1827 he established the "Youth's Companion," the first of the periodicals for the young, which he edited till in 1857.

Nathaniel P. Willis inherited all of his father's ability, which he increased many fold. He graduated at Yale College in 1827. His authorship commenced while he was in college by the publication of a series of "Scriptural Sketches" in verse, and other poems. These sketches appeared under the signature of "Roy." Upon graduating he was engaged at once by S. G. Goodrich, known as "Peter Parley," to edit the "Legendary" and the "Token." In 1828 he started for himself by establishing the "American Monthly Magazine," which was continued two years, then merged into the "New York Mirror." The "Mirror" had been established by George P. Morris, and Willis became associate editor. Soon after he visited Europe and wrote letters to that journal entitled "Pencillings by the Way;" these letters were collected into three volumes and published in London in 1835. In Paris he was made an attache of the American minister. After traveling through southern Europe, Turkey, and parts of Asia Minor he returned to England and in 1835 married a daughter of General Stace, commandant of the Woolwich arsenal. He also published "Melanie and Other Poems," in 1835; and "Inklings of Adventure" in three volumes, in 1836, being a series of tales and sketches which originally appeared in the "New Monthly Magazine" under the pseudonym "Philip Slingsby."

In 1837 he returned to the United States, and for two years lived in retirement on a small estate which he named Glenmary, on the Susquehanna, near Oswego, New York. In 1839 he became one of the editors of the "Corsair," a short-lived literary gazette published in New York. Later in the same year he revisited England, where appeared two dramas published together under the title "Two Ways of Dying for a Husband: 1. Dying to Keep Him, or Tortesa the Usurer; 2. Dying to Lose Him, or Bianca Visconti," in 1839; and "Letters from Under a Bridge, and Poems," 1840. Returning to New York he established, in 1844, in connection with George P. Morris, a daily newspaper called the "Evening Mirror;" but the death of his wife and his failing health led him to return to Europe. In this visit he published "Dashes at Life with a Free Pencil," in three volumes, in 1845, being a collection of magazine articles. On returning to New York in 1846 he married a daughter of the Hon. Joseph Grinnell, of New Bedford, and settled at a seat on the Hudson which he named Idlewild. In the same year he published a complete edition of his works in one large

volume, and with Mr. Morris established the "Home Journal," a weekly, to which he contributed till his death.

His other works include "Rural Letters, and Other Records of Thought and Leisure," published in 1849; "People I have Met," 1850; "Life Here and There," 1850; "Hurrygraphs," 1851; "Fun Jottings, or Laughs I have Taken a Pen to," 1853; "A Health Trip to the Tropics," 1853; "A Summer Cruise in the Mediterranean' in a United States Frigate," 1853; "Famous Persons and Places," 1854; "Out-Doors at Idlewild," 1854; "The Rag Bag," 1855; "Paul Fane, or Parts of a Life else Untold," 1856; and "The Convalescent," 1860. In all, he has published twenty-seven volumes of prose and poetry.

The beauty of his verse, both in thought and style, may be illustrated by his poem entitled

THIRTY-FIVE.

O weary heart! thou'rt half way home!
  We stand on life's meridian height—
As far from childhood's morning come,
  As to the grave's forgetful night.
Give Youth and Hope a parting tear,
  Look onward with a placid brow—
Hope promised but to bring us here,
  And Reason takes the guidance now—
One backward look—the last—the last!
One silent tear—for *Youth is past!*

Who goes with Hope and Passion back?
  Who comes with me and Memory on?
Oh, lonely looks the downward track—
  Joy's music hushed—Hope's roses gone!
To Pleasure and her giddy troop
  Farewell without a sigh or tear!
But heart gives way and spirits droop,
  To think that Love may leave us here!
Have we no charm when Youth is flown?
Midway to death left sad and lone!

Yet stay!—as 'twere a twilight star
  That sends its thread across the wave,

I see a brightening light, from far,
  Steal down a path beyond the grave!
And now—bless God! its golden line
  Comes o'er—and lights my shadowy way—
And shows the dear hand clasped in mine!
But list what those sweet voices say:
  "The better land's in sight,
    And, by its chastening light,
All love from life's midway is driven,
Save her whose clasped hand will bring thee on to heaven!"

WORDSWORTH.

WILLIAM WORDSWORTH was born at Cockermouth, Cumberland County, England, April 7, 1770, and he died on April 23, 1850. He was buried by the side of his daughter in the beautiful churchyard of Grasmere.

His father was law agent to Sir James Lowther, afterward Earl of Lonsdale, but he died when William was in his seventh year.

The poet attended school first at Hawkshead School, then at Cambridge University. William was also entered at St. John's in 1787. Having finished his academical course, Wordsworth, in 1790, in company with Mr. Robert James, a fellow-student, made a tour on the continent. With this friend Wordsworth made a tour in North Wales the following year, after taking his degree in college. He was again in France toward the close of the year 1791, and remained in that country about a twelvemonth. He had hailed the French Revolution with feelings of enthusiastic admiration.

    Bliss was it in that dawn to be *alive*
    But to be *young* was very heaven.

A young friend, Raisley Calvert, dying in 1795, left him a sum of

WILLIAM WORDSWORTH.

£900. A further sum of about £1,000 came to him as a part of the estate of his father, who died intestate; and with this small competence Wordsworth devoted himself to study and seclusion.

In 1793, in his twenty-third year, he appeared before the world as an author, in "Descriptive Sketches" and "The Evening Walk." The sketches were made from his tour in Switzerland with his friend, and the Walk was among the mountains of Westmoreland.

In 1795 Wordsworth and his sister were living at Racedown Lodge, in Somersetshire, where, in 1797, they were visited by Coleridge. The meeting was mutually pleasant, and a life-long friendship was the result. The intimate relations thus established induced Wordsworth and his sister to change their home for a residence near Coleridge, at Alfoxen, near Neither Stowey. In this new home the poet composed many of his lighter poems, also the "Borderers," a tragedy, which was rejected by the Covent Garden Theatre. In 1797 appeared his "Lyrical Ballads," which also contained Coleridge's "Ancient Mariner."

In 1798, in company with his sister and Coleridge, he went to Germany, where he spent some time at Hamburg, Ratzeburg and Goslar. Returning to England, he took up his residence at Grasmere, in Westmoreland. In 1800 he reprinted his "Lyrical Ballads" with some additions, making two volumes. Two years later he married Mary Hutchinson, to whom he addressed the beautiful lines, "She was a Phantom of Delight." In 1803, Wordsworth, with his sister and his friend Coleridge, visited Scotland. This visit formed one of the most important periods of his literary life, as it led to the composition of some of his finest lighter poems. In 1805 he completed the "Prelude, or Growth of my own Mind," a poem written in blank verse, but not published till after the author's death. In the same year he also wrote his "Waggoner," but did not publish it till in 1819. At this time he purchased a cottage and small estate at the head of Ulleswater, for £1,000, Lord Lonsdale generously assisting him. In 1807 he published two volumes of "Poems."

In the spring of 1813 he removed from Grasmere to Royal Mount, where he remained for the rest of his life, a period of thirty-seven years. Here were passed his brightest days. He enjoyed retirement and almost perfect happiness, as seen in his lines:

> Long have I loved what I behold,
> The night that calms, the day that cheers;
> The common growth of mother-earth
> Suffices me—her tears, her mirth,
> Her humblest mirth and tears.
>
> The dragon's wing, the magic ring,
> I shall not covet for my dower,
> If I along that lowly way
> With sympathetic heart may stray,
> And with a soul of power.

At the same time he commenced to write poems of a higher order, thus greatly extending the circle of his admirers. In 1814 he published "The Excursion," a philosophical poem in blank verse. By viewing man in connection with external nature, the poet blends his metaphysics with pictures of life and scenery. To build up and strengthen the powers of the mind, in contrast to the operations of sense, was ever his object. Like Bacon, Wordsworth would rather have believed all the fables in the Talmud and Alcoran, than that this universal frame is without a mind—or that mind does not, by its external symbols, speak to the human heart. He lived under the habitual sway of nature:

> To me the meanest flower that blows can give
> Thoughts that do often lie too deep for tears.

The removal of the poet to Rydal was marked by an incident of considerable importance in his personal history. Through the influence of the Earl of Lonsdale, he was appointed distributor of stamps in the county of Westmoreland, which added greatly to his income without engrossing all of his time. He was now placed beyond the frowns of Fortune—if Fortune can ever be said to have frowned on one so independent of her smiles. The subsequent works of the poet were numerous—"The White Doe of Rylstone," a romantic narrative poem, yet colored with his peculiar genius; "Sonnets on the River Duddon;" "The Waggoner;" "Peter Bell;" "Ecclesiastical Sketches;" "Yarrow Revisited," and others. His fame was extending rapidly. The universities of Durham and Oxford conferred academic honors upon him. Upon the death of his friend Southey, in 1843, he was made Poet Laureate of England, and the crown gave him a pension of £300 per annum. Thus his income was increased and honors were showered upon him, making glad the closing years of his life. But sadness found its way into his household in 1847, caused by the death of his only daughter, Dora, then Mrs. Quillinan. Wordsworth survived the shock but three years, having reached the advanced age of eighty, always enjoying robust health and writing his poems in the open air. He died in 1850, on the anniversary of St. George, the patron saint of England.

EDWARD YOUNG.

Dr. EDWARD YOUNG was born at Upham, in Hampshire, England, in 1684, and died in 1765, at the advanced age of eighty-one.

He commenced his education at Winchester School, and completed it at All Souls' College, Oxford. From the character of the schools attended, it will be seen that the poet had ample opportunities to acquire a thorough education. Young came forth from his studies a polished scholar, ambitious for both literary and political fame. His youth is said to have been passed in gayety and dissipation, like that of Byron, but he lived to overcome youthful follies and gain full control of his powerful intellect.

The poet published a satire on the "Universal Passion—the Love of Fame," which was at once keen and powerful. When upwards of fifty, Young entered the church, wrote a panegyric on the king, and was made one of his majesty's chaplains. In 1730 he obtained from his college the living of Welwyn, in Hertfordshire, where he was destined to close his days. The poet made a noble alliance with the daughter of the Earl of Lichfield, widow of Colonel Lee, which lasted ten years, and proved a happy union. The lady had two children by her first marriage, to whom Young was warmly attached. Both died; and when the mother also followed, Young composed his "Night Thoughts." Sixty years had strengthened and enriched his genius, and augmented even the brilliancy of his fancy. In 1761 the poet was made clerk of the closet to the princess-dowager of Wales, and died four years afterward at the advanced age of eighty-one.

It is seldom we find a man of Young's literary genius and industry, whose life like his, was filled with worldly anxieties. He appears in his "Night Thoughts" as a humble and penitent Christian, and an accomplished poetic artist. His works are numerous, but the best are the "Night Thoughts," the "Universal Passion," and the tragedy of "Revenge." The foundation of his great poem was family misfortune, for

> Insatiate archer! could not one suffice?
> Thy shafts flew thrice, and thrice my peace was slain;
> And thrice, ere thrice yon moon had filled her horn.

This rapid succession of bereavements was a poetical license, for in one case there was an interval of four years, and in another of seven months. The "Night Thoughts" were published from 1742 to 1744. The gay Lorenzo is overdrawn. It seems to us a mere fancy sketch. Like the character of Childe Harold in the hands of Byron, it afforded the poet scope for dark and powerful painting, and was made the vehicle for bursts of indignant virtue, sorrow, regret, and admonition. This artificial character pervades the whole poem. But it still leaves to our admiration many noble and sublime passages where the poet speaks as from inspiration of life, death, and immortality.

While we must look to "Night Thoughts" as the foundation of Young's fame, yet his satires, "Love of Fame, the Universal Passion, in Seven Characteristical Satires," published from 1725 to 1728, are poems of high merit.

www.ingramcontent.com/pod-product-compliance
Lightning Source LLC
Chambersburg PA
CBHW030601300426
44111CB00009B/1063